August, 1992

Travel Writer's Markets

Newspapers: no more than 1500

REVISED EDITION

Travel Writer's Markets

Where to Sell Your Travel Articles and Place Your Press Releases

ELAINE O'GARA

THE HARVARD COMMON PRESS
Harvard and Boston
Massachusetts

The Harvard Common Press
535 Albany Street
Boston, Massachusetts 02118

Copyright © 1989 by The Harvard Common Press

Printed in the United States of America.

Library of Congress Cataloging-in-Publication Data

O'Gara, Elaine.
    Travel writer's markets : where to sell your travel articles
and place your press releases / by Elaine O'Gara.—Rev. ed.
        p. cm.
    Includes index.
    ISBN 1-55832-009-1 : $16.95.—ISBN 1-55832-008-3
(pbk.) : $8.95
        1. Travel—Authorship—Handbooks, manuals, etc.
        2. Authorship—Marketing.   I. Title.
G151.0444   1989
070.5'2—dc19

Cover design by Jackie Schuman
Text design by Joyce C. Weston

10 9 8 7 6 5 4 3 2 1

Contents

Acknowledgments

MANY thanks to Alexandra Gautraud, for her innumerable, invaluable skills; Robert Scott Milne, for his encouragement over the years; and Robert B. Shapiro, for his computer know-how and emotional support.

Introduction

ONE great benefit of travel writing is the effect it has on your attitude. The fame and fortune *are* exciting, but in addition, your travels have a definite focus. Traveling as a travel writer is different from traveling as an "ordinary person." You are constantly aware of your experiences as potential ingredients for an article. You become a giant vacuum cleaner, sucking in myriad details, exotic facts, taking innumerable photos, overcoming shyness to talk to natives. Catastrophes become minor mishaps and often become material for a filler or article. An unfortunate nightclub tour could be the raw material of a humorous article. When you're a travel writer, you don't complain about inconveniences on a trip—you write an article about them, and turn disasters into dollars. One hitch: If you're traveling with others who aren't travel writers, they might find your constant note taking irritating and chide you for your rudeness.

Like any traveler, you have to be aware of local customs. Even though glasnost is spreading, there are still places where you don't take pictures in the Soviet Union. Also, in some countries the local inhabitants are getting organized and charging a set fee to have their pictures taken. In other cultures, someone taking photographs is thought to be stealing the subjects' souls.

Although some customs officials look askance at tape recorders, they're a great accessory for bus tours where you're being jostled too much to write legibly. They don't always work so well indoors in a quiet setting. I once took one along that had a loud switch, so as we followed our guide around a museum she was constantly aware that she was being taped.

Whatever you write about, remember that you do have a responsibility to your readers. Not as much responsibility as a brain surgeon, but people do read what you say and plan their trips accordingly. You're also in a position to give a needed promotional boost to deserving small businesses that don't have much money for advertising. One of my greatest thrills was to give some publicity to people who were offering a service I believed in. Several owners of inexpensive hotels I have written about said they had people clutching my article in their hands when they came in to register.

This book is not designed to tell you how to write travel articles. There are several books on travel writing, and you can also attend seminars and conferences on the subject around the country. (See the appendix, Resources for Travel Writers.) In chapter 1, I give you some tips on how to read a magazine to find out if it is appropriate for your piece, and I also give details on how to query an editor and submit material.

In the market listings (chapter 2), you'll find out how much magazines pay, what article lengths they prefer, and many other details on editorial policy. I also tell about those publications that are not good markets so you won't waste your time submitting to them. Chapters 3 and 4 contain similar information about newspapers and book publishers, and chapter 5 will help you deal with the business of travel writing.

I know you're eager to pack your bags and start seeing the world, but a travel writer's journey includes a lot of mental preparation before the trip begins. You'll do the first part of your research right in your own hometown. So prepare to exercise your brain cells before you don your walking shoes.

1

Marketing Your Travel Writing

Selling to Magazines

LET'S take a look at how you get an article published. The first step is selecting the right magazine for your query. Look through the market listings in this book, then write for the detailed writer's guidelines and look at sample copies. You can examine copies of a magazine at the library, buy them on a newsstand, or request them directly from the publisher. One clever (or devious) writer I know tells magazines he's thinking of running an ad in their publication and they send out a sample copy right away.

The listings in this book tell you which editor to send your queries to, but since editors are prone to move around, you should always check the editor's name on the masthead. Once you've selected the proper magazine and editor, send in a zingy query letter. The editor will write back as soon as humanly possible, but since editors sometimes receive several feet of mail a day, don't despair if you don't get an answer immediately. Their writer's guidelines may give a time period within which they try to reply to queries; if you don't hear back within this time, write a courteous follow-up letter, enclosing copies of your original correspondence.

If an editor hasn't worked with you before, you may be asked to submit an article on speculation. This means the editor likes your idea but can't guarantee that he or she will publish the final article. If you get an assignment, you'll get a contract spelling out the rights bought and the terms of payment. Some of the more common terms you might find in a contract are as follows:

All rights: Writer sells all rights to an article in its present form.
First serial rights: Writer sells the right to publish the article for the first time in any periodical anywhere in the world. All other

rights belong to the writer. This is also referred to simply as "first rights." First North American serial rights are the same as first rights except that they apply only to North American periodicals.

Kill fee: Fee for an assigned article that was written and submitted but not published.

Model release: Form signed by the subject of a photograph giving the photographer permission to use the photo.

One-time rights: Differs from first rights in that the article may have been published elsewhere previously.

Second rights: Writer sells the article for a second time after first rights have been sold and the article has appeared in print.

Work for hire: Writer signs away all rights and the copyright.

Articles are generally paid in two ways: on acceptance or on publication. Acceptance is much preferable because some magazines have editorial calendars stretching over a year so the writer will have to wait a long time to receive any money.

After you've established a track record as a writer, you might want to negotiate for a higher fee. This may work or it may not. Ask yourself, "What is the worst thing that can happen to me if I try to negotiate?" In most cases, the worst thing is that the editor will say no. If you have a one-of-a-kind article, such as "Backpacking with J. D. Salinger," your chances of writing your own ticket are much better. One writer has set her lowest acceptable pay for an article at $800. If the magazine won't pay that much, she won't write for them. However, she's been published in some of the top magazines and has a certain amount of name recognition. Another writer was offered $300 for a 1000-word piece in a major women's magazine. She said that was too low. The editor said, "Take it or leave it," so she took it, since her husband was out of work and she had to put food on the table.

If you feel you're not being treated fairly, speak up for your rights. Many writers, grateful for any type of publication, may be timid about asking for more. Perhaps someone should start giving assertiveness training sessions for writers. In the meantime, just remember that assertiveness is not the same as aggressiveness. Write down what you want, have logical reasons to back up your demands, and state your requests clearly and calmly. If the editor says no, at least you won't have made an enemy.

In any event, be sure you're clear about what rights the magazine is buying. Thus, even if you've sold first rights to an article overseas, you could still sell first North American serial rights. The principle also works in reverse: You can sell first North American serial rights and then sell the article to a magazine in England or Singapore.

Even if you've got a go-ahead, followed the editor's instructions down to the *n*th degree, and have prepared an immaculate manuscript, your article may still be rejected for any number of reasons. The magazine may have been sold. The editor may have quit. There may have been a revolution in the country you wrote about between the time you wrote the article and the time it landed on the editor's desk. In any event, do not despair. There are many other magazines to query.

To discern the differences in magazines, you have to study them carefully. The physical characteristics of a publication are the first thing to consider. Is it on glossy paper or newsprint? How many pages are in each issue?

Next, look at the masthead. Then look to see who wrote the articles. If all the articles were written by contributing editors, your chance of getting published is slim.

Look at the ads. Do you see luxury cars and jewelry? The readers are affluent and won't be interested in budget hotels. Are the ads full of computers and rental cars? The readers are probably business travelers.

Another factor in selling your travel articles is the genre, or form in which you decide to write. Here are a few examples:

- **Destination:** A comprehensive article on sightseeing, accommodations, restaurants, and nightlife.
- **How-to:** How to pack a suitcase, find low airfares, find a doctor overseas, travel with children, save money on hotels. I used to have insomnia while traveling but eventually learned a few tricks to make it easier to sleep. I shared my tips in a 700-word article, did a mass mailing to newspapers, and made $500.
- **Humor:** When things go bad, turn it into a humor piece. I've stayed in supposedly "quaint" bed and breakfast inns, where quaint meant a tiny and dirty room.
- **Roundup:** Eight favorite wine country inns, children's museums in Missouri.
- **Seasonal:** Oktoberfest, Christmas, fall foliage.
- **Newsworthy:** Anniversary celebrations, beginning of a new airline route, opening of a resort, introduction of a new service.
- **Adventure:** Trekking in the Andes, river rafting in Idaho.
- **Special audiences:** RVers, bicyclists, disabled travelers.
- **Revelation of secrets:** Where to find the best, cheapest.

Look at articles carefully, noting their length, type of photos used, number of facts, inclusion of anecdotes. Some publications want lots of concrete information, such as what airlines fly there, how much hotels cost, where to eat. This information may be part of the article or can be put in a sidebar. Are the articles written in first or third person? Some publications want negative as well as positive aspects of a place. Was the beauty of the countryside spoiled by an infestation of black flies in July and August? Let your readers know.

Some authors go through articles with colored pens, underlining or highlighting facts in one color, quotes in another, and so on. Thus they have a graphic picture of the editor's prejudices. When their article is finished, they can match the color code to see if it's a fit for the magazine. This may seem cold blooded and mechanical, but sometimes you have to do things like that if you want to make a buck. If you want your creativity to run rampant, you can always try writing the great American novel.

You've got the perfect article ready to go—or at least the perfect idea for a story. How do you get your foot in the editor's door? In most cases, you will need to write a preliminary letter, or query, before you send an editor an article. The query letter should be concise but informative, no more than one page in length if possible. You should clearly define your topic, mention what photos are available, and give an approximate word count.

Your query letter is your major sales presentation and should be an attention grabber. You might use the lead paragraph of your article as the lead paragraph of the query. Also, give some information on your background and why you're the one person in the world who should write the article. If the magazine has published an article on a similar theme, mention that fact to show that you read the magazine—and then point out why your story is different. Send queries well in advance for seasonal articles, and always include a self-addressed stamped envelope for the editor's reply.

After you've written your query and polished it to a high gloss, it's a good idea to get feedback from other writers. Here in San Francisco, I belong to a group that meets monthly to critique each other's queries and articles. It's amazing to find out how many errors someone else can find in your work. Of course, they may make suggestions you don't agree with. The final decision is yours.

Some writers are now using computers to generate query letters. This can save a lot of time, but there are pitfalls. Unless you customize each letter, your queries may not be as relevant to each magazine. Just don't forget to change the salutation, or a letter to Mr. Doe at *XYZ Magazine* may start out with "Dear Ms. Smith." The problem with computers is that they can't read your mind, so make sure you know how to use the form-letter function of your word-processing program before doing a mass mailing with it.

Some magazine editors state they want to see clips from writers they haven't published before. That poses a dilemma if you've never been published: How do you submit samples of your published work? Don't despair—you *can* get published *somewhere*. My first published writing was in the newsletter of our local library. I didn't get paid for the article, but it was typeset and had my byline, so it looked very professional as a published clip. Of course, if your query letter does its work, the editor may be so bowled over that clips are irrelevant. You may want to consider those marginal markets that pay very little in order to get a first article sale.

I've included phone numbers in the listings, but it's not a good idea to query by phone, because the work day of most editors is hectic enough without receiving calls out of the blue from writers they don't know. The only exceptions would be if you have a hot story or are unexpectedly leaving on a trip and there won't be time for the regular channels of correspondence.

That said, my last two assignments resulted from phone calls. In the first case, the editor called me because a mutual friend told him about my knowledge of the subject for which he needed an article. We chatted briefly and I asked him to send me a follow-up confirmation letter. For the other article, a friend who's a contributing editor to a financial publication called and said his editor was looking for a destination piece about the site of the magazine's next convention. My friend told me the rate of pay, the deadline date, the article length, and how long it took for them to pay. I called the editor on his 800 number, got an idea of the slant he wanted, and sent off the article the next week.

Some magazines will accept complete manuscripts instead of queries. Include a cover letter introducing yourself, since some magazines like to give a brief biographical sketch of their authors. Also give information about photos that are available, if this is appropriate.

The whole querying process can be circumvented if you know an editor. My sister Joan, who is a nursery school teacher and had never had an article published, got an assignment through a rather unorthodox method. The editor of a state tourist magazine had a son in Joan's class. One day Joan stuck a note on his locker asking the editor if she'd like an article on a nearby state park. The editor liked the idea and talked to my sister about it as they were putting on snowsuits at the end of the day.

As in many fields, it's easier to get assignments if editors know you. One of my friends had been working full time in a factory and writing in his spare time. He was determined to make it as a freelancer so he made a trip to New York just to meet editors. He asked for ten minutes of their time, had his clips neatly arranged, made a brief sales presentation, and left. Shortly afterward, he was able to quit his stultifying job and do what he wanted to do for a living: write. Editors often turn up at writer's conferences so attendance at the conference may be profitable beyond just learning better ways to write.

Many writers ask if it's OK to submit articles or queries to different publications at the same time. It's not a good idea for magazines that directly compete with each other. However, there are so many magazines published for so many special interest groups that you can submit simultaneously to those that don't compete. However, to be sure that an editor accepts this practice, mention in your query letter that you are submitting simultaneously to noncompeting publications. Magazines are segmented by religious denomination, age group, sex, region, and hundreds of other affiliations. The people who read *Susie Homemaker* magazine won't be reading *Macho Man*; city magazines in California aren't read by Minnesotans.

Some publications have a policy of not allowing writers to accept free or subsidized travel, so if part or all of your trip has been paid for by an airline, hotel, cruise line, or tourist board, the editors don't want to publish an article about that trip. If the publication has such a policy, I clearly state in my cover letter that my trip did not involve a freebie.

Selling to Newspapers

Most newspaper travel editors prefer to see a complete manuscript rather than just a query. Newspaper travel sections rarely run anything over 1500 words, and most articles are between 1000 and 1200 words. Some will give their length requirement in inches. A column inch is one column wide and one inch high. You'll have to look at a copy of the newspaper to translate column inches into number of words.

You can submit the same article to many different papers at the same time if the circulation areas do not overlap. Some writers use a hundred-mile distance as a rule of thumb, but newspapers such as the *New York Times*, *Washington Post*, and *Christian Science Monitor* have wider circulation areas. Also, some newspapers want travel articles only about their own region.

When making multiple submissions, type "First Rights Your Circulation Area" in the upper right-hand corner of the first page. When submitting articles without photos, I include a postcard for the editors' responses and indicate that they can toss the manuscripts away if they don't use them. This saves them the trouble of returning the articles and means I get a faster response. If I send in photos, I include a SASE.

Newspapers don't pay as well as magazines, but with multiple submissions you can increase your earnings. For the same 1000-word article with one black-and-white photo, I've been paid from $50 to $150. This is not very much per sale, but by selling to several different newspapers, the total income from that piece was almost $1000.

Writers sometimes would like to sell their work to newspaper syndicates, but it's extremely hard to do so unless you're a recognized name. By making multiple submissions, you're self-syndicating so you don't have to share the profits with anyone else.

Manuscript Submission

The moment has come: You got the assignment, did your work, and have your final draft in front of you. Your final task is to see that your manuscript is submitted in a professional format. Submissions should be typed double spaced on white 8-½-by-11 paper. Manuscripts should be free of grammatical errors, misspellings, typographical errors, and coffee stains. If you want your masterpiece returned, include a self-addressed stamped envelope (SASE) that's big enough for your manuscript and photos. When writing from the United States to a Canadian or other foreign publication, include an International Reply Coupon. These are available at your local post office.

Your name, address, day and evening phone numbers, and Social Security number should be in the upper left-hand corner of the first page of your manuscript. In the upper right-hand corner, give an approximate word count, what rights you are selling, and a copyright notice. About a third of the way down the page, center your title in capital letters. Two spaces down, type "By" and two spaces below that, center your name. Start the article three or four spaces below your name. On succeeding pages, type your name, abbreviation of the title (a "slug"), and page number in the upper right-hand corner. At the bottom of the last page, let the editor know it's the end by typing "- THE END -". On all other pages type "- MORE -" at the bottom. Margins should be at least one inch on all sides.

Some publications will have other specifications for their submissions, such as the use of a certain style book, like *The Chicago Manual of Style* or Strunk and White's *The Elements of Style*. Some want articles typed in 40-character columns; others want a 60-character line. Also, it's best not to hyphenate words at the end of a line, and some publications prefer that you not break paragraphs from one page to another. It's always best to move one line of a paragraph to be with the rest of the paragraph if the line would otherwise be alone at the beginning or end of a page.

Selling Photographs

Photographs can be a great help in selling your article. If you're not a photographer, there are many ways of obtaining pictures. State tourist bureaus, the National Park Service, photo agencies, and freelance photographers are good sources.

It used to be true that newspapers took only black-and-white photos but today more and more are using color. I recently did a multiple submission to 15 newspapers. Only five of them took only black-and-white; the rest would take either black-and-white or color. For those places taking black-and-white, an 8-by-10 glossy is preferred. On the back of the photo, put a label on which you have typed a caption and your name and address. Don't write on the back in pencil or pen; this can show on the front and the editor won't be able to use it.

Most magazines want 35mm Kodachrome 64 transparencies (slides), although some specify 2¼-inch-square or 4-by-5. The slower film speed means you miss some shots in low light, but the color reproduces much better.

Slides should be submitted in plastic sleeves encased in cardboard. You may purchase the plastic sleeves at most camera stores. Top-loading slide holders are easier to use, but be sure they're wrapped tightly in cardboard. I once spoke to a frustrated editor who'd just received a submission where all the slides had slipped out of the sleeves and were jumbled in the bottom of the envelope. Your name and address and a brief slug should be on each slide in case it gets lost. I have a rubber stamp with my name, address, phone number, and a copyright notice.

The stamp is small enough to fit on the cardboard area surrounding the slide. By hand I write in a description of the slide in one or two words ("Gobi—camels") and give it a number. This number matches a longer description on a caption sheet that I submit with the slides.

When shooting, be sure to vary your shutter speed and composition. Many editors specify vertical orientation for cover shots, with a space at the top for the magazine's logo. If you're undecided whether to shoot black-and-white or color, there are several solutions. One would be to take two cameras, one loaded with each type of film. Another would be to shoot only color and have inter-negatives made from your transparencies. This can be expensive if you have a lot of shots you want to change, since each inter-negative can cost $8 or $9.

There's a great deal of debate about model releases. I don't usually bother unless a photo will be used for a commercial purpose, such as in a catalog. However, some editors do require model releases.

Selling Travel Books

When choosing where to submit your book manuscript, look at the listings in this book and do some browsing in your local bookstore. I am constantly amazed at writers who just send a manuscript any-where without knowing a thing about the publisher. I originally self-published this book and never had any thought of publishing books by other people. However, since I had in effect established a publishing company, I got outlines or manuscripts on new ways of treating varicose veins, how to buy antiques, and a novel about vampires in Italy. The American Association for Retired Persons won't take a book on traveling with toddlers. Make sure you are sending your manuscript to a publisher who might be interested in publishing it.

The procedure for submitting a travel book proposal will vary from house to house, but most publishers like an outline and sample chapters. In addition, you may be asked to tell where and how your book will be marketed, how your book is different from others on the market, and what your qualifications are for writing the book. (This is some-thing a good author will have thought carefully about and may decide to volunteer in the first place.)

After the publisher has indicated an interest in publishing your book, you'll receive a copy of a contract in the mail. When I received my first book contract, I almost had a panic attack. It was a nine page document with 22 clauses about many things I'd never considered.

Was the publisher trying to pull a fast one, or was that the way things were done in the publishing business? Fortunately, our area has a service that refers artists and writers to lawyers equipped to handle intellectual property issues. The first thing my lawyer mentioned was that there is no such thing as a standard contract, and everything can be negotiated. Of course, the more the publisher wants your book, the more leverage you'll have.

Some of the possibilities you'll face will be who holds the copyright, how much your royalty and advance will be, when royalties will be paid, what the policy on returns from booksellers is, and when the manuscript will be published and how long it will be. Other clauses deal with subsidiary rights (which in my contract had 13 subclauses), whether the publisher would like to have an option to publish your next book, what the budgets for promotion and advertising will be, and how you will be involved in promoting the book (for example, by going on tour). *The Writer's Legal Companion* gives advice on contracts, as well as information on copyright, libel, taxes, and agents (see the appendix).

Some writers might see getting an agent as the way to break into book publishing. However, most travel books don't sell well enough to make it worthwhile for an agent to represent travel writers.

Some travel writers have bypassed the hassle of book contracts by becoming self-publishers. If you go this route you have to do much more than write. You'll have to learn about book production, marketing, and distribution. Also, there's no guarantee you'll make any money. Many self-publishers lose money for three or four years or more before breaking even. One of my friends self publishes a travel book that's updated every two years, and after six years she finally made $14,000 in one year. If you have a family to support, that's not going to make it. However, if the book creates a distinctive market niche, a large publisher may then decide to publish the book. The benefits of self-publishing are that you have total editorial control and get to keep more of the profits. Also, having a self-published book gives you a product to show agents and publishers. After my self-published book came out, I was approached by an agent and several publishers. The negative aspects of self-publishing are that your time is taken away from writing, you have to assume the financial risk, and you don't have the marketing and distribution power of most publishers. There are several excellent books on self publishing, and information on these is given in the appendix.

Other Markets

Other ways to make money in travel writing are to write newsletters for travel agents (these are sent out to an agency's clients as a way of promoting certain destinations or services), or to write press releases or brochures for specialty travel companies or for convention and visitors bureaus. One of my friends started in this field by approaching her neighborhood travel agents and pitching the idea of a newsletter as a marketing device. They liked the idea, and after producing the newsletter for them she had a sample of work to take around to other prospective clients in her city. But even if you don't live near a big city you can carry on this type of business through the mail. If you've gone on a rafting trip or been on a trek through the Himalayas, write to the tour organizer and offer your services. Point out to them that having you write brochures and press releases for them can be more cost effective than placing expensive advertisements in a number of travel magazines.

You may also write special magazine sections called advertorials. These are 8- to 16-page magazine inserts that look like articles but are really promotional pieces for a specific country or region. Advertorials are usually produced by public relations firms or freelance writers. The sponsoring organization (a tourist board, for example) would be the one to contact to get paid for this type of work. Advertorials are harder to break into since most have larger budgets than do your local travel agents. Other writers are branching out into audio and video tapes.

Sample Query Letter
Name
Address
Phone

April 4, 1989

Mr. John Doe
Editor
XYZ Magazine
123 Travel Street
Mishmash Falls, OH 00000

Dear Mr. Doe:

To many of your readers, the Gobi Desert may seem like one of those legendary places, along with El Dorado and Shangri-la, that exist only in the realm of imagination. However, the Gobi is indeed real, and the government of the Mongolian People's Republic has established a comfortable tourist camp there.

I've just returned from the Gobi, and found it has more to offer than sand dunes. The dunes are there, it's true, but the tourist camp is also located near the Altai Mountains. The Mongolia tourist agency, Zhuulchin, takes visitors on a daytrip to the mountains, which feature a variety of wildlife, wildflowers, and even a small glacier. The cooks from the camp set up a Mongolian barbecue that is the basis for a bountiful picnic.

Another daytime adventure is a jaunt to a camel-breeding farm where we had the opportunity to ride a camel. In the evenings there are volleyball games, movies, lectures on Mongolian costumes, and even a nightclub. We were fortunate enough to be there during a full moon so enjoyed taking a stroll across the open spaces.

Only several hundred Americans go to the Gobi each year so it is definitely an off-the-beaten-path destination. Would you be interested in a 1600-word feature on the Gobi Desert? I have been reading *XYZ Magazine* for many years so have an idea of the type of articles you publish. I shot numerous photos in the Gobi with Kodachrome 64 film.

I have been a travel writer for nine years and have had articles published in newspapers and magazines in the United States, Canada, New Zealand, and England. I am enclosing published clips of my work (these need not be returned).

I look forward to hearing from you.

Yours truly,

Sample Article to Show Article Format

Elaine O'Gara
P.O. Box 7548
Berkeley, CA 94707
(415) 767-1234
SS# 000-00-0000

First rights your area
About 700 words
Copyright 1988 Elaine O'Gara

"TOWN WITH A NAME FOR SOAKING AND SOARING"
By Elaine O'Gara

Calistoga, California, has been popular as a spa since 1859, and I found out first hand that it's a place that can really stick with you.

On my honeymoon I took a mud bath wearing my shiny new textured-gold wedding ring, and today the mud is still a part of the ring's pattern in spite of all efforts to dislodge it.

Robert Louis Stevenson was another (perhaps more famous) person who spent his honeymoon in Calistoga. He and his bride camped out in a bunkhouse that was abandoned after a silver mine played out.

The site is now a state park, with a trail to the mine, and a longer trail to the top of Mt. St. Helena, an extinct volcano that offers superb views of the San Francisco Bay Area, the Pacific Ocean, and the Sierra Nevada mountains.

The founding father of Calistoga was newspaperman Sam Brannan, who coined the town's name to shows its intended position as the "Saratoga of California." He built a resort hotel, race track, and golf course, and persuaded the railroad to build a branch line to the town.

The hotel and race track have disappeared, but the local museum has a model of Calistoga in the 1860s so that today's visitors can see what drew the 19th-century San Francisco elite.

In the 20th century the mineral and mud baths have continued to attract people, and many motels have complete schedules of massage and acupressure.

For those who want special accommodation, there are several special places to stay in the Calistoga area. Foothill House has three guest suites with handmade quilts made by innkeeper Susan Clow. Each room has a private bath and fireplace, and the Evergreen Suite has a whirlpool.

The Calistoga Inn has homey, reasonably priced rooms, a lively bar, an excellent restaurant and its own brew pub.

- MORE -

The elegant Mount View Hotel has the mood of the Riviera in the '20s and '30s, and maids in traditional uniforms turn down the beds each evening.

For outdoor lovers, there is no lack of camping grounds, both public and private. Bothe-Napa Valley State Park has camping, picnicking, a swimming pool, and hiking trails through redwoods, Douglas fir, tan oak, and wildflowers.

In the summer, rangers hold campfire programs on the plants, wildlife, and history of the Napa Valley.

At the east end of the main street is the Calistoga depot, which was a railway station from 1868 until 1963, and in 1978 was revived as the home of specialty shops and a restaurant and soda fountain. A passenger coach inside the depot now houses the wine shop, where visitors can learn about fine wines.

Down the block from the depot is the Soaring Center, which is popular for its glider rides. The air currents of the Napa Valley make gliding an exciting but safe adventure.

A favorite activity for visitors to Calistoga is discovering some of the 70 nearby wineries. Chateau Montelena is small and easily missed if you don't know its location on Tubbs Lane. Once you're there, the wines are excellent and there is a lake with islands for picnicking.

Another out-of-the-way winery is Pope Valley, with rusting farm equipment in front and the tasting room in a barn. Many of the other wineries are family run and require an appointment for tasting and tours.

Scenic attractions nearby include the Old Faithful Geyser and the Petrified Forest of California. The geyser is one of the few regularly erupting geysers in the world, spouting up to 60 feet at intervals of 50 minutes. The Petrified Forest consists of redwoods turned to stone, of which the largest is the Monarch, 126 feet long.

From the delights of soaring in the clouds to the earthiness of wallowing in the mud, Calistoga has something for everyone.

• THE END •

2

Magazine Markets

THE magazine market listings are based on questionnaires sent to editors in September 1988. If an editor did not return the questionnaire, the information was gathered from writer's guidelines previously received from the magazine. In all cases, I give the date I received the information. Some listings also include a brief description of the magazine's contents based on a perusal of sample copies.

If an editor did not answer a question, I've left the question out of that listing. For example, most editors still do not accept electronic submissions, so they didn't fill in that blank. Also, some did not state how long after acceptance they publish an article. If they do not pay a kill fee, then I made no mention of kill fees. Finally, some editors do not want their phone numbers listed since they don't want to receive phone calls from writers.

I use the following abbreviations in the listings in the interest of brevity. See chapter 1 for definitions of these terms.

AR all rights
ASMP American Society of Magazine Photographers
BW black-and-white photos
CM complete manuscript
ES electronic submissions
FL freelance
FL/year Number of freelance travel articles published per year
F(NAS)R first (North American serial) rights
ms(s) manuscript(s)
NA North American
OTR one-time rights
POA pays on acceptance
POB post office box

POP pays on publication
PPS previously published submissions
PQ phone queries
SAE self-addressed envelope
SASE self-addressed stamped envelope (no. 10 with first-class stamp,
  unless otherwise noted)
SC sample copy
SQ simultaneous queries
SR second rights
SS simultaneous submissions
WG writer's guidelines

ACTIVE MARKETS

AAA Maine Motorist, POB 3544, Portland, ME 04104.
Editor: Ellen Kornetsky. Phone: 207-774-6377, ext. 289. Reply
date: 10/28/88. Seven times/year. Circulation: 110,000. FL/year:
6-8. POP. Buys OTR. Replies to queries in 2 months. Lead time
for seasonal articles: 4 months. Accepts PPS. Subsidized trips OK.
Prefers features of 750-1000 words. Departments or columns: 250-
500 words. Pays 10 cents/word. SC, WG: Write editor. **Photos:**
Photo editor: Ellen Kornetsky. Uses BW, color. Pays $10/BW,
$30/color. Buys OTR. POP. **Editorial Slant:** Published by the
Maine Automobile Association.

AAA Today, 1380 Dublin Road, No. 109, Columbus, OH 43215.
Executive editor: Johanna Guzik. Phone: 614-481-8088. Reply date:
9/30/88. Six times/year. Circulation: 1.7 million. FL/year: 12. POP.
Buys FR. Replies to queries in 1 week to 2 months. Lead time for
seasonal articles: 6 months. Accepts CM, SQ, SS, PPS, PQ. Subsidized trips OK. Prefers features of 700-1000 words. Pays $100
for article and photo package. SC and WG available. **Photos:** Uses
BW, transparencies. Rarely uses photos without mss.

AAA World, 8111 Gatehouse Road, Falls Church, VA 22047-0001.
Managing editor: Douglas Damerst. Phone: 703-222-6386. Reply
date: 4/14/88. Bimonthly. Circulation: 2.2 million in 12 regional
editions. POA. Buys OTR and nonexclusive reprint rights. Kill fee:
25 percent. Replies to queries in 2-4 weeks. Lead time for seasonal
articles: 4-6 months. Accepts CM. Prefers features of 600-1500
words. Departments or columns: 400-800 words. Pays $250-$600

for features, $75-$150 for departments. **Editorial Slant:** Features articles on foreign and domestic travel and tourism, destinations, and leisure activities.

AAA World, 590 Queen Street, Honolulu, HI 96813.
General manager: Thomas R. Crosby, Jr. Phone: 808-528-2600. Reply date: 9/30/88. Bimonthly. Circulation: 35,000. POP. Replies to queries 1 day after receiving them. Articles published according to editorial need. Accepts CM, SQ, SS, PPS, PQ. Subsidized trips OK. Prefers features of approximately 1500 words. Pays 10 cents/ word. SC, WG: SASE to AAA Hawaii at above address. **Photos:** Photo editor: Thomas R. Crosby, Jr. Uses BW. Pays $25. POP. Photos purchased without mss. **Editorial Slant:** For AAA Hawaii members. Sample articles, 3/88: "Alaskan Dream Cruise," "A City of Contrasts" (Hong Kong), "Australia Throws a Party," "Visiting India in Style."

ABC Star Service, 131 Clarendon Street, Boston, MA 02116.
Managing editor: Kathy O'Regan. Phone: 617-262-5000. Reply date: 10/28/88. Quarterly. Circulation: 7,000. 100 percent freelance written. POP. Replies to queries in no longer than 2 weeks. Articles published a week to several months after acceptance. Accepts CM, SQ, SS, PQ (but prefers written). ES: WordPerfect 4.2. Subsidized trips OK. Pays base rate of $18/hotel report, $30/cruise ship report; 15 cents/word for newsletter articles. WG and sample reports available. **Photos:** No photos used. **Editorial Slant:** Hotel directory for travel agents. Hotel and ship reports based on on-site inspections. Editorial schedule available.

Aboard Inflight Magazines, 777 41st Street, POB 40-2763, Miami Beach, FL 33140.
Editor: Cristina Juri Arencibia. Phone: 305-673-8577. Reply date: 9/30/88. Six times/year. Circulation: 98,000. POP. Buys first West- ern Hemisphere rights and SR. Replies to queries in 7 working days. Prefers features of 1500-1600 words. Pays $150 for article and photo package. SC, WG: Send note and SASE. **Photos:** Uses color transparencies. Pays after publication. **Editorial Slant:** Bi- lingual in-flight magazine for travelers to and from Latin America.

Accent, 1720 Washington Boulevard, POB 10010, Ogden, UT 84409.
Editor: Libby Hyland. Reply date: 9/30/88. Monthly. Circulation: 400,000. FL/year: 36-40. POA. Buys FNASR, nonexclusive reprint

rights. Replies to queries in 6-8 weeks. Lead time for seasonal articles: 6-8 months. Articles published 8-12 months after acceptance. Accepts CM, SQ, SS, PPS. ES: WordPerfect (3-1/2-inch diskette). Subsidized trips OK. Prefers features of 1200 words. Departments or columns: 800 words. Pays 15 cents/word. SC: 10-by-13 SAE and $1. WG: SASE. **Photos:** Photo editor: Libby Hyland. Uses four-color. Pays $35/color, $50/cover. Buys FR, nonexclusive reprint rights. POA. Photos purchased without mss. **Editorial Slant:** Articles should be timeless, noncontroversial, upscale, and positive. Exciting travel destinations in the United States, Canada, and other countries. Travel by car, plane, and cruise lines. Focuses on expensive destinations—resorts, health retreats, sports vacations, and large cities—as well as national parks and historic sites, with emphasis on fine accommodations. Sample articles: North Carolina's Crystal Coast, houseboating, "Five of Europe's Grandest Hotels."

ACCENT on Living, POB 700, Bloomington, IL 61702.
Editor: Betty Garee. Phone: 309-378-2961. Reply date: 9/30/88. Four times/year. Circulation: About 20,000. FL/year: 4-8. POP. Usually buys FR. Replies to queries in 2-3 weeks. Lead time for seasonal articles: 6 months. Accepts CM, SQ, SS. Subsidized trips OK. Prefers features of 750-1000 words. Departments or columns: 500 words. Pays 10 cents/word. SC: $3. WG: SASE. **Photos:** Photo editor: Betty Garee. Uses photos showing disabled people engaging in activities or work. Pays $10/BW, $100/cover. Buys FR or OTR. Usually POP. Photos not usually purchased without mss. **Editorial Slant:** For disabled individuals throughout the United States and several foreign countries, parents of disabled children, and specialists and counselors in the field of rehabilitation.

Adirondack Life, POB 97, Jay, NY 12941.
Editor: Christopher Shaw. Phone: 518-946-2191. Reply date: 9/30/88. Six times/year. Circulation: 40,000. POA. Buys FNASR. Kill fee: $100 or half word count. Replies to queries in 30 days. Lead time for seasonal articles: Query 1 year in advance. Accepts CM, SQ. Prefers features of 2000-3000 words. Departments or columns: 1000-1200 words. Pays up to 25 cents/word. Pays expenses. SC: Send cover price. WG: SASE. **Photos:** Photo editor: Nathan Farb. Uses transparencies. Scenic and action shots. Pays $25/BW, $50/color, $300/cover. Buys FNASR. POP. Photos purchased without mss. **Editorial Slant:** Covers the Adirondack Moun-

tains of New York state and the agricultural and industrial valleys of the adjacent North Country.

Adventure Road, 360 Madison Avenue, 10th Floor, New York, NY 10017.
Editor: Marilyn Holstein. Phone: 212-880-2282. Reply date: 9/30/88. Bimonthly. Circulation: 1.5 million. FL/year: 24. POA. Buys FR. Kill fee: 25 percent. Replies to queries in 1 month. Lead time for seasonal articles: 1 year. Articles published 2 months after acceptance. Accepts SQ, PPS. Subsidized trips OK. Prefers features of 1500 words. Departments or columns: 800 words. Pays $350-$750. SC and WG available. **Photos:** Photo editor: Joan Kittredge. Uses stock. Buys OTR. Pays on receipt of invoice. Photos purchased without mss. **Editorial Slant:** For members of Amoco Motor Club. Sample articles, 11-12/88: "San Diego's North County," "Celebrating a Creole Christmas," "The Magic of Mexico."

Adventure Travel 1989, Rodale Press, 135 N. Sixth Street, Emmaus, PA 18098.
Managing editor: Mark Jenkins. Phone: 215-967-5171. Reply date: 9/30/88. Annual. Circulation: 160,000. FL/year: 20. POA. Buys AR. Kill fee: 25 percent. Replies to queries in 6 weeks. Lead time for seasonal articles: 4 months. Articles published 3-6 months after acceptance. Accepts CM, PQ (sometimes). ES: XyWrite 3.3 (modem). Prefers features of 3000 words. Departments or columns: 1200-1500 words. Pay varies. Sometimes pays expenses. SC available. **Photos:** Photo editor: Mike Shaw. Uses color slides. Pay varies. Buys OTR, FNASR. POP. Photos purchased without mss.

Alaska Airlines, 1932 First Avenue, No. 403, Seattle, WA 98101-1075.
Associate editor: Giselle Smith. Reply date: 4/14/88. Monthly. POP. Buys FR. Kill fee: One-third. Lead time for seasonal articles: 3 months. Prefers features of 2000 words or more. Columns: 1200-1500 words. Pays $400 for features, $300 for columns. **Editorial Slant:** Covers anywhere Alaska Airlines flies, including California, Pacific Northwest, Alaska. Looks for features with personal hooks and strong, vivid writing, ranging from investigative articles to service pieces. Columns include "Sports," "On Location," "Arts & Entertainment," "Meals & Lodging," and "Alaska Lore." Sample articles, 4/88: "Meet Me in Seattle," Ketchikan, Portland's art galleries.

ALASKA Magazine, 808 E Street, Suite 200, Anchorage, AK 99501. Managing editor: Barbara Brynko. Phone: 907-272-6070. Reply date: 9/30/88. Monthly. Circulation: 235,000. FL/year: 20 or more. POA. Buys OTR. Kill fee: 25 percent for assigned articles. Replies to queries in 30 days or less. Lead time for seasonal articles: 6 months. Articles usually published within 6 months of acceptance. Accepts CM, PPS. Articles based on subsidized trips considered on a case-by-case basis. Prefers features of up to 2000 words; less is better. Departments or columns: 500 words. Pays $300-$600 for features. Pays expenses. SC and WG available. **Photos:** Photo editor: Ron Dalby. Uses 35mm or larger transparencies. Pays $30-$100/ BW, $40-$150/color, $350/cover. Buys OTR. POP. Photos purchased without mss. **Editorial Slant:** Nearly 85 percent of readers live outside of Alaska. Features range from one page to lengthy research and historical pieces. First-person stories desired. Covers variety of Alaskan subjects: hunting, fishing, art, history, adventure, hiking, bicycling, canoeing, kayaking, climbing, skiing, lifestyle, culture.

ALOHA, The Magazine of Hawaii and the Pacific, POB 3260, Honolulu, HI 96801.
Editor: Cheryl Tsutsumi. Reply date: 9/30/88. Six times/year. Circulation: 65,000. FL/year: 4-6. POP. Buys FNASR. Replies to queries in 2 months. Editorial schedule is done 1½ years in advance, though changes are made. Articles published 1 year after acceptance. Accepts CM, SQ, PQ. Subsidized trips OK. Prefers features of 2000-3500 words. Departments or columns: 800 words. Pays $200-$400. SC: $2.95. WG: SASE with request. **Photos:** Photo editor: Lance Tominaga. Uses 35mm transparencies. Shots of Hawaii. Pays $25/ BW, $60-$125/color, $175/cover. Buys OTR. Pays within 30 days of publication. Photos purchased without mss. **Editorial Slant:** Covers arts, people, sports, destinations, history, Hawaiiana. Sample articles, 6/88: "Hawaiian Folk Mass," "The Big Island in Bloom," Kyoto.

America West Airlines Magazine, 7500 North Dreamy Draw Drive, Phoenix, AZ 85020.
Editor: Michael Derr. Phone: 602-997-7200. Reply date: 10/13/ 88. Monthly. Circulation: 110,000. FL/year: 100 or more. POP. Buys FNASR. Kill fee: 15 percent. Replies to queries in 2 weeks. Lead time for seasonal articles: 6 months. Articles published 2-3

Active Markets

23

months after acceptance. Accepts CM, SQ, SS. Prefers features of 1800-2200 words. Departments or columns: 1200-1400 words. Pays $350-$750. Pays expenses. SC: $2 check. WG: SASE. **Photos:** Photo editor: Elizabeth Krecker. Uses transparencies. Buys OTR. POP. Photos purchased without mss as photo essays. **Editorial Slant:** Examples of features: "Being There," profile of an America West destination (Denver as a blend of the Old West and the New, San Jose installing its first downtown, Chicago's lakefront bringing citizens together, Oakland emerging from San Francisco's shadow); "Click," photo essay on a regional topic. Examples of departments: "Dateline," profile of one aspect of travel in a city or region (San Diego's oceanside activities, Vietnam Veterans Memorial, Baltimore's Harborplace shopping center); "Main Events," public events in a destination city.

America's Civil War, 105 Loudoun Street, S.W., Leesburg, VA 22075.
Editor: Roy Morris, Jr. Phone: 703-771-9400. Reply date: 9/30/88. See Empire Press.

American Golf, 4500 South Lakeshore, Tempe, AZ 85282.
Editor: Mike Cox. Phone: 602-268-2737. Reply date: 9/30/88. Six times/year. Circulation: 75,000. FL/year: 10. POP. Buys FNASR. Replies to queries in 4 weeks. Lead time for seasonal articles: 4 months. Articles published 2-6 months after acceptance. Accepts CM, SQ, SS. ES: Macintosh, IBM (diskette, modem). Subsidized trips OK. Prefers features of 800-1500 words. Departments or columns: 600 words. Pays $50-$300. Pays some expenses. SC and WG available. **Photos:** Photo editor: Mike Cox. Uses color transparencies. Pays $150/cover. Buys FNASR. POP. Photos purchased without mss.

American Way, POB 619616, MD2G23, DFW Airport, TX 75261-9616.
Executive editor: Doug Crichton. Phone: 817-355-1583. Reply date: 11/23/88. Semimonthly. Circulation: 55,000. POA. Buys exclusive world rights. Kill fee: Paid if there is a contract; varies with fee that was to be paid. Replies to queries in 1-2 weeks. Lead time for seasonal articles: 2 months. Accepts SQ. Prefers features of 1600-2500 words. Pays $450 or more for features, $100 or more for short items. Pays expenses if negotiated in contract. SC, WG: SASE. **Photos:** Photo editor: Doug Crichton. Uses BW, 35mm color tran-

sparencies (no originals). Pay varies. Buys OTR. POP. Photos purchased without mss. **Editorial Slant:** In-flight magazine of American Airlines.

American West, 7000 East Tanque Verde Road, Suite 30, Tucson, AZ 85715. Managing editor: Mae Reid-Bills. Phone: 602-886-9959. Reply date: 9/30/88. Bimonthly. Circulation: Approximately 185,000. FL/year: Approximately 12. POA. Buys FNASR. Replies to queries in 1-4 weeks. Lead time for seasonal articles: Approximately 6 months. Accepts CM. Prefers features of approximately 2500 words. Departments or columns: 750-1000 words. Pays $200-$800. SC: Cover price. WG: SASE with request. **Photos:** Photo editor: Mae Reid-Bills. Uses BW prints, color transparencies. Pay varies depending on size used; pays $200/cover. Buys OTR. POP. **Editorial Slant:** Links the contemporary West with its historic past, emphasizing places to see and things to do for Western travelers from the Mississippi to the Pacific. Sample articles: "Trailing Lewis and Clark on the Missouri," "Decoration of the Missouri Capitol," "The City of Rock," dude ranch sampler.

Americana, 29 West 38th Street, New York, NY 10018. Editor: Sandra Wilmot. Phone: 212-398-1550. Reply date: 9/30/88. Bimonthly. Circulation: 300,000. FL/year: 10-15. POA. Kill fee: Paid for assigned articles. Replies to queries in 3-4 months. Lead time for seasonal articles: 6 months. Articles usually published immediately after acceptance. Accepts CM. Subsidized trips OK. Prefers features of 2500 words. Departments or columns: 2000 words. Pays $450-$700. Sometimes pays expenses. SC: $3. WG: SASE. **Photos:** Art director: Mervyn Clay. Uses BW, color transparencies. Pay varies. Buys FNASR. POP. Photos purchased without mss. **Editorial Slant:** Uses U.S. history to enhance readers' lifestyles. Travel emphasis is on places the reader can visit to relive some part of the past.

Americas, 1889 F Street, N.W., Washington, DC 20006. Managing editor: Catherine Healy. Reply date: 4/14/88. Bimonthly. Prefers features of up to 2500 words. Pays at least $200. **Photos:** Uses BW 8-by-10, color transparencies. **Editorial Slant:** Published by the Organization of American States, in English and Spanish editions. Seeks to advance mutual understanding among the peoples of the Western Hemisphere. Articles on anthropology, archeology, history, the visual arts, architecture, travel, wildlife.

Amtrak Express, 140 East Main, Huntington, NY 11743. Editor: Christopher Podgus. Phone: 516-385-9299. Reply date: 10/28/88. Bimonthly. Circulation: 380,000. FL/year: 6-8. Pays 2 months after acceptance. Buys FNASR. Kill fee: Payment depends on circumstances. Replies to queries in 6-10 weeks at most. Lead time for seasonal articles: 3-4 months. Accepts CM, SQ, SS, PPS, PQ (rarely). ES: IBM PC XT compatible; WordPerfect and WordStar after 7/89. Subsidized trips rarely acceptable. Prefers features of 1200-1800 words. Departments or columns: Up to 1000 words. Pays $400-$850. Pays expenses. SC: $2.50. WG available. **Photos:** Photo editor: Christopher Podgus. Pays $50-$80/BW, $80-$125/color, $800/cover. Buys NA serial rights. Pays for photos 3-4 months after acceptance of article. Photos almost never purchased without mss. **Editorial Slant:** General interest magazine distributed aboard Amtrak trains nationwide. Readers are business and professional people as well as leisure travelers. Articles on travel within Amtrak territory. Sample articles, 8-9/88: Washington's Union Station, dinosaurs, Pittsburgh.

Angling Adventures, POB 999, Brainerd, MN 56401-0999. Executive editor: Dave Csanda. Phone: 218-829-1648. Reply date: 6/24/88. Quarterly. POP. Lead time for seasonal articles: 6 months. Prefers features of 1000-2500 words. Departments or columns: 500-750 words. Pays $100-$500. **Photos:** Uses color transparencies. Superb full-color photography is essential to each and every article. **Editorial Slant:** Travel and lifestyle magazine geared to anglers, their families, and their friends. Stresses the local charm of destinations and the personality of the local people rather than technical fishing information. Sample articles, Winter 1988: "An Angling Adventure in the Adirondacks," "The Ventuari River" (Venezuela), "Trosa in Sweden."

Arizona Highways, 2039 West Lewis Avenue, Phoenix, AZ 85009-9988. Editor: Merrill Windsor. Phone: 602-271-5900. Reply date: 9/30/88. Monthly. Circulation: 415,000. FL/year: 25-30. POA. Buys FNASR. Replies to queries in 2-4 weeks. Lead time for seasonal articles: 7 months. Accepts CM, SQ, SS. Prefers features of 2000 words. Pays 35-50 cents/word. Pays expenses for assigned articles. SC, WG: Write. **Photos:** Photo editor: Peter Ensenberger. Uses four-color scenic shots. Pays $80-$350/color, $500/cover. Buys OTR. POP. Photos purchased without mss. **Editorial Slant:** Promotes travel to and through the state of Arizona. Also covers Mexico. Buys adventure, history, nature, arts and crafts, lifestyle articles.

Arizona Living, 5046 North Seventh Street, Phoenix, AZ 85014. Assistant managing editor: Kiana Dicker. Phone: 602-264-4295. Reply date: 9/30/88. Monthly. Circulation: 17,000. FL/year: 8-10. POP. Buys exclusive Arizona rights. Replies to queries in 2-4 weeks. Lead time for seasonal articles: 4 months or more. Articles published 2-3 months after acceptance. Subsidized trips OK. Prefers features of 1200-2000 words. Departments or columns: 80-800 words. Pays $35-$250. SC: $3.20. WG: SASE. **Photos:** Photo editor: Michael Green. Primarily uses BW; ask about color. Buys OTR. POP. Photos purchased without mss. **Editorial Slant:** The only statewide general interest magazine in Arizona. Subscribers are affluent Arizonans. Subject is primarily Arizona but also the rest of the Southwest if there is an Arizona angle.

AsiAm, 12100 Wilshire Boulevard, Suite 1050, Los Angeles, CA 90025. Query articles editor. Phone: 213-826-7818 (no PQ). Reply date: 9/30/88. Monthly. Circulation: 50,000. FL/year: 10-14. POP. Buys exclusive rights for 1 year. Kill fee: 25 percent. Replies to queries in 2-8 weeks. Lead time for seasonal articles: 5 months. Articles published 6-12 weeks after acceptance. Accepts CM, SQ, SS, PPS. Subsidized trips OK. Prefers features of 3000 words. Departments or columns: 1000 words. Pays $100-$700. SC: $4.50. WG: SASE with request. **Photos:** Submit photos to articles editor. Rarely uses BW prints. Uses color slides. Pay for photos is included in fee for article. Buys exclusive rights for 1 year. POP. **Editorial Slant:** For Asian Americans. Readers are college-educated professionals who like to do their own thinking.

ASU Travel Guide, 1325 Columbus Avenue, San Francisco, CA 94133. Managing editor: Brady Ennis. Phone: 415-441-5200. Reply date: 9/30/88. Quarterly. Circulation: 50,000. FL/year: 16. POP. Buys OTR. Replies to queries in 2-4 weeks. Lead time for seasonal articles: 3 months. Articles published 3 months after acceptance. Accepts

PPS. Subsidized trips OK. Prefers features of 1500-1800 words. Departments or columns: 250 words. Pays $200/article. SC available at editor's discretion. WG: SASE. **Photos:** Photo editor: Brady Ennis. Uses BW glossies, 35mm color slides (vertical format for cover). Pays up to $200/cover. POA. Buys OTR. Photos sometimes purchased without mss. **Editorial Slant:** For airline employees. Readers are interested in how to visit a destination inexpensively. Prefers on-the-beaten-track destinations.

Atlantic Salmon Journal, 1435 St. Alexandre, No. 1030, Montreal, Quebec, Canada H3A 2G4.
Managing editor: Terry Davis. Reply date: 3/1/88. Quarterly. Circulation: 20,000. Buys FR. Replies to queries in 6-8 weeks. Accepts SS and PPS, but these are not encouraged. Prefers features of 800-2500 words. Pays $100-$250. SC: Free. **Photos:** Uses BW, color. Bold action shots of Atlantic salmon fishing and management. Pays $30-$75/BW, $100-$250/color, up to $350/cover. **Editorial Slant:** Readers are dedicated salmon anglers and conservationists interested in new places to fish. Uses informative, lively features on foreign or domestic salmon fishing trips.

Backpacker, Rodale Press, 33 East Minor Street, Emmaus, PA 18098.
Managing editor: Tom Shealey. Phone: 215-967-5171. Reply date: 9/12/88 (WG were being revised). Bimonthly. Circulation: 165,000. POA. Buys AR or OTR. Replies to queries in 6-8 weeks. Lead time for seasonal articles: 4-5 months. Accepts CM. Prefers features of

AR	all rights	OTR	one-time rights
ASMP	American Society of	POA	pays on acceptance
	Magazine	POB	post office box
	Photographers	POP	pays on publication
BW	black-and-white photos	PPS	previously published
CM	complete manuscript		submissions
ES	electronic submissions	PQ	phone queries
FL	freelance	SAE	self-addressed envelope
FL/year	number of freelance travel	SASE	self-addressed stamped envelope
	articles published per	SC	sample copy
	year	SQ	simultaneous queries
F(NAS)R	first (North American serial)	SR	second rights
	rights	SS	simultaneous submissions
ms(s)	manuscript(s)	WG	writer's guidelines
NA	North American		

2000-3000 words. Departments or columns: 50-1500 words. Pays at least $350 for features, $25-$350 for departments. **Photos:** Photo editor: Mike Shaw. **Editorial Slant:** Articles focus on a wide range of self-propelled, self-contained outdoor activities in natural areas of North America and occasionally other continents. Topics include backpacking, climbing, mountaineering, canoe and kayak touring, mountain biking, off-track cross-country skiing. Sometimes covers caving, snowshoeing, paragliding, fishing, and birdwatching.

BC Outdoors, 202-1132 Hamilton Street, Vancouver, British Columbia, Canada V6B 2S2.
Phone: 604-687-1581. Reply date: 1/2/88. Ten times/year. Pays within 30 days of publication. Buys FNASR. Replies to queries in 4-6 weeks. Lead time for seasonal articles: 3 months. Accepts PPS. Prefers features of 750-2000 words. Pays up to $400. **Photos:** Uses BW 8-by-10 glossies, 35mm color negatives or slides, 2¼-inch transparencies. Pay for most photos is included in fee for article. For photos used alone, pays $30-$100/photo, $150/cover. Photos purchased without mss. **Editorial Slant:** More than 75 percent of readers fish, and more than 60 percent hunt. Where-to fishing, hunting, and camping articles constitute much of editorial material.

The Best Report, 140 East 45th Street, 36th Floor, New York, NY 10017.
Query Peter Filichia. Phone: 212-983-4320. Reply date: 9/30/88. Monthly. Circulation: 100,000. FL/year: 30-50. POA. Buys FNASR. Kill fee: 25 percent. Replies to queries in 1-3 weeks. Lead time for seasonal articles: 3 months. Articles published within 3 months of acceptance. Accepts CM, SQ. ES: Preferred; DOS, XyWrite. Subsidized trips OK. Prefers features of 1500 words. Departments or columns: 750 words. Pays 30 cents/word. SC: $3. WG: SASE. **Photos:** Photo editor: Dan Richards. Uses color slides. Pays $20/color. Buys FNASR. POA. Photos purchased without mss. **Editorial Slant:** Details high-quality travel in a concise, informative style. Background, where to go. Sample articles: "Luxury Rafting on the Rapids," "A Trip on the *Flying Scotsman.*"

Better Homes and Gardens, 1716 Locust Street, Des Moines, IA 50336.
Travel/pet editor: Mark Ingebretsen. Phone: 515-284-3000. Reply date: 10/1/88. Monthly. Circulation: 8 million. 10-15 percent freelance written. POA. Buys FR or AR. Kill fee: 25 percent. Replies

to queries in 3-4 weeks at most. Lead time for seasonal articles: 6 months. Accepts SQ, SS. Pay varies. Pays expenses. SC: On newsstands. WG: Write. **Photos:** Photo editor: Mark Ingebretsen or Jane Reiling. Uses color. Shots of families or children in scenic or regional settings. Pay varies depending on size used. Buys OTR; AR on assignments. Pays after copyright release is signed and returned with an invoice. **Editorial Slant:** Focuses on the home, community, and family. Sample article, 6/88: "Lake Michigan."

Bicycle Guide, 711 Boylston Street, Boston, MA 02116.
Managing editor: Karen Angeline. Phone: 617-236-1885. Reply date: 9/30/88. Nine times/year. Circulation: 175,000. FL/year: 5-6. POA or POP. Replies to queries in 2-4 weeks. Rarely accepts CM. Subsidized trips sometimes OK. Prefers features of 1000-1500 words. Pays $150-$400. Rarely pays expenses. SC: $3 check. WG: SASE. **Photos:** Art director: Cynthia Davis. Pay varies. **Editorial Slant:** Easiest way to get published is in "Rides" section, where articles report on 50- to 100-mile domestic bicycle rides in interesting and scenic areas, also covers foreign rides if story has an interesting angle.

Bicycling, Rodale Press, 33 East Minor Street, Emmaus, PA 18098.
Editor: James McCullagh. Phone: 215-967-5171. Reply date: 5/20/88. Ten times/year. Circulation: 250,000. POP. Buys AR. Lead time for seasonal articles: 4-5 months. Accepts CM only. Prefers features of 1000-2500 words. **Photos:** Uses BW Plus-X or Tri-X. Uses mostly color (35mm preferred, 2¼-inch acceptable; Kodachrome 64 or 25). Buys AR. POP. **Editorial Slant:** Articles on touring, containing local color mixed with anecdotes, suggested sightseeing stops, accommodations, primarily in the United States and Canada.

Bird Watcher's Digest, POB 110, Marietta, OH 45750.
Editor: Mary B. Bowers. Phone: 614-373-5285. Reply date: 11/19/88. Bimonthly. Circulation: 75,000. FL/year: 6. POP. Buys OTR. Replies to queries in 6-8 weeks. Lead time for seasonal articles: 12 weeks. Articles published 6-24 months after acceptance. Prefers CM; accepts PPS. Subsidized trips sometimes OK. Prefers features of 2000-2500 words. Pays at least $50 for originals, at least $25 for reprints. SC: $3. WG: SASE. **Photos:** Photo editor: William H. Thompson 3rd. Uses 35mm four-color transparencies. Pays at least $25. Buys OTR. POP. Photos purchased without mss. **Editorial Slant:** Advice about where to go to see birds.

Blue Ridge Country, POB 12567, Roanoke, VA 24026.
Editor: Kurt Rheinheimer. Phone: 703-989-6138. Reply date: 10/13/88. Bimonthly. Circulation: 30,000. FL/year: 6-12. POP. Buys FNASR. Replies to queries in 1-2 months. Lead time for seasonal articles: 4-6 months. Articles published 3-5 months after acceptance. Accepts CM, SQ. Prefers features of 1400 words. Departments or columns: 300 words. Pays $25-$200. Occasionally pays expenses. SC: SASE with $1.85 postage. WG: SASE. **Photos:** Photo editor: Kurt Rheinheimer. Uses color slides. Pays $25/color, $100/cover. Buys OTR. POP. Photos purchased without mss.

Boat Pennsylvania, POB 1673, Harrisburg, PA 17105-1673.
Editor: Art Michaels. Phone: 717-657-4520. Reply date: 5/19/88. Quarterly. POA. Buys AR; after publication, rights may be reassigned. Replies to queries in 1-2 weeks. Lead time for seasonal articles: 8 months. Accepts CM, PPS. Prefers features of up to 1500 words. Departments or columns: 150-300 words. Pays $50-$200 for article and photo package. **Photos:** Uses BW 5-by-7 or 8-by-10 glossies, 35mm and larger color transparencies (Kodachrome 64 and 25). For photos used alone, pays $5-$20/BW, $15-$50/color, $150/front cover, $50/back cover. Photos purchased without mss. **Editorial Slant:** The official voice of the Pennsylvania Fish Commission. Serves the state's powerboaters, canoeists, kayakers, rafters, water-skiers, and sailors. Articles include details on how to boat particular Pennsylvania waterways, facilities in the area, and technically accurate how-to information.

Boca Raton, Amtec Center, 6413 Congress Avenue, No. 100, Boca Raton, FL 33487.
Editor-in-chief: Debra Silver. Phone: 407-997-8683. Reply date: 10/12/88. Bimonthly. Circulation: 50,000. FL/year: 7-10. POA. Buys FNASR, reprint rights. Kill fee: Negotiable. Replies to queries in 2 months. Lead time for seasonal articles: 2 months. Accepts SQ, PPS. Subsidized trips OK. Prefers features of up to 2500 words. SC: $3.50 to Circulation Department. WG: Use SC as guidelines. **Photos:** Photo editor: Brian Black. Uses color slides. Pay negotiable. Pays 1 month before publication. Photos purchased without mss. **Editorial Slant:** Readers are affluent, college educated. Travel articles cover special destinations in Florida and around the country, from family getaways to romantic retreats.

Bon Appétit, 5900 Wilshire Boulevard, Los Angeles, CA 90036. Executive editor: Barbara Fairchild. Phone: 213-937-1025. Reply date: 10/3/88. Monthly. Circulation: 1.3 million. FL/year: 24. POA. Buys AR. Replies to queries in 4-6 weeks. Lead time for seasonal articles: 8-12 months. Subsidized trips OK. Prefers features of 1500 words. Departments or columns: 1500 words. Pays at least $800. SC: On newsstands. WG: SASE. **Photos:** All photography is assigned to a regular stable of freelance photographers. **Editorial Slant:** Gastronomically focused travel. Subject matter should have nationwide appeal.

Braniff, 9600 S.W. Oak Boulevard, No. 310, Portland, OR 97223. Editor: Terri J. Wallo. Phone: 503-244-2299. Reply date: 4/14/88. See Skies America. Hub cities for Braniff are Dallas, Orlando, and Kansas City. Sample articles, 9/88: Albuquerque, "Santa Fe's Focus on Photography."

Bridal Trends, 1720 Washington Boulevard, POB 10010, Ogden, UT 84409.
Phone: 801-394-9446. Reply date: 10/2/88. Monthly. POA. Buys FR, SR, nonexclusive reprint rights. Replies to queries in 6 weeks. Lead time for seasonal articles: 6-8 months. Accepts PPS. Prefers features of 1200 words. Pays 15 cents/word for FR. SC: 9-by-12 SAE and $1. WG: SASE. **Photos:** Prefers 4-by-5 or 2¼-inch color transparencies; accepts color prints. Pays $35/inside, $50/cover. Buys FR and nonexclusive reprint rights. **Editorial Slant:** Honeymoon destinations.

British Travel Letter, 11846 Balboa Boulevard, No. 285, Granada Hills, CA 91344.
Editor: Neil Saunders. Phone: 818-368-7567. Reply date: 10/28/88. Monthly newsletter. FL/year: Numerous. POP. Buys AR. Replies to queries in 1-2 weeks. Lead time for seasonal articles: 2-3 months. Articles usually published 1-2 months after acceptance. Accepts SQ, SS, PPS, PQ. ES: Macintosh, preferably Microsoft Word. Subsidized trips OK. Prefers features of 1000-2500 words. Departments or columns: 250-1000 words. Pays $20-$200. Pays British contributors 10-120 pounds. Pays postage. SC: $3. WG: SASE. **Photos:** Uses no photos. Uses line illustrations. **Editorial Slant:** Provides frequent American visitors to Great Britain with recommendations, suggestions, and tips on things to see and do, including a special emphasis on traveling off the beaten track.

Business Travel News, 600 Community Drive, Manhasset, NY 11030. Editor: Jim Alkon. Phone: 516-562-5000. Reply date: 9/30/88. 32 times/year. Circulation: 54,000. FL/year: 120. POA. Kill fee: Negotiable. Accepts PQ, ES. Pays $10/column inch. Pays expenses. **Editorial Slant:** For qualified travel arrangers.

Business Traveler International, 41 East 42nd Street, No. 1512, New York, NY 10017. Editor: Terence Murphy. Phone: 212-697-1700. Reply date: 9/30/88. Monthly. Circulation: 40,000. FL/year: 10-25. POA. Buys AR for 2 years. Kill fee: 5-7 percent. Replies to queries in 1 month. Lead time for seasonal articles: 4 months. Articles published 90 days after acceptance. ES: WordPerfect (diskette). Prefers features of 1500-2500 words. Departments or columns: 750-1000 words. Pays up to 50 cents/word. Pays expenses. SC available.

Camp-orama, 7077 South Tamiami Trail, Sarasota, FL 34231. Editor: Carole Yellen. Phone: 813-922-2111. Reply date: 9/30/88. Monthly. Circulation: 29,000. FL/year: Over 40. POP. Buys first Florida rights for RV publications. Replies to queries in 1-2 weeks. Lead time for seasonal articles: 2-3 months. Articles published within 4-6 months of acceptance. Accepts CM, some SS, PPS, PQ. Prefers features of 500-1000 words. Departments or columns: 500-1000 words. Pays 5 cents/word, $25/reprint. SC: $2. WG: Write or phone. **Photos:** Photo editor: Carole Yellen. Uses BW. Pays $5/BW, $25/cover. Buys first Florida rights for RV publications. POP. Photos purchased without mss. **Editorial Slant:** One of the largest newspapers on camping and RVs, circulated in Florida and the Southeast. Articles cover interesting places to go and things to do in Florida and the Southeast, the RV lifestyle, and camping or outdoor trips.

Camperways, 1108 North Bethlehem Pike, POB 460, Spring House, PA 19477. Editor: Donna S. Miller. Phone: 215-643-2058. Reply date: 9/30/88. 10 times/year. Circulation: 35,000. FL/year: Approximately 90. POP. Buys first regional rights and second (reprint) regional rights. Replies to queries in 1 month. Lead time for seasonal articles: 3 months. Articles published as soon as possible after acceptance. Accepts CM, SQ, SS, PPS. Subsidized trips OK. Prefers features of 1200-2000 words. Pays up to $80 for first rights for 57 column inches. SC: $2 check. WG: SASE. **Photos:** Photo editor: Donna S.

Miller. Uses BW. Pays $10/BW if author's photo, $5/BW if obtained by author from other source, $25/cover. Buys first regional and second (reprint) regional rights. Pays after publication. **Editorial Slant:** Regional camping publication serving a seven-state area from New York to Virginia. Emphasis is on places to go and things to do on close-to-home camping trips for campers living in and near the metropolitan corridor that runs from the lower Hudson Valley to Northern Virginia. Publishes annual snowbird issue in October featuring articles on Florida and other Sunbelt states.

Campus USA, 1801 Rockville Pike, No. 216, Rockville, MD 20852. Editor: Gerald S. Snyder. Phone: 301-468-1010. Reply date: 9/30/88. Five times/year. Circulation: 600,000. FL/year: 10. POP. Buys AR. Replies to queries in 2-3 weeks. Lead time for seasonal articles: 3 months. Articles published 2-3 months after acceptance. Accepts CM, SQ, SS. Subsidized trips OK. Prefers features of 1200-1500 words. Departments or columns: 800 words. Pays $150-$500. Sometimes pays expenses. SC: SASE with $1.45 postage. WG available. **Photos:** Uses photos only with articles.

Canadian Geographic, 488 Wilbrod Street, Ottawa, Ontario, Canada K1N 6M8. Editor: Ross Smith. Phone: 613-236-7493. Reply date: 6/8/88. Bimonthly. Circulation: 141,000. Buys AR for assigned articles, FR for others. Prefers features of 2000-3000 words. Pays 30 cents/word. **Photos:** Pays $50-$200/color, $400/cover. Photos purchased without mss. **Editorial Slant:** Published by the Royal Canadian Geographical Society. Welcomes articles of a high caliber on appropriate Canadian subjects. Topics include geography, anthropology, archeology, architecture, wilderness exploration, wildlife, national and provincial parks, scenic wonders and natural beauty, mountains and mountaineering, natural phenomena. Sample articles, 4-5/88: "Mennonites Break New Ground in Northern Alberta," right whales along Canada's east coast, "Old Fort Franklin."

Canadian Magazine, 1705 10th Avenue, S.W., Calgary, Alberta, Canada T3C 0K1. Editor: Frann Harris. Phone: 403-244-7516. Reply date: 10/12/88. Monthly. Circulation: Approximately 90,000. FL/year: 12. POA. Buys FNASR. Kill fee varies. Lead time for seasonal articles: 4-6 months. Articles published 3-4 months after acceptance. Accepts SQ, SS. Subsidized trips sometimes OK. Prefers features of 2000-

2500 words. Departments or columns: 800-1000 words. Pays 35 cents/word. Pays expenses if agreed on in advance. SC: Request by phone. WG: Not yet available as editor is new. **Photos:** Art director: Karin Schrik. Uses transparencies. Pays $200/full page color, $400/ cover. Buys OTR. POP. Photos purchased without mss. **Editorial Slant:** In-flight magazine of Canadian Airlines. Sample articles, 10/ 88: "New Zealand, Island of Surprises," skiing in Alberta and Quebec.

Canoe, POB 3146, Kirkland, WA 98083.
Query Bart Parrot. Phone: 206-827-6363. Reply date: 9/30/88. Six times/year. Circulation: 55,000. FL/year: 40. POP. Buys FR and reprint rights. Kill fee: One-third (paid very infrequently). Replies to queries in 30 days. Lead time for seasonal articles: 3 months. Articles published 2 months after acceptance. Accepts CM. ES: MS-DOS, ASCII (5¼-inch diskette). Subsidized trips OK. Prefers features of 2000-4000 words. Departments or columns: 1500 words. Pays $5/column inch. SC and WG available. **Photos:** Photo editor: Bart Parrot. Uses BW prints, color transparencies. Pays $25-$100/ BW, $50-$100/color, $250/cover. Buys FNASR, OTR. POP. Photos infrequently purchased without mss. **Editorial Slant:** "Destinations" features tell the story of a special place to take a canoe or kayak. "Short Strokes" department reports on interesting but easily accessible canoe trips, not over three or four days in duration.

Cape Cod Compass, POB 375, Chatham, MA 02633.
Editor/publisher: Andrew Scherding. Reply date: 4/14/88. POA. Buys FR, one-year exclusivity. Kill fee: Up to 25 percent. Replies to queries in 2-6 weeks. Articles published up to 1 year after acceptance. Pays $250-$800 for assigned articles, $200-$500 for non-assigned articles. Pays some expenses.

Cape Cod Life, POB 222, Osterville, MA 02655.
Phone: 508-428-5706. Reply date: 4/29/88. Six times/year. Pays within 30 days of publication. Buys FNASR and reprint rights. Kill fee: 20 percent. Replies to queries in 1 month. Lead time for seasonal articles: 5 months. Accepts CM. Prefers features of 1500-3000 words. Pays 10 cents/word. Pays expenses for some writers on assignment. **Photos:** Uses BW prints or proof sheets, 35mm or larger color transparencies. Pays $7.50-$15/BW, $10-$20/color. Buys FR, reprint rights. **Editorial Slant:** Regional magazine about Cape Cod, Martha's Vineyard, and Nantucket designed to appeal to year-round

and seasonal residents as well as to repeat visitors. Areas of interest: activities, the arts, history, legends, the environment.

Caribbean Travel and Life, 8403 Colesville Road, Silver Spring, MD 20910. Editor: Veronica Stoddart. Phone: 301-588-2300. Reply date: 9/30/88. Bimonthly. Circulation: 80,000. FL/year: 70. POP. Buys FNASR. Kill fee: 25 percent. Replies to queries in 2 months. Lead time for seasonal articles: 6-8 months. Articles usually published 2-3 months after acceptance. Accepts CM, SQ. Subsidized trips OK. Prefers features of 2500 words. Departments or columns: 1000-1500 words. Pays $550 for features, $200 for departments. SC: SASE with $1.08 postage. WG: SASE. **Photos:** Photo editor: Sharon Jaffe. Uses 35mm or larger color transparencies. Pays $75-$150/color, $400/cover. Buys OTR. POP. Photos purchased without mss. **Editorial Slant:** Devoted exclusively to the unique vacation, travel, recreational, cultural, and investment opportunities offered by the diverse islands of the Caribbean, the Bahamas, and Bermuda. Readers are sophisticated and upscale. Features, which deal with specific aspects of travel and life in the Caribbean, include travelogues and destination pieces, stories of cultural and historical interest, articles about sports and recreational vacations, reports on special events, and service pieces on shopping, dining, and cruises.

Cascades East, POB 5784, Bend, OR 97708. Editor: Geoff Hill. Phone: 503-382-0127. Reply date: 10/12/88. Quarterly. Circulation: 11,000. FL/year: 10. POP. Usually buys OTR; sometimes buys AR. Replies to queries in 2 months. Lead time for seasonal articles: 6 months or more. Articles published 6 months to 1 year after acceptance. Accepts CM, SQ, SS, PPS, PQ. Prefers features of 1000-2000 words. Departments or columns: 500-1000 words. Pays 3-10 cents/word. SC: $3.50. WG available. **Photos:** Photo editor: Geoff Hill. Uses BW glossies, transparencies. Pays $8-$25/BW, $10-$35/color, $75/cover. Buys OTR. POP. Photos purchased without mss. **Editorial Slant:** Central Oregon's recreational quarterly. Uses first-person accounts of outdoor activities.

Chevy Outdoors, 3221 West Big Beaver, No. 110, Troy, MI 48084. Editor: Michael Brudenell. Phone: 313-643-7050. Reply date: 10/13/88. Quarterly. Circulation: 1.1 million. FL/year: Approximately 50. POA. Buys mainly FNASR. Kill fee: 25 percent. Replies to queries in 3-4 weeks. Lead time for seasonal articles: 3 months.

Articles published 3-9 months after acceptance. Accepts CM, SQ, SS, PPS. Subsidized trips OK. Prefers features of 1000-1500 words. Departments or columns: 800-1000 words. Pays $600-$750 for features, $600 for departments. SC, WG: Write editor. **Photos:** Photo editor: Leonard Loria. Uses transparencies, color prints. Pays at least $250/color, at least $500/cover. Buys mainly FNASR. POA. Photos purchased without mss. **Editorial Slant:** Primarily for outdoors enthusiasts who own recreational vehicles. Editor looks for the atypical in destination pieces.

Cincinnati Magazine, 409 Broadway, Cincinnati, OH 45202.
Editor: Lilia Brady. Phone: 513-421-4300. Reply date: 9/30/88. Monthly. Circulation: 32,000. FL/year: 7-10. POA. Buys FR. Replies to queries in 3-4 weeks. Lead time for seasonal articles: 2 months. Articles published 2-3 months after acceptance. Accepts CM. Subsidized trips OK. Prefers features of 1000-1500 words. Pays $100-$200. SC and WG available. **Photos:** Photo editor: Thomas Hawley. Uses BW glossies. Pays $25/BW. POP. **Editorial Slant:** A city magazine for readers who are college educated, have a high income, and work as professionals or managers.

City Sports, POB 3693, San Francisco, CA 94119.
Editor: Jane McConnell. Phone: 415-546-6150. Reply date: 9/30/88. Monthly. Circulation: 330,000. FL/year: 12-25. POP. Buys FNASR. Kill fee: One-third. Replies to queries in 4-8 weeks. Lead time for seasonal articles: 4 months. Articles published 2-3 months after acceptance. Accepts SQ, SS. Subsidized trips OK. Prefers features of 1200-1500 words. Departments or columns: 500-1000 words. Pays $150-$650. SC: $3. WG: SASE. **Photos:** Photo editor: Rico Mendez. Uses BW, color. Pays $50-$150/BW, $75-$200/color, $200-$400/cover. Buys FR. POP. Photos purchased without mss. **Editorial Slant:** Nationwide publication covering participatory sports, including running, bicycling, tennis, skiing, golf, the outdoors, walking, travel. Publishes four editions: Northern California, Southern California, New York, and Boston.

Coast & Country, 644 Humphrey Street, No. 43, Swampscott, MA 01907.
Editor: Robert Hastings. Phone: 617-592-0160. Reply date: 9/30/88. Six times/year. Circulation: 75,000. FL/year: 5. POA. Buys FNASR. Kill fee varies. Replies to queries in 4-6 weeks. Lead time for seasonal articles: 2-3 months. Articles published 2 months after

acceptance. Accepts CM, SQ, SS, PPS. Subsidized trips OK. Prefers
features of 1000-1800 words. Departments or columns: 800-1000
words. Pays 15-20 cents/word. SC: $2.50. WG: Write or phone.
Photos: Photo editor: Susan Barrow-Williams. Uses BW, color.
Buys FR. POP. **Editorial Slant:** Travel department features geta-
ways near and far. 1989 schedule includes "Sporting Vacations" and
"An-Hour-Away Getaways" in July-August and "The Best Leaf-
Looking Spots" in September-October.

Colorado Homes & Lifestyles, 2550 31st Street, No. 154, Denver,
CO 80216.
Managing editor: Beth Ewen. Phone: 303-455-1944. Reply date:
9/30/88. Bimonthly. Circulation: 25,000. FL/year: 6. POA. Buys
FR. Kill fee: 10 percent. Replies to queries in 1 month. Lead time
for seasonal articles: 8 weeks. Articles published 6 weeks after acceptance. Accepts CM, SQ, SS. Subsidized trips OK. Prefers features
of 1200-1500 words. Pays 10 cents/word. **Photos:** Photo editor:
Karen Polaski. Uses BW, color. Pays $15/BW, $25/color, $50/
cover. POA. **Editorial Slant:** "Away from Home" department deals
with travel in Colorado and Colorado resorts.

Condé Nast Traveler, 360 Madison Avenue, New York, NY 10017.
Features editor: Margaret Simmons. Phone: 212-880-8800. Reply
date: 11/23/88. Monthly. Circulation: Over 800,000. FL/year: Mostly
commissioned. POP. Buys OTR. Kill fee: 25 percent. Replies to
queries in 3 weeks. Accepts ES. No subsidized trips. Prefers features

AR	all rights	OTR	one-time rights
ASMP	American Society of	POA	pays on acceptance
	Magazine	POB	post office box
	Photographers	POP	pays on publication
BW	black-and-white photos	PPS	previously published
CM	complete manuscript		submissions
ES	electronic submissions	PQ	phone queries
FL	freelance	SAE	self-addressed envelope
FL/year	number of freelance travel	SASE	self-addressed stamped envelope
	articles published per	SC	sample copy
	year	SQ	simultaneous queries
F(NAS)R	first (North American serial)	SR	second rights
	rights	SS	simultaneous submissions
ms(s)	manuscript(s)	WG	writer's guidelines
NA	North American		

of 2500-3000 words. Departments or columns: 500 words. Pays $1/word, less for first-timers. Pays expenses. SC: On newsstands. No WG; study recent issues. **Photos:** Photo editor: Kathleen Klech. Uses BW, color. Buys OTR. Photos purchased without mss. **Editorial Slant:** Sophisticated, affluent audience. Gives negative as well as positive aspects in stories.

Connecticut Traveler, 2276 Whitney Avenue, Hamden, CT 06518. Managing director: Elke P. Martin. Phone: 203-281-7505. Reply date: 9/30/88. Bimonthly. Circulation: 144,000. POA. Buys OTR or reprint rights. Kill fee: 25 percent. Replies to queries in 2-5 weeks. Lead time for seasonal articles: 6 months. Accepts CM, SQ, SS, PPS. Subsidized trips OK. Prefers features of 1000 words. Departments or columns written in house. Pays $100-$250. SC: 9-by-12 SASE with 45 cents postage. WG: Sent with sample copy. **Photos:** Uses BW 5-by-7 or 8-by-10, four-color transparencies. Photos purchased with ms. Pays $250-$400/cover. **Editorial Slant:** Publication of the Connecticut Motor Club. Publishes three types of travel articles: Weekending, on destinations within fairly easy driving distance of Connecticut; regional travel features, on daytrips or extended vacations in the Northeast; and national and international features, which focus on destinations as outlined in the editorial calendar.

Cross Country Skier, Rodale Press, 33 East Minor Street, Emmaus, PA 18049.
Managing editor: Virginia Hostetter. Phone: 215-967-5171. Reply date: 6/13/88. Monthly October to February. POP. Buys AR. Prefers features of 2000-4000 words. Departments or columns: 100-2000 words. Pays $450-$750 for destination features, $50-$350 for departments. **Photos:** Uses BW, color transparencies (35mm, 2¼-inch, or 4-by-5, Kodachrome preferred). Pays $35-$100/BW, $75-$200/color, $200-$400/cover. Photos purchased without mss. **Editorial Slant:** Destination articles should evoke the special personality of the area in which the skiing takes place. "Shortswings" department features brief pieces on destinations that are easily accessible, day or weekend trips located in North America.

Cruise Industry News, 441 Lexington Avenue, No. 1209A, New York, NY 10017.
Publisher: Oivind Mathisen. Phone: 212-986-1025. Reply date: 10/18/88. Semimonthly. Circulation: 2,000. FL/year: 10. POA. Buys

FR. Replies to queries immediately. Lead time for seasonal articles: None. Articles published immediately after acceptance. Accepts CM, SQ, PQ. Subsidized trips OK. Prefers features of 1000 words. "Going freelance rate is $50 for at least a column of copy, up to one full page." SC: Write or phone. **Editorial Slant:** Writing for this industry newsletter for cruise line executives requires high level of expertise. Covers news on cruise ships, destinations, shipyards, financing of cruise ships, market trends. Also advertising and PR campaigns and other sales and marketing angles.

Cruise Magazine, POB 1289, Gulf Breeze, FL 32561.
Editor: Andy Myers. Phone: 904-932-0711. Reply date: 11/22/88. Bimonthly. Circulation: 82,000. FL/year: 25-35. POP. Buys FR. Kill fee: 33 percent. Replies to queries in 14-21 days. Lead time for seasonal articles: 120 days. Writers are given specific publication date on acceptance. Accepts CM, SQ, SS. Subsidized trips OK. Prefers features of 1200-1500 words. Departments or columns: 300-500 words. Pays 12 cents/word. SC, WG: Write editor. **Photos:** Uses original 35mm slides or 2¼-inch transparencies. Pays $35/ color. Buys OTR unless some other arrangement is made. POP. Photos purchased without mss. **Editorial Slant:** Covers cruise ship lines, individual cruise ships, captains of these vessels, cruise line cuisine, new or unique cruise itineraries, plans for new vessels, cruise industry executives, etc. Sample articles, 9-10/88: Sailing on a Soviet ship, Lido decks, private yachts.

Discovery, One North Arlington, 1500 Shure Drive, 7th Floor, Arlington Heights, IL 60004.
Editor: Claire McCrea. Reply date: 6/8/88. Quarterly. Circulation: 1.5 million. Buys FNASR and one-time anthology rights. Lead time for seasonal articles: 6-14 months. Prefers features of 1500-2000 words. Pays $800-$1500. Pays expenses for original assigned articles. SC: 9-by-12 SASE with $1 postage. **Photos:** Pays for photographers' time: $450/day, $300/half day. **Editorial Slant:** Official publication of the Allstate Motor Club. Magazine's purpose is to give readers a better look at the United States through travel features. Wants travel ideas that have a personality hook and promise insight as well as entertainment.

Diver, 10991 Shellbridge Way, No. 295, Richmond, British Columbia, Canada V6X 3C6.
Editor: Neil McDaniel. Phone: 604-273-4333. Reply date: 6/8/88.

Nine times/year. Circulation: 25,000. Pays within 6 weeks of publication. Accepts PPS if so advised. Prefers features of 1000-2500 words. Pays $2.50/column inch. **Photos:** Uses BW 5-by-7 or 8-by-10 glossies, high-quality color transparencies. Pays at least $7/ BW, at least $15/color, $100/cover. **Editorial Slant:** Uses well-illustrated articles on dive regions with up-to-date service information as well as personal experience and travel destination articles. Sample articles, 6/88: "The Louisbourg Shipwrecks," inflatables.

Diversion, 60 East 42nd Street, No. 2424, New York, NY 10165. Executive editor: Claire Hardiman. Phone: 212-682-3710. Reply date: 5/22/88. Monthly. Circulation: 180,000. Pays 12 weeks after ms submission. Kill fee: 25 percent. Replies to queries in 3 weeks. Lead time for seasonal articles: 3-4 months. Prefers features of 1800 words. Departments or columns: 1000-1200 words. Pays $700 for features, $450 for columns. SC available. **Editorial Slant:** A travel and leisure magazine for physicians. Articles on vacation destinations, resorts, food, wine, participatory and spectator sports. Sample articles, 5/88: China's religious shrines; cruises around New York City; mountain biking; Mineral Point, Wisconsin.

Down East, POB 679, Camden, ME 04843. Phone: 207-594-9544. Mss to manuscript editor. Reply date: 4/14/ 88. Monthly. POA. Buys FR for unsolicited articles. Prefers features of 1500-3000 words. "Traveling Down East" department: Up to 1500 words. Pays 15 cents/word for articles; $250 for "Traveling Down East" items. SC: $3.50 to Subscription Department. **Photos:** Photos to art director. Uses 35mm or larger color transparencies. Pays $100/page. Buys OTR. **Editorial Slant:** "Traveling Down East" is a travelogue that depicts the unique character of a particular town, route, or area anywhere in Maine, while highlighting places, people, or events of local interest.

Early American Life, POB 8200, Harrisburg, PA 17105-8200. Editor: Frances Carnahan. Phone: 717-657-9555. Reply date: 5/19/ 88. POA. ES: MS-DOS, ASCII, Microsoft Word, Office Writer, Multimate, DisplayWrite, WordPerfect, WordStar. Prefers features of 1000-3000 words. **Editorial Slant:** Designed to bring something of the warmth and beauty of early America into readers' lives. Accurate information on traveling to historic sites and restorations. Time period generally 1700-1900.

Empire Press, 105 Loudoun Street, S.W., Leesburg, VA 22075.
Executive editor: C. Brian Kelly; query editor of the particular
magazine you're interested in. Phone: 703-771-9400. Reply date:
10/1/88. Publishes 3 bimonthly magazines that include travel departments: *Military History (MH)*, *Wild West (WW)*, and *America's
Civil War (ACW)*. Circulation: *MH*, 210,000; *WW, ACW,* 100,000.
FL/year: 6 in each magazine. POP. Buys FNASR. Replies to queries
in 1-2 months. Articles published 6 months to 2 years after acceptance. Accepts CM. Subsidized trips OK. Prefers articles of 1500-
2000 words for travel departments. *MH* pays $200; *WW* and *ACW*
pay $150. SC: *MH*, $3.50; *WW* and *ACW*, $3.95. WG: SASE;
same WG apply to all magazines. **Photos:** Often obtain photos
themselves or regard photos as part of the article package. **Editorial
Slant:** *MH* covers military history world wide, any period. *WW* is
the U.S. West; *ACW* is self-explanatory. All magazines emphasize
history, with some expository material on what there is to see today.
Future schedule for *MH* includes travel articles on Fredericksburg,
Virginia; Luxembourg; Washington Naval Yard; Bastogne; HMS
Belfast. *WW* will cover the Seattle Underground and stagecoach
stops in California. *ACW* recently has featured central Missouri,
Vicksburg, and a Gettysburg tour.

Equinox, 7 Queen Victoria Road, Camden East, Ontario, Canada K0K
1J0.
Assistant editor: Jody Morgan. Phone: 613-378-6661. Reply date:
7/30/88. Six times/year. Circulation: 165,000. Uses 30-36 feature
articles per year. Pays within 30 days of receipt of ms. Buys FNASR.
Kill fee: 50 percent. Replies to queries in 6 weeks. Lead time for
seasonal articles: 1 year. Prefers features of 2000-4000 words. Departments or columns: 100-1000 words. Pays $1250-$2000 for
features, $200-$350 for departments. Pays expenses. SC: $5. WG:
SASE. **Photos:** Uses mostly color (Kodachrome preferred). Pays
$100-$300/photo, $350/cover. Buys OTR. **Editorial Slant:** Articles
on geography, biology, the arts, travel, architecture, and adventure.
Sample articles: Royal Winnipeg Ballet, Jamaica's Maroons, "Orca,
the Sociable Whale," Canada's smallest railroad, Saskatchewan's
grasslands.

Essence, 1500 Broadway, New York, NY 10036.
Senior editor: Valerie Wilson Wesley. Phone: 212-647-0600. Reply
date: 10/7/88. Monthly. Circulation: 800,000. FL/year: 12 or more.

POA. Buys FNASR. Kill fee: 25 percent. Replies to queries in 6-8 weeks. Lead time for seasonal articles: 4-6 months. Articles published within 1 year of acceptance. Accepts CM, SQ, SS. Subsidized trips OK. Prefers features of 3000 words. Departments or columns: 1000 words. Pays $200-$600. Pays expenses. SC: Write. WG: SASE. **Photos:** Photo editor: Sharon Pryor. Uses BW, color slides. POP. Photos purchased without mss. **Editorial Slant:** Lifestyle and service magazine for Black women.

Explore, 410-301 14th Street, N.W., Calgary, Alberta, Canada T2N 2A1.
Editor: Peter Thompson. Phone: 403-270-8890. Reply date: 7/10/88. Pays 30 days after publication. Buys Canadian serial rights, SR. Accepts SS. ES: IBM compatible. Prefers features of 1000-1500 words. Departments or columns: 600-1000 words. Pays 10-17 cents/word. **Photos:** Uses BW prints 5-by-7 or larger, transparencies 35mm or larger, color prints 5-by-7 or larger. Pays $15-$90/BW, $20-$130/color, $200/cover. Pays 30 days after publication. Photos purchased without mss. **Editorial Slant:** Canada's adventure magazine for active outdoorsy people. Goal is to encourage and inform readers, whether they be novice skiers, mountain bikers, or world-traveled backpackers. Sample articles, 5-6/88: Bicycling in the United Kingdom and Japan, Eastern Canadian mountain parks, ocean kayaking, adventure yacht chartering.

Family, POB 4993, Walnut Creek, CA 94596.
Executive editor: Janet A. Venturino. Reply date: 9/30/88. Monthly. Circulation: 550,000. FL/year: 10. POP. Buys FNASR. Kill fee: 25 percent for assigned articles. Replies to queries in 2-3 weeks. Lead time for seasonal articles: 6 months. Articles published 6 months or more after acceptance. Accepts CM, SQ, SS, PPS. Prefers features of up to 2000 words. Departments written in house. Pays $100-$300. SC: $1.25 check. WG: SASE. **Photos:** Photo editor: Janet A. Venturino. Uses BW prints, color slides and transparencies. Pays $25/BW, $50/color, $150/cover. POP. Photos purchased without mss. **Editorial Slant:** Caters to the U.S. military wife. Distributed at U.S. commissaries around the world. Travel stories should appeal to military wives.

Family Motor Coaching, 8291 Clough Pike, Cincinnati, OH 45244.
Associate editor: Robbin Maue. Phone: 513-474-3622. Reply date: 10/28/88. Monthly. Circulation: 72,500. FL/year: 180-200. POA.

Buys FNASR. Replies to queries in 2-4 weeks. Lead time for seasonal articles: 120 days. Articles published 4-8 months after acceptance. Accepts CM. Prefers features of 1500-2000 words. Departments or columns: 800-1000 words. Pays $125-$225 for standard travel articles. SC: $2.50. WG: SASE. **Photos:** Query travel editor. Uses BW glossies, 35mm or larger color transparencies. Photos purchased as package with ms. Buys OTR. Photos rarely purchased without mss. **Editorial Slant:** For members of the Family Motor Coaching Association. Travel articles should give information on camping accommodations, recreational and scenic features, geography and history. Sample articles, 3/88: "A Shopper's Guide to San Diego," "Lake George Rediscovered," "Mobile and the Southern Riviera," "Favorite Seashore Parks in Maine."

Far East Traveler, 1-4-28, Moto-Azabu, Minato-ku, Tokyo, Japan 106.
Managing editor: William Ross. Phone: 03-452-0705. Reply date: 6/8/88. Pays 1 month after publication. Buys first Asian rights. Prefers CM. Prefers features of 1200-2500 words. Pays 10 cents/word. SC: 6 International Reply Coupons. **Photos:** Pays $40/photo, $100/cover. Pays 1 month after publication. **Editorial Slant:** Consumer magazine distributed to hotel guests in over 50 of the top hotels in Asia, particularly in Japan, Hong Kong, Seoul, and Taipei. Features one country per issue, with four to six stories on the main country and two to four supporting articles on other destinations. Sample articles, 6/88: Singapore, Japanese armor-making in the 1980s, Kagoshima, Truk islands.

Field and Stream, 380 Madison Avenue, New York, NY 10017.
Editor: Duncan Barnes. Phone: 212-719-6565. Reply date: 5/23/88. Monthly. POA. Buys first world rights. Replies to queries within 60 days. Prefers features of 2000-2500 words. Departments or columns: 300-700 words. Pays $500 or more for features, $250-$350 for departments. WG: SASE. **Photos:** Uses BW 8-by-10 prints, 35mm or 2¼-inch color transparencies. Pays $75/page/BW, $450/page/color, $1000 or more/cover. Buys first world rights. **Editorial Slant:** Deals in hunting and fishing. Has regional sections for Northeast, Midwest, Far West, West, and South.

Fishing World, 51 Atlantic Avenue, Floral Park, NY 11001.
Editor-in-chief: Keith Gardner. Phone: 516-352-9700. Reply date: 9/30/88. Bimonthly. Circulation: 350,000. FL/year: 36. POA. Buys

FNASR. Kill fee: 50 percent. Replies to queries in 1 week. Accepts CM. Subsidized trips OK. Prefers features of 1500-2500 words. Pays $150-$300. SC and WG available. **Photos:** Query editor-in-chief. Uses color. Pays $300/cover. Buys FNASR. POA. Cover and centerfold purchased without mss. **Editorial Slant:** Subject matter can be where-to on a hot fishing site, or a story on one lake or an entire region, either freshwater or salt.

Florida Wildlife, 620 South Meridian Street, Tallahassee, FL 32399-1600.
Editor: Andrea Blount. Phone: 904-488-1960. Reply date: 10/8/88. Bimonthly. Circulation: 28,000. Buys OTR. Replies to queries in 1 month. Accepts SS and PPS if so advised. Prefers features of 800-2000 words. Pays $50-$400. **Photos:** Uses BW 5-by-7 or 8-by-10, 35mm or larger color transparencies. Pays $15-$50/color, $50/back cover, $100/front cover. Buys OTR. **Editorial Slant:** An environmental and conservation magazine concerned with game and freshwater fish. Travel writers are not regular contributors, but a travel story could be structured to conform to the publication.

Fly Fisherman, 2245 Kohn Road, POB 8200, Harrisburg, PA 17105.
Editor/publisher: John Randolph. Phone: 717-540-8175. Reply date: 10/18/88. Six times/year. Circulation: 144,000. FL/year: 5. POA. Buys FNASR. Replies to queries in 4-6 weeks. Lead time for seasonal articles: 8 months. Articles published 6 months to 2 years after acceptance. Accepts CM, SQ. ES: ASCII (diskette). Subsidized trips OK. Prefers features of 2000-3000 words. Departments or columns: 1500 words. Pays $200-$600. SC, WG: Write or phone. **Photos:** Art director: Rod Bond. Uses BW prints, color slides. Shots related to fly-fishing. Pays $30-$100/BW, $30-$200/color, $500/cover. Buys FNASR. POP. Photos purchased without mss. **Editorial Slant:** The nation's largest consumer magazine devoted solely to the sport of fly-fishing. Sample articles, 7/88: "Colorado's South Platte," "Mississippi Headwaters," "Labrador Brookies."

The Flyfisher, 1387 Cambridge Drive, Idaho Falls, ID 83401.
Editor: Dennis Bitton. Phone: 208-523-7300. Reply date: 5/19/88. Circulation: 10,000. Pays after publication. Prefers features of 1000-1500 words. Pays $50-$200. SC: $3 to FFF, POB 1088, West Yellowstone, MT 59758. **Photos:** Uses BW 8-by-10 prints, negatives; 35mm, 2¼-inch, or 4-by-5 color transparencies. Photos purchased with mss. **Editorial Slant:** Official publication of the Federation

of Fly Fishers. Articles on places of interest to fly-fishers. Sample articles, Winter 1988: "Idaho's South Fork of the Snake River," "Texas' Stock Tank Bass."

Food & Wine, 1120 Avenue of the Americas, New York, NY 10036. Senior editor: Catherine Bigwood. Phone: 212-382-5600 (no PQ). Reply date: 10/12/88. Monthly. Circulation: 750,000. FL/year: 12. POA. Buys first world rights. Kill fee: 25 percent. Replies to queries in 2-3 weeks. Lead time for seasonal articles: 5-6 months. Accepts CM, SQ. Prefers features of 2500-3000 words. Departments or columns: 2500-3000 words. Pays $1500 for first-time contributors. Pays expenses. SC: $2.50 to Circulation Department, 20th Floor, same address as above. WG: Write senior editor. **Photos:** Photo editor: Jim Brown. Uses 35mm or 8-by-10 transparencies. Pays $100/color, $1000/cover. Buys first world rights. POA. Photos purchased without mss. **Editorial Slant:** Seeks to engage readers in all the rewarding aspects of dining and entertaining. Monthly features and columns on restaurants and travel.

Ford Times, 111 East Wacker Drive, No. 1700, Chicago, IL 60601. Editor: John Fink. Phone: 312-819-1330. Reply date: 9/30/88. Monthly. Circulation: 1.2 million. FL/year: 75. POA. Buys FR. Kill fee: One-third. Replies to queries in 1 month. Lead time for seasonal articles: 9 months. Articles published 6-18 months after acceptance. Accepts SQ, SS. Subsidized trips OK. Prefers features of 1500 words. Departments or columns: 200 words for departments, 1000 words for humor. Pays $400-$800. Pays expenses up to $200. SC, WG: SASE. **Photos:** Photo editor: Jim Prendergast. Uses four-color transparencies. Pays $150/less than full page, $350/full page, $500/cover. Buys FR. POP. Photos purchased without mss. **Editorial Slant:** Published by Ford Motor Company for a family audience. Anything that relates to current life in North America that is upbeat and in good taste. Most readers ages 18-35. Articles on places of interest, such as guesthouses of New Orleans; first-person accounts of unusual vacation trips or real-life travel adventures.

Frequent Flyer, 888 Seventh Avenue, New York, NY 10106. Managing editor: Jane Levere. Phone: 212-977-8300. Reply date: 10/28/88. Monthly. Circulation: 350,000. FL/year: 4-6. POA. Kill fee varies. Replies to queries in 1-3 months. Lead time for seasonal articles: 2-4 months. Subsidized trips OK. Prefers features of 1500-

2000 words. Pays $500 on average. Pays some expenses. SC and WG available. **Photos:** Photo editor: Susan Comolli. Uses all types, preferably color. POA. Photos purchased without mss. **Editorial Slant:** Published by Official Airline Guide. Most readers are corporate executives, entrepreneurs, or professionals with household incomes over $100,000. Has published articles on in-flight health risks, overseas job markets, hotel surcharges. Sample topics, 1989: "New York: Host to the World" (June), "Hawaii: Business and Pleasure" (August), "Business Guide to Switzerland" (September), "Guide to International Hotels" and "Business/Leisure Guide to Mexico" (October).

Friendly Exchange, Locust at 17th, Des Moines, IA 50336.
Editor: Adele Malott. Reply date: 10/21/88. Quarterly. Circulation: 4.5 million. FL/year: 35-40. POA. Buys AR. Kill fee: 25 percent. Replies to queries in 4-6 weeks. Lead time for seasonal articles: 12-15 months. Articles published 5-6 months after acceptance. Accepts CM, SQ, SS. Accepts ES for assigned stories. Subsidized trips OK. Prefers features of 1000-1800 words. Departments or columns: 400-800 words. All departments are composed of reader-generated material. Pays $400 or more. Sometimes pays expenses. SC: 9-by-12 envelope with 5 first-class stamps. WG: SASE. **Photos:** Photo editor: Peggy Fisher. Uses people-oriented travel and leisure topics. Pays $50/BW, at least $150/color; pay for cover is negotiable. Buys FR. POP. Photos purchased without mss. Requires model releases, particularly for covers. **Editorial Slant:** Published by Farmers Insurance Group and distributed to its policyholders living in 24 states from Ohio to California. Explores travel and leisure topics of interest to active Western and Midwestern families.

Friends, 30400 Van Dyke Boulevard, Warren, MI 48093.
Editor: Thomas Morrisey. Phone: 313-575-9400, 800-232-6266. Reply date: 6/4/88. Monthly. Circulation: 1 million. Prefers features of 800-2000 words. Pays $300-$750. **Photos:** Uses color transparencies. Photos are important. **Editorial Slant:** Readers are Chevrolet owners residing in the United States. Editorial coverage is limited to North America and Hawaii. Readers like to discover new travel trends and new activities. Sample stories: "Four-Star in the Forest," about luxury hotels in or near national parks.

Fuller-Weissmann Report, 810 St. William Avenue, Round Rock, TX 78681.

Editor: Arnie Weissmann. Phone: 512-244-1658. Reply date: 10/11/88. Quarterly. FL/year: 80. POA. Buys AR. Replies to queries in 8 weeks. Articles published 2 months after acceptance. Accepts SQ, PQ. Pay negotiable. SC and WG available. **Photos:** No photos used. **Editorial Slant:** Does not publish articles per se. Has already-written country profiles for most countries of the world which are continuously being updated. Looking for writers who are traveling and can review material to ensure its continued accuracy. Country profiles are used primarily by travel agents, not consumers. Writers should submit detailed itineraries of their nonsubsidized trips.

Fur-Fish-Game, 2878 East Main Street, Columbus, OH 43209.
Editor: Mitch Cox. Phone: 614-231-9585. Reply date: 9/30/88. Monthly. Circulation: 130,000. FL/year: 6-12. POA. Buys FNASR. Replies to queries in 2-4 weeks. Lead time for seasonal articles: 6 months. Accepts SQ. Subsidized trips OK under certain conditions. Prefers features of 1500-3000 words. Pays $50-$150. SC: SASE with $1. WG: SASE. **Photos:** Uses BW prints, color slides. Photos considered part of article package. Buys OTR. **Editorial Slant:** An outdoor magazine interested only in outdoor vacation and adventure articles. "Some camping. *Nothing else, please.*"

Game & Fish Publications, POB 741, Marietta, GA 30061; 2250 Newmarket Parkway, Suite 110, Marietta, GA 30067.
Editor: Chris Dorsey. Phone: 404-953-9222. Reply date: 9/30/88. Publishes 31 monthly magazines, each focusing on a different state.

AR	all rights	OTR	one-time rights
ASMP	American Society of	POA	pays on acceptance
	Magazine	POB	post office box
	Photographers	POP	pays on publication
BW	black-and-white photos	PPS	previously published
CM	complete manuscript		submissions
ES	electronic submissions	PQ	phone queries
FL	freelance	SAE	self-addressed envelope
FL/year	number of freelance travel	SASE	self-addressed stamped envelope
	articles published per	SC	sample copy
	year	SQ	simultaneous queries
F(NAS)R	first (North American serial)	SR	second rights
	rights	SS	simultaneous submissions
ms(s)	manuscript(s)	WG	writer's guidelines
NA	North American		

Buys OTR. Reads queries every 3 months. Lead time for seasonal articles: 8 months. Accepts SQ. Prefers features of 2200-2400 words. Pays $150-$300. SC: $2.50. WG: SASE. **Photos:** Uses BW 8-by-10 glossies, color transparencies (preferably Kodachrome). Pays $25/BW, $75/color, $250/cover. **Editorial Slant:** Magazines are information-oriented, with a focus on hunting, fishing, and outdoor recreation related to hunting and fishing. Uses articles on a certain state or several states.

GlobeHopper, 57 Berkeley Street, Toronto, Ontario, Canada M5A 2W5.
Managing editor: Joanna Ebbutt. Phone: 416-368-0944. Reply date: 6/13/88. Bimonthly. FL/year: 30. POP. Buys first Canadian rights. Lead time for seasonal articles: 6 months. Prefers features of 1500-2000 words. Pays $175-$275. WG: SASE. **Photos:** Uses slides. Pays $25/color. **Editorial Slant:** Articles on faraway destinations: remote Canada, sunny areas, offbeat vacations, Europe, and "Cityscape." Sample articles, 4-5/88: Egypt, Switzerland, "Cruising through Canada," "Summer in the Mountains," Lisbon.

Golden State, 555 19th Street, San Francisco, CA 94107.
Editor: Anne Evers. Phone: 415-621-0220. Reply date: 9/30/88. Quarterly. Circulation: Over 600,000. FL/year: 20. POA. Buys FNASR, some SR. Kill fee: 20 percent. Replies to queries in 1-2 months. Lead time for seasonal articles: 3 months. Accepts CM, SQ, SS, PPS. Prefers features of 1800 words. Pays 20 cents/word. Pays phone expenses. SC, WG: SASE. **Photos:** Uses no photos. **Editorial Slant:** Distributed to out-of-state vehicles at California's 16 border stations. Articles can be statewide in scope or focus on a particular region.

The Golf Club, 16 Forest Street, 2nd Floor, New Canaan, CT 06840.
Managing editor: E. Michael Johnson. Phone: 203-972-3892. Reply date: 9/30/88. Bimonthly. Circulation: 120,000. FL/year: Approximately 10. Buys FNASR. Replies to queries in 1-2 weeks. Lead time for seasonal articles: 2 months. Articles usually published 2 months after acceptance. Accepts CM, SQ, SS. Subsidized trips OK. Prefers features of 1500-2000 words. Pay varies. Pays expenses. SC: Write or phone. WG given at time of assignment. **Photos:** Photo editor: E. MacFarlan Moore. Uses 35mm. Golf courses, people, architecture of clubhouses. Pay varies for color; pays $300/cover.

Buys OTR. POP. Photos purchased without mss. **Editorial Slant:** For members of private golf clubs.

Golf Magazine, 380 Madison Avenue, New York, NY 10017.
Senior editor: Brian McCallen. Phone: 212-687-3000. Reply date: 9/30/88. Monthly. Circulation: 950,000. FL/year: 5-8. POA. Buys NA rights. Replies to queries in 2-3 months. Lead time for seasonal articles: 4-6 months. Articles published 6-12 months after acceptance. Subsidized trips OK. Prefers features of 1800 words. Pays $800-$1200. Pays expenses. SC: Write. **Photos:** Photo editor: Brian McCallen. Uses color (Kodachrome 64). Photos purchased without mss. **Editorial Slant:** For golfers who are serious about the game and all its elements. Travel articles should cover places to play golf around the world.

Gourmet, 560 Lexington Avenue, New York, NY 10022.
Travel editor: Patricia Bell. Phone: 212-371-1330. Reply date: 6/8/88. POA. Replies to queries in 2 months. Prefers features of 2500 words, 3000 words if there are recipes. Pay varies. **Photos:** Sometimes uses color photos. **Editorial Slant:** Magazine's readers are well-to-do, educated, and widely traveled, with a considerable knowledge of food. Articles on travel, fishing, or hunting experiences dealing in some way with food or drink, written in a light, sophisticated manner. Likes first person. Sample articles, 6/88: Restaurants in New York and California, "A Flower Trail through the Alps," Beatrix Potter's home near Lake Windermere.

Great Lakes Fisherman, 921 Eastwind Drive, No. 101, Westerville, OH 43081.
Editor: Ottie M. Snyder, Jr. Phone: 614-882-5653. Reply date: 5/19/88. Also publishes *Ohio Fisherman* and *Tri-State Bass Fisherman.* Pays on or near the 15th of the month before issue date. Lead time for seasonal articles: 1 year. Prefers features of 1500-2000 words. Departments or columns: 3 double-spaced pages. Pays $135-$200 for article and BW photos. WG: SASE. **Photos:** Uses BW, color. Pay for BW included in pay for article; pays $50-$75/color, $150/cover. Buys FR, SR. Photos purchased without mss. Sample article, 4/88: "Top Ports for Early Salmon and Trout."

Guam & Micronesia Glimpses, POB 8066, Tamuning, Guam 96911.
Editor: Phyllis Koontz. Phone: 671-646-5135, 671-477-3483. Reply date: 9/30/88. Quarterly. Circulation: 3,000. FL/year: 20-25.

POP. Buys FR. Kill fee: 10 percent. Replies to queries in 1 month. Lead time for seasonal articles: 6 months. Articles published 6-18 months after acceptance. Accepts CM, SQ, SS, PPS (if not published in a Pacific regional publication), PQ. Subsidized trips OK but plugs will be edited out. Prefers features of 1000-1500 words. Departments or columns: 400-600 words. Pays $2.50/column inch for first-time contributors, $3.50/column inch afterward. SC: $3. **Photos:** Photo editor: Phyllis Koontz. Uses BW historical photos, otherwise color transparencies. Articles must be accompanied by photos. Pays $10/BW or color, $75/cover. Buys FR. POP. **Editorial Slant:** General interest nonfiction articles about Guam and Micronesia: people, lifestyles, traditions, history, culture, the arts.

Hawaii—Gateway to the Pacific, POB 6050, Mission Viejo, CA 92690.
Editor: Dennis Shattuck. Phone: 714-855-8822. Reply date: 9/30/88. Six times/year. Circulation: 45,000. FL/year: 24. POP. Buys FNASR, OTR. Replies to queries in 15-45 days. Lead time for seasonal articles: 6 months. Articles published 2-6 months after acceptance. Accepts CM, PPS. Prefers features of 1000-2000 words. Pays 7.5 cents/word. SC: $3. WG available. **Photos:** Photo editor: Dennis Shattuck. Uses BW, color. Pays $25/color, $250/cover. Buys OTR. POP. Photos purchased without mss. **Editorial Slant:** Articles that appeal to both island residents and mainland visitors.

High Times, 211 East 43rd Street, 20th Floor, New York, NY 10017.
Executive editor: John Holmstrom. Phone: 212-972-8484. Reply date: 9/30/88. Monthly. Circulation: 250,000. FL/year: 7-12. POP. Buys rights to publish in "Best of" anthologies, calendar. Kill fee: 20 percent. Replies to queries in 1 month or more. Lead time for seasonal articles: 3 months. Articles published 3-5 months after acceptance. Accepts CM, PPS. ES: "Maybe soon." Subsidized trips OK. Prefers features of 1500-2500 words. Pays $100-$600. Sometimes pays expenses. SC, WG: Write. **Photos:** Photo editor: Elin Wilder. Uses BW, color slides. POP. Photos purchased without mss. **Editorial Slant:** Travel stories detailing the use of mind-expanding drugs by other cultures.

Highlights for Children, 803 Church Street, Honesdale, PA 18431.
Editor: Kent L. Brown, Jr. Phone: 717-253-1080. Reply date: 11/22/88. Monthly, except July-August. Circulation: 2.5 million. POA. Buys AR. Kill fee: 50 percent. Replies to queries in 1-3 weeks.

Accepts CM, SQ. Subsidized trips OK. Prefers features of 900 words. Pays at least 14 cents/word. SC, WG: Write. **Photos:** Photo editor: Larry Rosler. Uses BW prints, color transparencies. Buys AR. POA. **Editorial Slant:** For children ages 2-12. Does not publish travel articles as such; looks for fiction and nonfiction on foreign subjects. Wants authors who write from first-hand experiences and can interpret the ways of life, especially of children, in other countries; who show appreciation of cultural differences; and who don't leave the impression that the ways of North Americans are always the best.

Historic Preservation, 1785 Massachusetts Avenue, N.W., Washington, DC 20036.
Query editor. Phone: 202-673-4065. Reply date: 7/24/88. Bimonthly. Circulation: 200,000. FL/year: At least 6. Buys FR. Prefers features of 750-4000 words. Pays $150-$800. WG: SASE. **Photos:** Buys FR. **Editorial Slant:** Published by the National Trust for Historic Preservation. Travel to colorful and historic destinations is an area of growing interest to readers.

Horizon.
See Skies America. In-flight magazine of Horizon Air. Hub cities are Seattle, Portland, Boise, Spokane.

Illinois Magazine, POB 40, Litchfield, IL 62056.
Editor: Peggy Kuethe. Phone: 217-324-3425. Reply date: 10/28/88. Bimonthly. Circulation: 7500. FL/year: 6-10. POP. Buys FNASR. Replies to queries in 6-8 weeks. Lead time for seasonal articles: 6 months. Articles published within 1 year of acceptance. Accepts CM, SQ, PPS, PQ. Prefers features of up to 2000 words. Pays $10-$250. SC: SASE and $1. WG available. **Photos:** Photo editor: Peggy Kuethe. Uses BW glossies, 35mm color slides. Pays $10-$15/BW, $20-$50/color, $50/cover. Buys FNASR. POP.

Indianapolis Monthly, 8425 Keystone Crossing, No. 225, Indianapolis, IN 46240.
Managing editor: Sam Stall. Phone: 317-259-8222. Reply date: 11/3/88. Monthly. Circulation: 45,000. FL/year: 3-6. POP. Buys FR. Kill fee: 50 percent. Replies to queries in 6-8 weeks. Lead time for seasonal articles: 3 months. Articles published 2-3 months after acceptance. Accepts CM. Prefers features of 1500-3000 words. Departments or columns: 1000 words. Pays $150-$400. SC: SASE and

$3.05. WG: SASE. **Photos:** Photo editor: Marie Cronin. Uses BW glossies; 35mm, 2¼-inch, or 4-by-5 color transparencies; color prints. Pays $25/BW, $35/color. Buys OTR. POP. **Editorial Slant:** Subject matter of interest to people living in central Indiana. Weekend travel in Indiana, no first person.

International Living, 824 East Baltimore Street, Baltimore, MD 21202. Editor: Bruce Totaro. Phone: 301-234-0515. Reply date: 9/30/88. Monthly. Circulation: 50,000. FL/year: 100-120. POP. Buys AR. Replies to queries in 4 weeks. Lead time for seasonal articles: 5 months. Articles published 1 month to 1 year after acceptance. Accepts CM, SQ. ES: IBM compatible, WordStar, Multimate. Subsidized trips OK. Prefers features of 1500 words. Departments or columns: 500-1000 words. Pays $50-$300. SC: $2.50. WG: SASE. **Photos:** Photo editor: Bruce Totaro. Uses BW prints only. Pays $50-$75/BW. Buys OTR. POP. Photos purchased without mss. **Editorial Slant:** Uses material on travel, lifestyle, shopping, real estate, employment, and education overseas only. Never uses material on destinations in the United States.

International Wildlife, 8925 Leesburg Pike, Vienna, VA 22184. Managing editor: Jonathan Fisher. Reply date: 10/7/88. Six times/ year. Circulation: 550,000. FL/year: 50. POA. Buys AR. Kill fee: One-third. Replies to queries in 3 weeks. Lead time for seasonal articles: 8 months. Articles published 8-12 months after acceptance. Accepts SQ. Subsidized trips OK. Prefers features of 2000-2500 words. Pays $1000-$2000. Sometimes pays expenses. SC, WG: Write. **Photos:** Photo editor: John Nuhn. Uses 35mm color slides. Pays at least $255/color, $750/front cover. Buys OTR. POA. Photos purchased without mss. **Editorial Slant:** Published by the National Wildlife Federation.

The Iowan, 108 Third Street, Suite 350, Des Moines, IA 50309. Editor: Charles W. Roberts. Phone: 515-282-8220. Reply date: 4/ 27/88. Quarterly. POP. Replies to queries in 4-6 weeks. Lead time for seasonal articles: 9-12 months. Accepts CM. Prefers features of 1500 words. Pays $200-$300. WG: SASE. **Photos:** Uses BW, 35mm or larger color transparencies. Pays $25/BW, $50/color. Buys OTR. Photos purchased without mss. **Editorial Slant:** General interest magazine dedicated to presenting, through outstanding color and exciting features, all that is extraordinary about Iowa. Sample articles, Fall 1987: "The Urban Pioneers of Sherman Hill," autumn color, "Wartburg's Commitment to Caring."

Islands, 3886 State Street, Santa Barbara, CA 93105.
Editor: Joan Tapper. Phone: 805-682-7177. Reply date: 10/18/88. Bimonthly. Circulation: 150,000. FL/year: 30. Pays half on acceptance and half on publication. Buys first world serial rights and reprint rights. Kill fee: 25 percent. Replies to queries in 6 weeks. Lead time for seasonal articles: 1 year. Articles published within 1 year of acceptance. Accepts CM, SQ, SS. Subsidized trips OK. Prefers features of 3500 words. Departments or columns: 1000 words. Pays 25 cents to $1/word. Pays expenses. SC: $5.25. WG: SASE.
Photos: Photo editor: Suzette Curtis. Uses photos evocative of place: scenics, architecture, people. Pays $75-$250/color, $300/cover. Buys OTR. Pays 30 days after publication. Photos purchased without mss. **Editorial Slant:** Focuses on islands around the world, whether urban, tropical, developed, or rural. Varying perspectives: historical, geological, spiritual, cultural. Departments on the arts, foods, people, and recreation.

The Itinerary, POB 1084, Bayonne, NJ 07002-1084.
Editor: Robert S. Zywicki. Phone: 201-858-3400. Reply date: 10/7/88. Bimonthly. Circulation: 10,500. FL/year: 20. POP. Buys AR. Replies to queries in 6 weeks. Lead time for seasonal articles: 6 months. Articles published 3-12 months after acceptance. Accepts CM, SQ, SS. Prefers features of 1200-1700 words. Departments or columns: 800-1000 words. Pays $50-$150. Pays expenses for assigned stories. SC, WG: 9-by-12 envelope and 4 first-class stamps. **Photos:** Photo editor: Robert S. Zywicki. Uses BW, preferably 5-by-7. Buys any rights. POP. Photos rarely purchased without mss. **Editorial Slant:** Uses articles relating specifically to travel for the disabled, including travelogues, how-to features, access reports, data on travel resources, reviews of travel books or guides in which information is provided for the disabled, new products and services designed to make travel easier for the disabled.

Jacksonville Today, 1325 San Marco Boulevard, No. 900, Jacksonville, FL 32207.
Managing editor: Rejeanne Davis Ashley. Phone: 904-396-8666. Reply date: 9/30/88. POP. Replies to queries in 4 weeks. Prefers features of 2000-3000 words. Departments or columns: 1000-1500

words. Pays $250-$500 for features, $100-$250 for departments. **Editorial Slant:** City lifestyle magazine relating to Jacksonville and North Florida, including St. Augustine, Gainesville, and Fernandina. Sample topics, 1989: Summer celebration (July); theaters, museums, and galleries (September).

The Jewish Journal of Greater Los Angeles, 3660 Wilshire Boulevard, No. 204, Los Angeles, CA 90010.
Travel editor: Marilyn Zeitlin. Phone: 213-738-7778. Reply date: 7/30/88. Circulation: 150,000. Pays $50. **Photos:** Pays $20 for original photos. **Editorial Slant:** Wants stories on something or some place Jewish. Personal accounts and what to see, do, buy, eat. Sample articles, 7/22/88: Restaurant review, "The Sybaritic Pleasures of the Napa Valley Wine Country."

The Jewish Monthly, 1640 Rhode Island Avenue, N.W., Washington, DC 20036.
Editor: Marc Silver. Reply date: 9/30/88. Ten times/year. Circulation: 180,000. FL/year: 6. POP. Buys FNASR. Kill fee varies. Replies to queries in 1 month. Lead time for seasonal articles: 6 months. Articles published 2-6 months after acceptance. Accepts CM, SQ, ES. Subsidized trips OK. Prefers features of 1000-2500 words. Pays 25 cents/word. SC: $1. WG: SASE. **Photos:** Pays $25-$250/photo, depending on usage. Buys OTR. POP. **Editorial Slant:** Concentrates on people. Articles on politics, religion, current events, history, culture, and social issues.

Kansas!, 400 West Eighth Street, 5th Floor, Topeka, KS 66603.
Editor: Andrea Glenn. Phone: 913-296-3479. Reply date: 9/30/88. Quarterly. Circulation: 46,500. FL/year: Approximately 65. POA. Buys FR. Replies to queries in 2 weeks to 1 month. Lead time for seasonal articles: 1 year. Articles published 1 year after acceptance. Accepts CM, SQ. Prefers features of 3-5 double-spaced typed pages. Pays $150-$250. SC: Write. WG: SASE. **Photos:** Photo editor: Andrea Glenn. Uses color transparencies. Pays $35-$75/color, $100-$200/cover. Buys FR. POA. A few photos purchased without mss. **Editorial Slant:** Published by the Kansas Department of Commerce to promote the beauty and economy of the state.

KCET Magazine, 5900 Wilshire Boulevard, Los Angeles, CA 90036.
Managing editor: Norman Kolpas. Phone: 213-936-0445 (no PQ). Reply date: 9/30/88. Monthly. Circulation: 250,000. FL/year: 12-

16. POA. Buys FNASR. Kill fee: 20 percent. Replies to queries in 2-4 weeks. Lead time for seasonal articles: at least 4 months. Articles published 2-3 months after acceptance. Accepts SQ. ES: ASCII (diskette with hard copy). Prefers features of 1500-3000 words. Departments or columns: 1200-1500 words. Pays $500-$1000, depending on length. SC: Write. WG: Study the magazine. **Photos:** Art director: Lisa Wrigley. Uses four-color original transparencies, no duplicates. Buys OTR. POA. Photos purchased without mss. **Editorial Slant:** For contributors to KCET public television station. Sample articles, 7/88: The Queen Mary, local musical events, the Monterey Peninsula.

L.A. West, 919 Santa Monica Boulevard, No. 245, Santa Monica, CA 90401.
Editor: Jan Loomis. Phone: 213-458-3376. Reply date: 9/30/88. Monthly. Circulation: 60,000. FL/year: 150. POA. Buys AR or FNASR. Replies to queries in 2 months. Lead time for seasonal articles: 6 months. Articles published 6 months to 1 year after acceptance. Accepts CM. Subsidized trips OK. Prefers features of 800-1000 words. Pays $75-$500. SC: SASE. WG: SASE. **Photos:** Photo editor: Jan Loomis. Uses photos of hotels and travel destinations. Pays $50/BW, $75/color, $150/cover. Buys AR. POP. Photos purchased without mss. **Editorial Slant:** Uses travel articles about both foreign and domestic destinations. Include sidebar with information about facilities, shopping, touring, etc.

The Lady, 39-40 Bedford Street, The Strand, London WC2E 9ER, England.
Editor: Joan L. Grahame. Phone: 01-379-4717. Reply date: 9/30/88. Pays at the end of the month in which publication appears. Buys first British serial rights. Prefers features of 800-1600 words. Pays 40 pounds/1000 words. **Photos:** Uses BW. Pays 12-14 pounds/photo. Travel articles may be illustrated or unillustrated. Sample articles, 9/6/88: "Bridgeman on the Gloucester to Sharpness Canal," "The Sacred Promontory of Portugal," St. Abb's Head in Scotland.

Lake Superior Magazine, 325 Lake Avenue South, No. 100, Duluth, MN 55802.
Editor: Paul Hayden. Phone: 218-722-5002. Reply date: 6/8/88. Six times/year. Circulation: 15,000. Pays within 30 days of publication. Buys FNASR, SR. Prefers CM. ES: Diskette and modem.

Pays up to $400. WG: SASE. **Photos:** Uses BW 5-by-7 or 8-by-10 glossies; 35mm, 4-by-5, or 8-by-10 color transparencies preferred. Pays $20/BW, $30/color. Buys FNASR. **Editorial Slant:** Upscale readers. Every issue contains stories about Michigan, Wisconsin, Minnesota, and Ontario. Coffee table quality.

Lakeland Boating, 1600 Orrington Avenue, Suite 500, Evanston, IL 60201.
Editor: Douglas Seibold. Phone: 312-869-5400. Reply date: 10/14/88. Eleven times/year. Circulation: 40,000. FL/year: 10-12. POA. Buys FNASR. Kill fee: 25 percent. Replies to queries in 1-4 weeks. Lead time for seasonal articles: 3-6 months. Articles published 1-12 months after acceptance. Accepts SQ. Prefers features of 2000 words. Pays $400-$600 for 2000-word feature. SC: Write. **Editorial Slant:** For powerboat and sailboat owners on the Great Lakes and major inland rivers.

Life in the Times, The Times Journal Co., Springfield, VA 22159-0200.
Query Roger Hyneman. Phone: 703-750-8671. Reply date: 10/28/88. Weekly. Circulation: 320,000. FL/year: 50. POA. Buys FNASR. Replies to queries in 1-2 weeks. Lead time for seasonal articles: 2 months. Articles published up to 1 year after acceptance. Accepts SQ, SS. Prefers features of 2500-3000 words. Departments or columns: 400 words. SC, WG: Write. **Photos:** Photo editor: Louis Atkins. Uses BW prints, color slides and prints. Pays $35/BW or color; pay for cover varies. Buys FR. POP. **Editorial Slant:** Weekly lifestyle section of *Army Times, Navy Times,* and *Air Force Times.* Articles on duty stations. Special travel sections on spring-summer travel in May and fall-winter travel in September.

Long Island Monthly, 600 Community Drive, Manhasset, NY 11030.
Editorial assistant: Trudy Balch. Phone: 516-562-5952. Reply date: 9/30/88. Monthly. Circulation: 70,000. FL/year: 6. Pays within 60 days of acceptance. Buys FNASR on assigned articles. Kill fee: 25 percent. Replies to queries in 6 weeks. Lead time for seasonal articles: 4 months. Accepts CM, SQ, SS, PPS. ES: ASCII (1200 baud modem, with hard copy). Pays 10 cents to $1/word. Pays expenses. SC: $3.50. WG: SASE. **Photos:** Art director: Rick Fiala. Uses BW, color. Buys OTR. Photos sometimes purchased without mss. **Editorial Slant:** For educated readers in Nassau and Suffolk counties.

Los Angeles, 1888 Century Park East, No. 920, Los Angeles, CA 90067.
Executive editor: Lew Harris. Phone: 213-557-7569. Reply date: 5/18/88. Circulation: 162,000. POA. Buys FNASR. Kill fee: 30 percent. Replies to queries in 3 weeks. Accepts CM. Prefers departments of 1500 words. Pays $300. **Editorial Slant:** Guide to getting the most out of life in the Los Angeles area.

Los Angeles Reader, 12224 Victory Boulevard, North Hollywood, CA 91606.
Editor: Lana H. Johnson. Phone: 818-763-3555. Reply date: 6/28/88. 70 percent freelance written. Pays in the week following publication. Buys FR. Prefers CM. Prefers features of 1000-3000 words. Departments or columns: 250-750 words. Pays $250 for features. **Editorial Slant:** The arts, entertainment, and features about Los Angeles and Southern California.

Main Line Style, POB 350, Wayne, PA 19087.
Editor-in-chief: Charles H. Thomas. Phone: 215-687-5997. Reply date: 4/18/88. Also publishes *Chester County Living*. Pays 30 days after publication. Usually buys FNASR. Lead time for seasonal articles: 6 months. Accepts PPS if they have not appeared in readership area. Prefers features of 100-1400 words. Pays 15 cents/word. WG: SASE. **Photos:** Uses BW glossies, 35mm color slides. Pays $10/BW. **Editorial Slant:** For readers in southeastern Pennsylvania

AR	all rights	OTR	one-time rights
ASMP	American Society of	POA	pays on acceptance
	Magazine	POB	post office box
	Photographers	POP	pays on publication
BW	black-and-white photos	PPS	previously published
CM	complete manuscript		submissions
ES	electronic submissions	PQ	phone queries
FL	freelance	SAE	self-addressed envelope
FL/year	number of freelance travel	SASE	self-addressed stamped envelope
	articles published per	SC	sample copy
	year	SQ	simultaneous queries
F(NAS)R	first (North American serial)	SR	second rights
	rights	SS	simultaneous submissions
ms(s)	manuscript(s)	WG	writer's guidelines
NA	North American		

who are 45-54 years old, well educated, with a household income of $65,000 or more.

Marlin, POB 12902, Pensacola, FL 32576.
Editor: Margaret Fifield. Phone: 904-434-5571. Reply date: 9/30/ 88. Bimonthly. Circulation: 15,000. FL/year: 12-15. POA. Buys FNASR. Kill fee: 30 percent. Replies to queries in 2-4 weeks. Lead time for seasonal articles: 4 months. Accepts CM, SQ, SS, PQ. Prefers features of 1500-2000 words. Departments or columns: 500- 800 words. Pays $250-$300 for features, $100-$200 for departments. SC, WG: Write. **Photos:** Art director: Janet Willett. Uses BW prints, color slides. Pays $50-$75/photo, $300/cover. Buys rights for 1 year. POP. Photos purchased without mss. **Editorial Slant:** Articles relating to offshore big game fishing.

Maryland, 217 East Redwood Street, 9th Floor, Baltimore, MD 21202.
Editor: Bonnie Joe Ayers. Phone: 301-333-6600. Reply date: 10/ 28/88. Quarterly. Circulation: 45,000. FL/year: 6-12. Buys AR. Kill fee: 25 percent. Replies to queries in 3-10 weeks. Lead time for seasonal articles: 6 months to 1 year. Articles published in next issue to 2 years after acceptance. Accepts CM, PQ (but prefers written). ES: Fax. Prefers features of 1500-2200 words. Departments or columns: 850-1000 words. Pays $150-$450. Pays expenses with prior approval. SC available. WG: SASE. **Photos:** Publisher: D. Patrick Hornberger. Uses BW prints, color slides and transparencies. Pay varies depending on type of assignment. Buys AR for shots used; OTR for stock shots. POA. Photos purchased without mss. **Editorial Slant:** Submissions must have a Maryland orientation, invite reader participation whenever possible. Stories are contemporary and historical, informational and entertaining.

The Mature Traveler, POB 50820, Reno, NV 89513.
Editor: Gene Malott. Phone: 702-786-7419. Reply date: 9/30/88. Monthly. Circulation: Over 1400. FL/year: 6-10. POA. Buys FR. Replies to queries in 3 weeks. Lead time for seasonal articles: 3 months. Articles published 1-6 months after acceptance. Accepts CM, PPS. Subsidized trips OK. Prefers features of 500-1000 words. Departments or columns: 200-400 words. Pays $100 for major articles, $10-$50 for others. Pays expenses. SC: $1. WG available. **Photos:** Photo editor: Gene Malott. Uses photos showing 49ers-plus having a good time. Pays $5/BW. Buys FR. POA. **Editorial Slant:** Readers are active and inquisitive people over 49 who are

avid travelers. Editor interested in major destination pieces about potential retirement spots, special discoveries off the beaten track, cruising, RVing, special interest trips (birding, bridge cruises, genealogy, golf weekends, antiquing, wine tasting).

Mauian Magazine, POB 10669, Lahaina, Maui, HI 96761.
Editor: D. Hunter Bishop. Phone: 808-661-5844. Reply date: 4/14/88. Bimonthly. POP. Buys FR. Articles published up to 6 months after acceptance. Prefers features of 2000 words. Pays $50-$500. SC: $3. WG: SASE. **Photos:** Uses BW, slides, transparencies. Pays $25/photo. **Editorial Slant:** The only regional magazine serving Maui and its neighboring islands of Lanai, Kaho'olwe, and Molokai. Designed to inform and enlighten the residents of Maui while also appealing to the millions of people who annually visit the island.

McCall's, 230 Park Avenue, New York, NY 10169.
Travel editor: Lydia Moss. Phone: 212-551-9500. Reply date: 10/7/88. Monthly. Circulation: 5 million. FL/year: 8. POA. Kill fee: 20 percent. Replies to queries in 2 weeks to 2 months. Lead time for seasonal articles: 3-4 months. Articles published 4 months to 1 year after acceptance. Accepts CM, SQ, PQ. Subsidized trips OK. Prefers features of 1000-1200 words. Pays $650-$1000. Pays phone expenses. SC available. **Editorial Slant:** Travel appears in "Silver Edition" section created for the million-plus readers between 50 and 65. Travel articles give a closer look at fabulous places readers have always dreamed of visiting and can finally afford.

MD, 3 East 54th Street, New York, NY 10022.
Editor: Sharon AvRutick. Phone: 212-355-5432. Reply date: 9/30/88. Monthly. Circulation: 130,000. FL/year: 15-20. POA. Buys FNASR. Kill fee: One-third. Replies to queries in 1 month. Lead time for seasonal articles: 3-6 months. Accepts CM, SQ, SS, PPS. Subsidized trips OK. Prefers features of 1500 words. Departments or columns: 1200 words. Pays $350-$750. Pays expenses. SC: SASE and $2. WG: SASE. **Photos:** Photo editor: Keith Goldstein. Uses 35mm color slides. Buys OTR. POP. Photos purchased without mss. **Editorial Slant:** Readers are physicians. Sample articles: Ballooning in France, pack trip in Wyoming.

Men's Health, Rodale Press, 33 East Minor Drive, Emmaus, PA 18098.

Executive editor: Michael Lafavore. Phone: 215-967-5171. Reply date: 9/30/88. Quarterly. Circulation: 250,000. FL/year: 4-6. POA. Buys FR. Pays kill fee. Replies to queries in 2 weeks. Lead time for seasonal articles: 6 months. Articles published 3 months after acceptance. Accepts CM, SQ, PPS. Subsidized trips sometimes OK. Prefers features of 1500 words. Pays 50 cents/word. SC: $2.95. WG not yet available. **Photos:** Photo editor: Margaret Skrouanek. Uses color transparencies. Pay varies. Buys FR. POA.

Mexico Magazine, POB 700, 502 Main Street, No. 305, Carbondale, CO 81623.
Managing editor: Harlan Feder. Phone: 303-963-2330. Reply date: 10/12/88. Quarterly. Circulation: 20,000. FL/year: Approximately 50. POP. Buys first NA and Mexican serial rights. Replies to queries in 2 months. Lead time for seasonal articles: 4 months. Articles published about 5 months after acceptance. Accepts CM, SQ, SS, PPS, PQ (if writer has previously been published in magazine). Subsidized trips may be OK if writer lets editor know the circumstances. Prefers features of up to 1500 words. Departments or columns: 400-800 words. Pays $125/page (about 1200 words). SC: $1. WG available with editorial schedule and response form. **Photos:** Photo editor: Rebecca Young. Uses color slides. Pays at least $50/color, depending on size; pays $200/cover (negotiable). Buys FR or reprint rights. POP. Photos purchased without mss. **Editorial Slant:** Preference given to material that presents Mexico's uniqueness and culture as differences to be appreciated; material that helps travelers understand, accept, and cope with these differences respectfully; and material that reflects a genuine concern, caring acceptance, or love of Mexico on the part of the writer.

Michigan Living, 17000 Executive Plaza Drive, Dearborn, MI 48126.
Managing editor: Jo-Anne Harman. Phone: 313-336-1506. Reply date: 10/13/88. Circulation: 1 million. FL/year: 40-50. POA. Buys FR. Replies to queries in 4-6 weeks. Lead time for seasonal articles: 6 months. Articles published 1-2 years after acceptance. Accepts CM, SQ, SS. Subsidized trips OK. Prefers features of 500-700 words. Pays $150-$385. SC, WG: Write. **Photos:** Photo editor: Jo-Anne Harman. Uses BW, color. Pays $25/BW, $60-$200/color, $385/cover. POP. Photos sometimes purchased without mss. Always looking for superior covers. **Editorial Slant:** Always in the market for pieces on Michigan. Foreign travel articles other than

Canada are almost always staff written. Sections on Florida and other warm areas in December, Canada (particularly eastern areas) in May, and Michigan in the summer months.

Michigan Out-of-Doors, POB 30235, Lansing, MI 48909.

Editor: Kenneth S. Lowe. Phone: 517-371-1041. Reply date: 9/30/88. Monthly. Circulation: 125,000. FL/year: Approximately 6. POA. Buys FNASR. Replies to queries within 2 weeks. Lead time for seasonal articles: 6 months to 1 year. Articles published 3 months to 1 year after acceptance. Accepts CM, PQ. Prefers features of 2000-2500 words. Pays $75-$150 for feature stories. SC: $1.50. WG available. **Photos:** Photo editor: Kenneth S. Lowe. Uses color photos for cover. Pays $60/cover. Buys FNASR. POA. Photos purchased without mss only for covers. **Editorial Slant:** Published by Michigan United Conservation Clubs. Interested in outdoor recreation, with special emphasis on hunting and fishing, conservation, and environmental affairs.

Mid-Atlantic Country, 300 North Washington Street, No. 305, Alexandria, VA 22314.

Executive editor: Anne Elizabeth Powell. Phone: 703-548-6177. Reply date: 9/30/88. Circulation: 120,000. FL/year: Approximately 25. POP. Buys FR. Kill fee: Up to 25 percent. Replies to queries in 8 weeks at most. Lead time for seasonal articles: 6 months to 1 year. Articles usually published within 2 months of acceptance. Accepts CM. Prefers features of 2500-3000 words. Departments or columns: 800-1000 words. Pays up to $500 for feature-length pieces. Pays expenses only if preapproved. SC, WG: SASE. **Photos:** Art director: Jeff Roth. Uses BW, color. Pays $25-$100/BW or color, up to $300/cover. Buys OTR. POP. Photos purchased without mss. **Editorial Slant:** Focuses on the Mid-Atlantic region, covering outdoor sports, history, arts and crafts. Uses human interest stories, photo essays.

Midway.

See Skies America. In-flight magazine of Midway Airlines. Hub city is Chicago.

The Midwest Motorist, 12901 North Forty Drive, St. Louis, MO 63141.

Managing editor: Jean Kennedy. Phone: 314-576-7350. Reply date: 9/30/88. Bimonthly. Circulation: 385,000. FL/year: 30-40. POA.

Buys OTR, reprint rights. Replies to queries in 2-4 weeks if accompanied by SASE. Lead time for seasonal articles: 6 months. Articles published 6-8 months after acceptance. Accepts CM, SQ, SS, PPS. Subsidized trips OK. Prefers features of 1000 words. Pays $50-$350. SC: 9-by-11 SASE. WG: SASE. **Photos:** Photo editor: Jean Kennedy. Uses BW, 35mm color slides. Pays $50-$150/BW or color, at least $100/cover. Buys OTR. POA. Photos purchased without mss. **Editorial Slant:** Published by the AAA-Auto Club of Missouri. Goal is to provide members with a variety of useful information on travel.

Military History, 105 Loudoun Street, S.W., Leesburg, VA 22075. Phone: 703-771-9400. Reply date: 9/30/88. See Empire Press.

Military Lifestyle, 1732 Wisconsin Avenue, N.W., Washington, DC 20007.
Editor: Hope Daniels. Reply date: 8/28/88. Ten times/year. 90 percent freelance written. POP unless article will be held for more than 6 months, then POA. Buys FNASR. Replies to queries in 8 weeks. Lead time for seasonal articles: 6 months. Prefers features of 1800 words. Departments or columns: 1200 words. Pays $100-$650. SC: $1.50 for current issue or $2 for back issue to Magazine Requests. WG: SASE. **Editorial Slant:** Published in two editions, United States and overseas. Readers are primarily military spouses or members of the service between the ages of 18 and 38. Articles must be slanted to military families. Readers travel extensively and move frequently. Sample articles, 3/88: Texas dude ranch, skiing, cycling vacations, military FAMCAMPS, offbeat vacations, spring training.

Modern Bride, 475 Park Avenue South, New York, NY 10016.
Travel editor: Risa Weinreb. Phone: 212-779-1999. Reply date: 9/30/88. Six times/year. Circulation: 350,000. FL/year: 50. POA. Buys FR. Replies to queries in 2 months. Articles published 6 months after acceptance. Accepts SQ. Subsidized trips OK. Pays $900-$1100. Pays expenses. SC: On newsstands. **Photos:** Photo editor: Beth Traunfeld. Uses 35mm, 2¼-inch, and 4-by-5 color transparencies. Pays $300/page/color. Buys OTR. POP. Photos purchased without mss.

Montana, POB 5630, Helena, MT 59604.
Editor: Carolyn Cunningham. Phone: 406-443-2842. Reply date:

9/30/88. Bimonthly. Circulation: 69,000. FL/year: 6-8. POP. Buys OTR. Kill fee: Occasionally paid for assigned articles. Replies to queries in 4-6 weeks. Lead time for seasonal articles: 3 months. Articles published within 1 year of acceptance. Accepts CM, SQ, SS, PPS (depending on crossover readership). ES: Diskette with hard copy. Subsidized trips OK. Prefers features of 2000 words. Departments or columns: 800-1000 words. Pays $75-$500. Occasionally pays expenses for assigned articles. SC: $2. WG available. **Photos:** Photo editor: Carolyn Cunningham. Uses BW prints, transparencies. On Montana subjects only. Pays $25/BW, $50/color, $75/cover. POP. Photos purchased without mss. **Editorial Slant:** Montana topics only. Articles on people, geography, history, cities, small towns, wildlife, recreational opportunities, places to dine, byways, and infrequently explored country.

Motor Club News, 484 Central Avenue, Newark, NJ 07107.
Managing editor: Marlene Timm. Phone: 201-733-4033. Reply date: 9/30/88. Bimonthly. Circulation: 40,000-50,000. FL/year: 24 or more. POA. Buys AR. Replies to queries only when interested. Lead time for seasonal articles: 2 months. Articles published 1-6 months after acceptance. Accepts CM, SQ, PPS (depending on circumstances). ES: Macintosh (modem). Subsidized trips OK. Prefers features of 12,000 characters or 7 double-spaced pages. Pays $250-$350 depending on art. SC and WG available. **Photos:** Photo editor: Marlene Timm. Uses BW, color, slides. Pay varies. POA. Photos purchased without mss.

MotorHome, 29901 Agoura Road, Agoura, CA 91301.
Editor: Bob Livingston. Phone: 213-991-4980. Reply date: 4/14/88. Monthly. FL/year: 24 or more. Buys FNASR. Replies to queries in 30-45 days. Lead time for seasonal articles: 4 months. Prefers features of 1000-2000 words. Pays $75-$350. WG: SASE. **Photos:** Uses BW 8-by-10 glossies, color transparencies. Photos purchased without mss. **Editorial Slant:** Travel destinations, virtually unlimited as long as they are accessible by motor home, range from Canada to Mexico and around the world, in addition to the United States. Each travel story needs a map detailing routes, campgrounds, and specific sights mentioned in the copy. Descriptions of little-known attractions and activities are good elements for an article, as are personal observations on the character of a specific area and its inhabitants. Wide variety of quality color slides is essential for a

travel feature and at least one or two must include a motor home in the appropriate setting. Sample articles, 4/88: Wisconsin's Maple Sugar Festival; New Mexico fiesta; South Dakota; King's Landing, New Brunswick.

Motour, 15 West Central Parkway, Cincinnati, OH 45202.
Articles editor: Terri Hamer. Reply date: 10/8/88. Monthly except December. Circulation: 160,000. FL/year: 22. POP. Buys FR in AAA membership territory. Replies to queries in 4-8 weeks. Lead time for seasonal articles: At least 3 months. Articles published 2 months after acceptance. Accepts CM, SQ, SS, PPS. Subsidized trips OK. Prefers features of 1200-1500 words. Pays $100-$250. Pays expenses. SC: SASE and $1. WG: SASE. **Photos:** Uses BW prints, color slides. Pay included with articles. Buys exclusive rights in their market. Pays with article payment or on publication. Photos purchased without mss. **Editorial Slant:** Topics include foreign, domestic, and local travel.

National Geographic Traveler, 17th and M streets, N.W., Washington, DC 20036.
Editorial director: Richard Busch. Reply date: 9/30/88. Bimonthly. Circulation: 800,000. FL/year: 50. POA. Buys AR. Kill fee: 50 percent. Replies to queries within 1 month. Lead time for seasonal articles: 9 months. Articles published 6-18 months after acceptance. Accepts CM. Prefers features of 2000-3000 words. Departments or columns: 750-1500 words. Pays approximately $1 per word. Pays expenses. SC: $5.60 to Robert Dove. WG: SASE. **Photos:** Query editor. Uses color transparencies. Pays $300/page/color, $500/cover. Buys OTR. POA. Photos rarely purchased without mss. **Editorial Slant:** Published by the National Geographic Society. Highlights mostly U.S. and Canadian subjects, but about 20 percent of articles cover other destinations, most often Europe, Mexico, and the Caribbean, occasionally the Pacific.

National Parks, 1015 31st Street, N.W., Washington, DC 20007.
Editor: Michele Strutin. Phone: 202-944-8530. Reply date: 9/30/88. Bimonthly. Circulation: 80,000. FL/year: Approximately 20. POP. Buys FR. Replies to queries in 2-6 weeks. Articles published 1-12 months after acceptance. Prefers features of 1800 words. Pays $100-$300. SC: $3. WG: SASE. **Photos:** Photo editor: Michele Strutin. Uses BW, color. Pays $50-$300. Buys FR. POP. Photos purchased without mss. **Editorial Slant:** Published by the National

Parks and Conservation Association. Subjects include proposed new areas, threats to parks, park wildlife, new trends in park use and enjoyment, legislative issues, descriptive accounts, adventure with a new angle, and endangered species of plants or animals relevant to national parks.

National Wildlife, 8925 Leesburg Pike, Vienna, VA 22184.
Managing editor: Mark Wexler. Reply date: 6/8/88. Six times/year. Circulation: 900,000. POA. Lead time for seasonal articles: 10 months. Prefers features of 800-2500 words. WG: SASE. **Photos:** Photo editor: John Nuhn. Uses BW, 35mm and larger color transparencies (Kodachrome or Fuji 50 or 100 slide film). Photos purchased without mss. **Editorial Slant:** Published by the National Wildlife Federation. Uses nature essays and articles about adventure travel. Sample articles, 6-7/88: Forest Service special agents, feral swine, nature sculptor Kent Ullberg, damming the Platte River, barn owls in the Midwest.

Nevada, 101 South Fall Street, Carson City, NV 89710-0005.
Associate editor: Cliff Glover. Phone: 702-885-5416. Reply date: 10/21/88. POP. Buys FNASR. ES: Macintosh, Microsoft Word. Prefers features of 500-1800 words. Pays $50-$300. **Photos:** Art director: Brian Buckley. Uses BW 8-by-10 glossies, 35mm color transparencies, some color prints. Pays at least $20/photo, $100/cover. POP. **Editorial Slant:** Published by Nevada Commission on Tourism. Subjects include Nevada's people, history, recreation, entertainment, towns, and scenery.

New England Senior Citizen/Senior American News, 470 Boston Post Road, Weston, MA 02193.
Editor-in-chief: Eileen DeVito. Phone: 617-899-2702. Reply date: 9/30/88. Monthly tabloid newspaper. FL/year: 48-60 or more. POP. Buys FR. Replies to queries in 6 months at most. Lead time for seasonal articles: 6 months. Accepts CM. Prefers features of 1000-1500 words. Departments or columns: 600-800 words. Pays $25-$100. SC: 50 cents. WG: SASE. **Photos:** Query editor. Uses BW 5-by-7 or 8-by-10 glossies. Pays for photos when payment for manuscript is made.

New Hampshire Profiles, 90 Fleet Street, POB 4638, Portsmouth, NH 03801.
Editor: Jack Savage. Phone: 603-433-1551. Reply date: 9/30/88.

Monthly. Circulation: 24,000. FL/year: 6-10. POP. Buys FR. Kill fee: 25 percent. Replies to queries in 2 months. Lead time for seasonal articles: 6 months. Articles published 3 months after acceptance. Accepts CM, SQ, SS, PPS. Subsidized trips OK. Prefers features of 2000 words. Departments or columns: 1200-1500 words. Pays $100-$275. Pays expenses. SC: $3. WG: SASE. **Photos:** Photo editor: Jack Savage. Uses primarily color slides. Pays $35/BW, $50/color, $150/cover. Buys OTR. POP. Photos purchased without mss. **Editorial Slant:** Magazine covers the people, towns, history, natural environment, and lifestyles of New Hampshire.

New Mexico, 1100 St. Francis Drive, Santa Fe, NM 87503.
Editor: Emily Drabanski. Phone: 505-827-0220. Reply date: 4/14/88. Monthly. Circulation: 100,000. FL/issue: 7-10. POA. Replies to queries in 4 to 6 weeks. Lead time for seasonal articles: 6-12 months. Prefers articles of 250-2500 words. Pays $60-$350. SC: $1.95. WG: SASE. **Photos:** Art director: Mary Sweitzer. Uses BW, 35mm to 8-by-10 color transparencies. Pays $50 and up/assigned BW, $30-$50/nonassigned color, $50-$200/assigned color. POP. Buys FNASR, OTR. **Editorial Slant:** Examines the people, culture, arts, history, and landscape of New Mexico for an educated readership, two-thirds of whom live outside the state.

New York Alive, 152 Washington Avenue, Albany, NY 12210.
Editor: Mary G. Stoll. Phone: 518-465-7511. Reply date: 4/18/88. Six times/year. Pays within 60 days of acceptance. Kill fee: 25 percent. Replies to queries in 12-14 weeks. Prefers features of 2500-3000 words. "Great Escapes" travel column: 1000-2000 words. Pays $200-$350 for features, $50-$150 for departments. Pays expenses. SC: $2.50. WG: SASE. **Editorial Slant:** Published by the Business Council of New York State to increase knowledge and appreciation of the state.

Nightlife, 1770 Deer Park Avenue, Deer Park, NY 11729.
Query Michael Watt. Phone: 516-242-7722. Reply date: 9/30/88. Monthly. Circulation: 100,000. FL/year: 10-12. POP. Replies to queries in a week. Lead time for seasonal articles: 2 months. Accepts CM, SQ, SS, PPS. Subsidized trips OK. Prefers features of 3-4 pages. Pays $50-$125. SC: On newsstands. **Photos:** Prefers slides. **Editorial Slant:** Uses travel articles on skiing and the Caribbean. Also cruises out of Florida and New York, amusement parks, European travel packages, U.S. vacations, Atlantic City.

Nissan Discovery, POB 4617, North Hollywood, CA 91607.
Editor: Wayne Thoms. Phone: 818-506-4081. Reply date: 9/30/88. Six times/year. Circulation: 500,000. FL/year: 25. POA. Buys FR and reprint rights. Replies to queries in 2-4 weeks. Lead time for seasonal articles: 6-8 weeks. Articles published 1-3 months after acceptance. Accepts CM, SQ, PPS. Subsidized trips OK. Prefers features of 1500-1800 words. Pays $300-$1000. SC: SASE and $1.50 in stamps or coin. WG: SASE. **Photos:** Photo editor: Wayne Thoms. Uses color. Pay for photos is part of story package. Buys FR. **Editorial Slant:** A general interest family magazine covering travel, lifestyle, sports—offbeat but not too far out. Good art is the key to acceptance.

North Shore Magazine/Sandwich Islands, POB 1320, Hanalei, Kauai, HI 96714.
Editor: Myles Ludwig. Phone: 808-826-9588. Reply date: 11/7/88. Quarterly. Circulation: 20,000. FL/year: 8. POP. Buys FR. Kill fee: 50 percent. Replies to queries in 2 weeks. Lead time for seasonal articles: 3 months. Accepts SQ, PPS, PQ. Subsidized trips OK. Prefers features of 1000-2000 words. Departments or columns: 1000 words. Pays $100-$200. Pays expenses. SC available. **Photos:** Photo editor: Myles Ludwig. Uses all types of photos. Pays $25-$50/BW or color. Buys FR, SR. POP. Photos purchased without mss. **Editorial Slant:** Magazine is about the beauty, excitement, and tradition of Kauai.

AR	all rights	OTR	one-time rights
ASMP	American Society of	POA	pays on acceptance
	Magazine	POB	post office box
	Photographers	POP	pays on publication
BW	black-and-white photos	PPS	previously published
CM	complete manuscript		submissions
ES	electronic submissions	PQ	phone queries
FL	freelance	SAE	self-addressed envelope
FL/year	number of freelance travel	SASE	self-addressed stamped envelope
	articles published per	SC	sample copy
	year	SQ	simultaneous queries
F(NAS)R	first (North American serial)	SR	second rights
	rights	SS	simultaneous submissions
ms(s)	manuscript(s)	WG	writer's guidelines
NA	North American		

Northeast Outdoors, POB 2180, Waterbury, CT 06722-2180.
Editor: Camilo Falcon. Phone: 203-755-0158. Reply date: 9/30/
88. Monthly. Circulation: 26,000. FL/year: 50-70. POP. Buys OTR.
Kill fee: 50 percent. Replies to queries in 1 month. Lead time for
seasonal articles: 3 months. Articles published 2-6 months after
acceptance. Accepts CM, SQ, SS, PPS. Prefers features of 1000-
1500 words. Departments or columns: 500-1000 words. Pays $40-
$60 for features, $60-$80 for features with photos. SC: $1.50. WG:
SASE. **Photos:** Photo editor: Camilo Falcon. Photos rarely purchased
without mss. **Editorial Slant:** Interested in articles and photographs
about camping and outdoor activities in the Northeast: New England, New York, New Jersey, and Pennsylvania. Greatest need is
advice on good campgrounds and destinations throughout the region
to aid in vacation planning. Likes first-person approach.

Northern California Home & Garden, 2317 Broadway, Suite 330,
Redwood City, CA 94063.
Editor: Rachael Grossman. Phone: 415-368-8800. Reply date: 9/
30/88. Monthly. Pays up to 6 weeks after invoice. ES: IBM compatible. Prefers features of 2000-3000 words. Departments or columns: Up to 1500 words. Pays $250-$500 for features, $150-$250
for departments. WG: SASE. **Photos:** Art director: Dana Irwin.
Editorial Slant: Stories must appeal to a sophisticated Northern
California audience. Annual travel issue in March.

Northwest Living!, 130 Second Avenue South, Edmonds, WA 98020.
Editor: Terry W. Sheely. Phone: 206-774-4111. Reply date: 9/30/
88. Bimonthly. Circulation: 25,000. FL/year: 17. POP. Buys OTR.
Replies to queries in 4 weeks. Lead time for seasonal articles: 6
months. Articles published 6 months to 1 year after acceptance.
Accepts CM, PPS. Subsidized trips OK. Prefers features of 800-
1200 words. Pays $200-$300 for article and photo package. SC:
SASE. **Photos:** Uses BW, 35mm color slides (prefers Kodachrome
64). Pays $50-$100/color, $200/cover. Buys OTR. POP. Photos
purchased without mss. **Editorial Slant:** Covers Washington, Oregon, Idaho, Montana, Alaska, British Columbia, Alberta, and the
Yukon Territory. Interested in people, natural science, history, homes,
foods, outdoor recreation, regional travel, wildlife.

Oceans, 2001 West Main Street, Stamford, CT 06902.
Editor: Michael Robbins. Phone: 203-359-8626. Reply date: 11/6/
88. Bimonthly. Circulation: 50,000. FL/year: 8-10. POP. Buys

FNASR. Kill fee: $200. Replies to queries in 2 weeks to 1 month. Lead time for seasonal articles: 4 months. Articles published 2-6 months after acceptance. Accepts CM, SQ. Subsidized trips OK. Prefers features of 2500-3000 words. Departments or columns: 800 words. Pays $800-$2000. Pays expenses. SC and WG available. **Photos:** Photo editor: Terry Nyhan. Uses 35mm color slides. Pays ASMP rates/BW or color; pay negotiable for cover. Buys OTR. POP. Photos purchased without mss. **Editorial Slant:** Articles on sea-related adventures.

Off Duty Europe, Escherheimer Landstrasse 69, Frankfurt/M1, West Germany 6000.

Editor: J. C. Couch. Phone: 069-590805. Reply date: 10/18/88. Monthly. Circulation: 125,000. FL/year: Over 50. POA. Buys FR in European military market. Replies to queries in 2-3 weeks. Lead time for seasonal articles: 6 months. Articles published immediately to 1 year after acceptance. Accepts CM, SQ, PPS. Subsidized trips OK. Prefers features of 800-1800 words. Pays 10-12 cents/word. SC, WG. International Reply Coupon with request. **Photos:** Query editor. Uses BW prints, color transparencies. Pays $25/BW, $50/color, $200/cover. Buys FR in the European military market. POP. Photos purchased without mss.

Off Duty Pacific, 14/F Park Commercial Center, 8 Shelter Street, Causeway Bay, Hong Kong.

Editor: Jim Shaw. Phone: 852-5-777215. Reply date: 11/21/88. Monthly. Circulation: 83,000. FL/year: 50. POA. Buys FR. Replies to queries in 6 weeks. Lead time for seasonal articles: 3 months. Accepts CM, SQ, PPS. ES: Diskette. Subsidized trips OK. Prefers features of under 2000 words. Departments or columns: 800-1000 words. Pays 10 cents/word. SC, WG: Write. **Photos:** Photo editor: Jim Shaw. Prefers transparencies. Pays $25/BW, at least $25/color, $150-$200/cover. Buys OTR. POP. Photos not usually purchased without mss. **Editorial Slant:** For military personnel stationed in the Pacific.

Off-Road, 12100 Wilshire Boulevard, No. 250, Los Angeles, CA 90025.

Editor: Duane Elliott. Phone: 213-820-3601. Reply date: 9/30/88. Monthly. Circulation: 100,000. FL/year: 40. POP. Pays kill fee under prearranged terms. Replies to queries in 2 weeks. Lead time for seasonal articles: 3 months. Articles published as soon as possible after acceptance. Accepts CM, SQ, SS, PPS. ES: Fax (213-207-9388). Subsidized trips OK. Pays $125 per published page. SC: On newsstands. **Photos:** Photo editor: Duane Elliott. Uses 35mm or larger color transparencies. POP. Photos purchased without mss.

Offshore, 220-9 Reservoir Street, Needham Heights, MA 02194. Managing editor: Richard Booth. Phone: 617-449-6204. Reply date: 9/30/88. Monthly. Circulation: 40,000. FL/year: 12. Pays 1 week before publication. Buys FR. Kill fee: $35-$50. Replies to queries within 1 month. Lead time for seasonal articles: 6 to 8 weeks. Accepts CM, SQ, SS, PPS, PQ. ES: Modem XTC. Prefers features of 1200-2500 words. Departments or columns: 1000-1200 words. Pays $150-$350. Pays expenses on assignments. SC, WG: Write. **Photos:** Art director: David Dauer. Uses BW. Pay for most photos included in article package. Pays $15/assigned photo, $200/cover. Pays before publication. Buys FR. **Editorial Slant:** A boating publication with two editions: New England and Northeast (New York and New Jersey).

Ohio Magazine, 40 South 3rd Street, Columbus, OH 43215. Managing editor: Ellen Stein Burbach. Phone: 614-461-5083. Reply date: 10/7/88. Monthly. Circulation: 102,000. Buys OTR. Replies to queries in 2-6 weeks. Lead time for seasonal articles: 6 months. Articles published 1 month to 1 year after acceptance. Accepts CM, PPS. Subsidized trips sometimes OK if editor is told. Prefers features of 300-2000 words. Departments or columns: 200-1200 words. Pays $15-$850. Sometimes pays expenses. SC: $3.50. WG: SASE. **Photos:** Photo editor: Brooke Wenstrup or Ellen Stein Burbach. Uses BW, four-color. Pays $25 or more. Buys OTR. Pays on acceptance or 2-3 months after. Photos purchased without mss. **Editorial Slant:** Articles on Ohio's country life, city life, sports, dining, arts, events.

Oklahoma TODAY, POB 25125, Oklahoma City, OK 73152. Managing editor: Susan Tomlinson. Phone: 405-521-2496. Reply date: 9/30/88. Bimonthly. Circulation: 38,000. FL/year: 12. POA. Buys FR. Kill fee: $50. Replies to queries in up to 2 months. Lead time for seasonal articles: 1 year. Articles published up to 1 year after acceptance. Accepts CM. Subsidized trips OK. Prefers features of 1400-2500 words. Departments or columns: 1200 words. Pays $250-$500 for features, $200 for departments. SC: $2.50. WG: SASE. **Photos:** Photo editor: Felton Stroud. Uses some BW prints, mostly color transparencies. Pays $50-$125/BW or color, $200/cover. Buys OTR. POP. Photos purchased without mss. **Editorial Slant:** Official magazine of the state of Oklahoma. Most stories are about travel and outdoor recreation. Fishing, hiking, bicycling, museums, special events, lakes and parks, art, theater, music, sports, unusual restaurants.

Omni, 1965 Broadway, New York, NY 10023-5965.
Associate editor: Kevin McKinney. Phone: 212-496-6100. Reply date: 9/30/88. Monthly. Circulation: 950,000. FL/year: Varies. Buys AR. Kill fee: 25 percent. Replies to queries in 2-4 weeks, sometimes longer. Accepts PQ if writer has previously written for magazine. Subsidized trips OK. Prefers columns of 900-1200 words. Pays $900. Pays expenses if discussed beforehand. SC, WG: Write or phone. **Photos:** Photo editor: Hilde Kron. Uses slides, transparencies. Pays $450/color. Buys OTR. POP. **Editorial Slant:** Travel has a broad definition. Previous articles have been on Florida's Stonehenge and travel inside an active volcano. Other possible topics are future family expeditions, such as adventures in space, high-tech treasure hunting, archeological and anthropological fieldwork and discoveries.

Ontario OUT OF DOORS, 227 Front Street East, Toronto, Ontario, Canada M5A 1E8.
Editor: Burton J. Myers. Phone: 416-596-2655. Reply date: 9/30/88. POA. Buys FNASR. Replies to queries in 6 weeks. Prefers features of 1500-2000 words. Pays $35-$350. WG: SASE. **Photos:** Uses BW glossies, color transparencies. Pays $300-$500/cover. **Editorial Slant:** How-to and where-to articles relating to hunting and fishing, plus camping, boating, recreational vehicles, photography, and target shooting as they relate to angling and hunting.

Orange Coast, 245-D Fischer, Suite 8, Costa Mesa, CA 92626.
Editor: John Morell. Phone: 714-545-1900. Reply date: 10/28/88. Monthly. Circulation: 35,000. FL/year: Over 24. POA. Buys FNASR. Replies to queries in 2 months. Lead time for seasonal articles: 4 months. Articles published 4 months to 1 year after acceptance. Accepts CM. Subsidized trips OK. Prefers features of at least 2000 words. Departments or columns: 1500 words. Pays $150 for features, $100 for departments. SC and WG available. **Photos:** Photo editor: Leslie Lawicki. Uses scenic travel shots specific to a destination. No pay for photos. Buys FR. **Editorial Slant:** For wealthy

Orange County residents. Travel articles on international destinations as well as weekend getaways.

Out West, POB 19894, Sacramento, CA 95819.
Editor: Chuck Woodbury. Reply date: 9/30/88. Quarterly. Circulation: 2,500. FL/year: 25-40. POP, sometimes POA. Buys OTR. Kill fee: 50 percent. Replies to queries in 1-6 weeks. Lead time for seasonal articles: 6 weeks. Articles usually published 1 to 6 months after acceptance. Accepts CM, SQ, SS, PPS. Prefers features of 500-1000 words. Departments or columns: 600 words. Pays $20-$75. SC: $1.50. WG: SASE. **Photos:** Photo editor: Chuck Woodbury. Uses BW. Pays $10-$15/BW. Buys OTR. POP. Photos purchased without mss. **Editorial Slant:** Travel about offbeat places: lodges, lakes, ghost towns, little-known state and national parks and monuments, B&Bs, historic sites, desert boomtowns, museums, cafes, small-town festivals, Indian reservations.

Outdoor Canada, 801 York Mills Road, No. 301, Don Mills, Ontario, Canada M3B 1X7.
Editor: Teddi Brown. Phone: 416-443-8888. Reply date: 7/25/88. Nine times/year. POP. Prefers features of 1500-2500 words. Departments or columns: 100-500 words. "Sportsman's Journal" section pays $6/inch. **Photos:** Art director: Maria Mastromarco. Uses BW negatives and contact sheets, 35mm color slides (Kodachrome 64). **Editorial Slant:** One issue per year devoted to fishing, another to hunting. Other issues focus generally on fishing, canoeing, hiking, camping, hunting, photography, wildlife, and cross-country skiing. "Destinations" department contains profiles of outdoor places. Sample articles, Summer 1988: Wildlife photography, fishing tournaments.

Outdoor Life, 380 Madison Avenue, 7th Floor, New York, NY 10017.
Executive editor: Vin T. Sparano. Phone: 212-687-3000. Reply date: 10/18/88. Monthly. Circulation: "National." Buys FNASR. Rarely pays kill fee. Replies to queries in 1 month. Lead time for seasonal articles: 6 months to 1 year. Accepts CM. Subsidized trips sometimes OK. Prefers features of 2500-3000 words. Departments or columns: 1500 words. Pays $800-$1100 for features, $300-$500 for regional articles. SC and WG available. **Photos:** Art director: Jim Eckes. Uses BW 8-by-10 glossies with negatives, 35mm color slides. Pays $35-$200. Buys FNASR. Pays after publication. Photos sometimes purchased without mss. **Editorial Slant:** Emphasizes fish-

ing, hunting, camping, boating, and conservation. Regional articles focus on "lakes, rivers, specific geographic locations, counties, shorelines, and sometimes whole states or multistate regions that are of special interest to hunters and fishermen."

Outside, 1165 North Clark Street, Chicago, IL 60610.
Editor: John Rasmus. Phone: 312-951-0990. Reply date: 4/14/88. Twelve times/year. Uses 5-7 features and 5 columns per issue. POP. Kill fee: 25 percent. Replies to queries in 4-6 weeks. Prefers features of 2000-4000 words. Departments or columns of 200-2000 words. Pays $75-$1500. **Editorial Slant:** For active, educated, upscale adults who love the outdoors and are concerned about its preservation. "Destinations" column covers activity-oriented travel ideas with a national scope.

Overseas!, Kolpingstrasse 1, 6906 Leimen, West Germany.
Managing editor: Greg Ballinger. Phone: 06224-706-50. Reply date: 6/8/88. Circulation: 83,000. POA. Prefers features of 1500-2500 words. Pays 10 cents/word. **Photos:** Uses BW, color. **Editorial Slant:** Leisure-time and lifestyle magazine for the US military stationed in Europe. Average reader is male, age 24. Sample articles: "The 10 Best Beers in Germany," "A Nightlife Guide to London," "The Top Beaches of Italy."

Palm Springs Life, 303 North Indian Avenue, Palm Springs, CA 92262.
Editor: Rebecca Kurtz. Phone: 619-325-2333. Reply date: 8/15/88. Monthly. POP. Buys AR. ES: Modem. Prefers features up to 2000 words. Pays $150-$200 for features. **Photos:** Pays $25/BW, $50-$100/color, $250/cover. **Editorial Slant:** Luxury lifestyle magazine for affluent residents of Palm Springs. Articles on travel, beauty, health, sports, and lifestyles of the powerful, rich, and famous.

Parenting, 501 2nd Street, No. 110, San Francisco, CA 94107.
Articles editor: Rebecca Poole. Phone: 415-546-7575. Reply date: 10/12/88. Monthly. Circulation: 400,000. FL/year: 10-20. POA. Kill fee: 25 percent. Replies to queries in 4-8 weeks. Lead time for seasonal articles: 4 months. Accepts CM, SQ, SS. Prefers features of 2000-3000 words. Departments or columns: 500-1500 words. Pays $750-$2000 for features, $50-$100 for shorter pieces. Pays expenses. SC, WG: Write Dana Sullivan, Assistant to Editor. **Photos:** Photo editor: Tripp Mikich. Uses all kinds of photos. Photos

purchased without mss. **Editorial Slant:** For parents of children from birth to ten years old, with most emphasis put on the under-sixes.

The Peak Magazine, 1-13 D-Aguilar Street, Central, Hong Kong. Editor-in-chief: Bill Cranfield. Reply date: 9/30/88. Bimonthly. POP. Buys SR. Prefers features of 1500-2000 words. Pays $500-$600 for article and photo package, $200-$350 for story alone. **Photos:** Pays $350 for a photo package. **Editorial Slant:** Lifestyle magazine for Hong Kong's most affluent citizens. Travel interests: the exotic, esoteric, expensive, exclusive. Europe and the States tend to be of more appeal than Asia.

Peninsula, 2317 Broadway, Suite 330, Redwood City, CA 94063. Editor: David Gorn. Phone: 415-368-8800. Reply date: 8/23/88. Pays within 15 days of publication. Buys OTR. ES: Diskette or modem. Prefers features of 3000-4000 words. Pays up to $600 for features, $100-$200 for departments. **Editorial Slant:** For the affluent, well-educated residents of the San Francisco peninsula. Travel is California only.

Peninsula Magazine, POB 2259, Sequim, WA 98382. Phone: 206-683-5421. Reply date: 10/21/88. Three times/year. POP. Buys FR. Kill fee: 20 percent. Prefers features of 1000-1500 words. Departments or columns: 400-1000 words. Pays $150-$350 for features; 10 cents/word for shorts. **Editorial Slant:** Presents a picture of life on the Olympic Peninsula. Outdoor activities: camping, skiing, kayaking, beachcombing, fishing, boating.

Pennsylvania Angler, POB 1673, Harrisburg, PA 17105-1673. Editor: Art Michaels. Phone: 717-657-4520. Reply date: 5/19/88. Monthly. Circulation: 65,000. FL/year: Over 100-120 features. POA. Buys AR. Replies to queries in 1-2 weeks. Lead time for seasonal articles: 8 months. Accepts CM, PPS (rarely). Prefers features of up to 2500 words. Departments or columns: 150-300 words. Pays $25-$300 for article and photo package. WG: SASE. **Photos:** Uses BW 5-by-7 or 8-by-10 glossies; 35mm and larger color transparencies (Kodachrome 25 or 64). Pays $10-$50/BW, $15-$50/color, $50-$100/back cover, up to $300/front cover. **Editorial Slant:** Official voice of the Pennsylvania Fish Commission. Uses where-to's that include details on how to fish specific Pennsylvania waterways, times of day best for action, and technically accurate how-to information.

Pennsylvania Heritage, POB 1026, Harrisburg, PA 17108-1026.
Editor: Michael O'Malley 3rd. Phone: 717-787-1396. Reply date:
5/2/88. Quarterly. POA. Replies to queries in 2-3 weeks. Accepts
CM. Prefers features of 3000-3500 words. Pays $100 and up. WG:
SASE. **Photos:** Uses BW 5-by-7 or 8-by-10 glossies; 35mm or
larger color transparencies (preferably Ektachrome 200). Pays $5-
$10/BW, $25/color, $25-$50/back cover, $100/front cover. Buys
AR. **Editorial Slant:** Articles relating to Pennsylvania's history and
culture. Fine and decorative arts, architecture, archeology, exhibits,
natural history, historic sites, and travel.

Pennsylvania Magazine, POB 576, Camp Hill, PA 17011.
Editor/publisher: A. E. Holliday. Phone: 717-761-6620. Reply date:
9/30/88. Bimonthly. Circulation: Over 35,000. FL/year: Over 30.
POP if assigned, POA if unsolicited. Buys OTR. Kill fee: 25 percent
for assigned articles. Replies to queries in 2-4 weeks. Lead time for
seasonal articles: 6-8 months. Accepts CM, SQ. Subsidized trips
OK if so stated. Prefers features of 1000-2500 with illustrations.
Pays 10-15 cents/word. Pays expenses if discussed in advance. SC:
$3. WG: SASE. **Photos:** Photo editor: A. E. Holliday. Uses photos
related to article. Pays $100/cover. Buys OTR. Pays for photos at
same time as for mss. Photos purchased without mss. **Editorial
Slant:** Topics covered include people and personalities, history, travel,
family life, and leisure time, all related directly to Pennsylvania.

Personal Marketing, Inc., 8520 Sweetwater, Suite F57, Houston,
TX 77037.
Senior editor: Pam Roark. Phone: 713-591-6015, 800-231-0440.
Reply date: 10/12/88. Publishes 25 different four-color real estate
newsletters. Monthly. Circulation: 3 million (combined). FL/year:
20. POA. Buys FNASR. Replies to queries in 4-6 weeks. Lead time
for seasonal articles: 6 months. Accepts CM, SQ, SS, PPS. Prefers
features of 300-350 words. Pays 20 cents/word. SC, WG: SASE.
Photos: Photo editor: Anne Roberts. Uses 35mm slides, transparencies. Pays $25/color. Buys FR. POA. Photos purchased without
mss. **Editorial Slant:** Travel articles on interesting, offbeat places;
activities such as ballooning and adventure camps; Elderhostel programs; walking the Appalachian Trail; birdwatching; vacationing
in inns; motorhome trips.

Petersen's FISHING, 8490 Sunset Boulevard, Los Angeles, CA 90069.
Editor: Robert Robb. Phone: 213-854-2723. Reply date: 8/20/88.

Buys AR. Prefers features of 2000-2500 words. Pays $300-$400 for article and BW photos. **Photos:** Art director: Greg Hollobaugh. Uses BW 8-by-10, color (Kodachrome and Fujichrome). Pays $35/ BW, $150/page/color, $500/cover. Buys AR or OTR. **Editorial Slant:** Subject matter relating to the interests of the North American angler, mostly on North American spots, but some international features.

Petersen's HUNTING, 8490 Sunset Boulevard, Los Angeles, CA 90069.
Editor: Craig Boddington. Phone: 213-854-2222. Reply date: 1/7/ 88. Prefers features of 2000-2500 words. Pays $100-$400. **Photos:** Art director: C. A. Yeseta. Uses BW glossies, color slides (Kodachrome). Pays $35/BW, $75-$150/color, $350/cover. Buys AR, OTR. **Editorial Slant:** Subject matter tailored to the interests of North American hunters.

Pleasure Boating, 1995 N.E. 150th Street, North Miami, FL 33181.
Managing editor: Gord Lomer. Phone: 305-945-7403. Reply date: 10/21/88. Monthly. Circulation: 25,000. FL/year: 12-15. POP. Buys FNASR. Replies to queries in 1-2 weeks. Lead time for seasonal articles: 2 months. Articles published 2-3 months after acceptance. Accepts CM, SQ, PPS, PQ. Subsidized trips OK. Prefers features of 1800-2500 words. Pays $200-$250 and up. SC and WG available. **Photos:** Photo editor: Terri Johnson. Pays $25/BW, at least $50/ color, at least $100/cover. Buys OTR. Pays 30 days after publication. Photos purchased without mss.

Portland Magazine, 816 S.W. First Avenue, Portland, OR 97204.
Editor: David Gemma. Phone: 503-274-7640. Reply date: 8/15/ 88. POP. ES: WordPerfect (5¼-inch diskette). Prefers features of 1500-4000 words. Departments or columns: 750-1500 words. Pays 10 cents/word for unsolicited articles, 15 cents/word for solicited articles. **Editorial Slant:** Articles on Portland's restaurants, architecture, recreation opportunities, and the arts.

A Positive Approach, 1600 Malone Street, Millville, NJ 08332.
Publisher/editor: Patricia Johnson. Phone: 609-327-4040. Reply date: 6/8/88. Bimonthly. POP. Prefers features of 1000 words. Travel column: 500 words. Pays 10 cents/word. SC: $2. **Photos:** Uses 35mm. Pays $5/BW. **Editorial Slant:** Nonfiction articles on all aspects of the positive-thinking disabled person's private and business life.

Powder, POB 1028, Dana Point, CA 92629.

Managing editor: Pat Cochran. Phone: 714-496-5922. Reply date: 9/30/88. Seven times/year. Circulation: 150,000. FL/year: 30-40. POA if assigned, otherwise POP. Buys FR. Kill fee: 50 percent. Replies to queries in 6-8 weeks. Lead time for seasonal articles: 4-5 months. Accepts CM, PQ. ES: Call for information. Subsidized trips OK. Prefers features of 1500 words plus sidebar. Departments and columns are staff written. Pays $500 on average. Pays expenses. SC: $2. WG: Write Jackie Mathys, Associate Editor. **Photos:** Photo editor: James Cassimus. Uses color slides only. Pay for photos depends on size. Buys FR. POP. Photos purchased without mss. **Editorial Slant:** Articles on nearly every facet of skiing: downhill racing, backcountry experiences, heli-skiing, cross-country treks, freestyle, speed skiing, recreational racing, and snowboarding. Audience is composed of advanced to expert skiers.

Prime Times, 2802 International Lane, Suite 120, Madison, WI 53704.

Managing editor: Russell Grote. Reply date: 10/3/88. Quarterly. FL/year: "Many." POP. Buys FR or reprint rights. Replies to queries in several weeks. Lead time for seasonal articles: 90 days. Accepts CM, SQ, SS, PPS. ES: ASCII. Prefers features of 1000-1500 words. Departments or columns: 1000 words. Pays $125-$1000 for full-length articles. SC: 9-by-12 SASE and $2.50. WG: SASE. **Photos:** Uses BW, color. Pays $50/less than half page, $100/half page, $250/

AR	all rights	OTR	one-time rights
ASMP	American Society of	POA	pays on acceptance
	Magazine	POB	post office box
	Photographers	POP	pays on publication
BW	black-and-white photos	PPS	previously published
CM	complete manuscript		submissions
ES	electronic submissions	PQ	phone queries
FL	freelance	SAE	self-addressed envelope
FL/year	number of freelance travel	SASE	self-addressed stamped envelope
	articles published per	SC	sample copy
	year	SQ	simultaneous queries
F(NAS)R	first (North American serial)	SR	second rights
	rights	SS	simultaneous submissions
ms(s)	manuscript(s)	WG	writer's guidelines
NA	North American		

page. Buys OTR. POP. **Editorial Slant:** For credit union members who are retired or over 50. Travel department open to freelancers.

Private Clubs, 2711 LBJ Freeway, No. 800, Dallas, TX 75234. Editor: Julie J. Bain. Phone: 214-888-7547. Reply date: 11/21/87. Circulation: 200,000. POA. Kill fee: 25 percent. Pays at least 50 cents/word. Pays expenses. WG: SASE. **Editorial Slant:** For members of private city, country, athletic, and resort clubs associated with Club Corporation of America. Readers are 88 percent male with an average annual income of $144,000, 73 percent of whom have indicated they are interested in travel. Does not accept unsolicited queries or manuscripts. Writers should send in samples and a brief note outlining areas of expertise.

Quarante, POB 2875, Crystal City, Arlington, VA 22202. Editor: Michele Linden. Phone: 703-920-3333. Reply date: 10/23/88. Four times/year. Circulation: 50,000. FL/year: 25. POP. Buys OTR. Usually replies to queries in 6 weeks at most. Lead time for seasonal articles: 3-6 months. Accepts CM, SQ, SS, PPS. Subsidized trips sometimes OK. Prefers features of under 2500 words. Departments or columns: 800 words or more. Pays $0-$250. SC: SASE and $3. WG: SASE. **Photos:** Photo editor: Jutta Kobia. Uses BW glossies, color transparencies. **Editorial Slant:** For educated, affluent women over 30. Covers cuisine, culture, world problems.

Radiance, POB 31703, Oakland, CA 94604. Editor-publisher: Alice Ansfield. Phone: 415-482-0680. Reply date: 5/19/88. Quarterly. Circulation: 10,000. POP. Prefers features of 800-1500 words. Pays $25-$100. **Photos:** Pays $15/photo, $50-$100/cover. **Editorial Slant:** For American women who wear a size 16 or larger. Travel department covers spas, resorts, bed and breakfasts, and other places where the larger person is welcome and comfortable. Sample articles, Summer 1988 (travel issue): "Breaking the Ice in Siberia," cruises, "When Irish Isles are Beguiling," "Escape to Egypt," "Confessions of a Brazil Nut."

Ranger Rick, 8925 Leesburg Pike, Vienna, VA 22184-0001. Address the editors. Phone: 202-797-6800. Reply date: 6/23/88. Prefers to buy all world rights. Lead time for seasonal articles: 10 months. Prefers features of 900 words. Pays up to $550. **Editorial Slant:** Published by the National Wildlife Federation for children ages 6-12. Articles on any aspect of wildlife, nature, outdoor adventure and discovery, conservation. Sample articles, 2/88: Making maple syrup in Vermont, the Mozambique spitting cobra.

Real Travel, 410-301 14th Street, N.W., Calgary, Alberta, Canada T2N 2A1.
Associate editor: Kate Yorga. Phone: 403-270-8633. Reply date: 7/26/88. Quarterly. Pays within 30 days of receipt of ms. Buys FNASR. Kill fee: 50 percent. Replies to queries in 3-4 weeks. Prefers features of 1000-1800 words. Departments or columns: 100-200 words. Pays $250-$500 for features, $35-$50 for departments. Pays phone expenses. WG: SAE with International Reply Coupon. **Photos:** Prefers 35mm Kodachrome (Ektachrome OK). Pays $25-$75/photo, $250/cover. Buys OTR. **Editorial Slant:** For the sophisticated adventure traveler. Articles on untouched corners of the globe, cultural tips, practical information on choosing an outfitter.

Recreation News, POB 32335, Washington, DC 20007.
Editor: Annette Licitra. Phone: 202-965-6960. Reply date: 9/30/88. Monthly. Circulation: 108,000. FL/year: 12. Buys FR or SR. Kill fee: 20 percent after third acceptance. Replies to queries in 1-3 months. Lead time for seasonal articles: at least 6 months. Articles published at least 6 months after acceptance. Accepts CM, SQ, SS, PPS, PQ. Prefers features of 1000-1500 words. Pays $50-$100 for travel features. SC, WG: SASE with 90 cents postage. **Photos:** Photo editor: Karen Hannigan. Uses mostly BW, rarely color. Pays $30/BW, $75/color or cover. Buys FR or SR. POP. Photos rarely purchased without mss. **Editorial Slant:** Articles on recreation for federal employees living in Washington, D.C., area.

Regent, 1-13 D-Aguilar Street, Central, Hong Kong.
Editor-in-chief: Bill Cranfield. Reply date: 9/30/88. Quarterly. POP. Buys SR. Prefers features of 1500-2000 words. Pays $500-$600 for article and photo package, $200-$350 for article alone. **Photos:** Pays $350 for photo package. **Editorial Slant:** Hotel magazine for Regent International group of deluxe properties. Travel interests are upscale and offbeat.

Retired Officer, 201 North Washington Street, Alexandria, VA 22314-2529.
Editor: Col. M. L. Wilson, Jr., USA-Ret. Phone: 703-549-2311. Reply date: 5/19/88. Monthly. Circulation: 360,000. POA. Buys FR. Replies to queries in 6 weeks. Lead time for seasonal articles:

6 months. Prefers features of 750-2000 words. Pays up to $500 for unsolicited ms. SC: 9-by-12 SASE. WG: SASE. **Photos:** Uses BW 5-by-7 or 8-by-10 glossies. Pays $20/BW, $50-$100/color, $175/ cover. **Editorial Slant:** Audience is commissioned and warrant officers and families, widows, and widowers of members of the seven uniformed services. Uses optimistic and upbeat themes.

Rice—The Premier Asian-American Pacific Rim Magazine, 11022 Santa Monica Boulevard, No. 100, Los Angeles, CA 90025.
Travel editor: Marian Kwon. Phone: 213-312-6696. Reply date: 9/ 30/88. Monthly. Circulation: 75,000. FL/year: Approximately 12. POA. Kill fee: 15 percent. Replies to queries in 4-6 weeks. Lead time for seasonal articles: at least 3 months. Articles published 1- 2 months after acceptance. Accepts CM, SQ, SS. Subsidized trips OK. Prefers features of 1500-3000 words. Departments or columns: 750-1500 words. Pays expenses. SC: Write or phone. **Photos:** Query art director. Uses BW, color. Pays for photos in 30-60 days. Photos purchased without mss. **Editorial Slant:** Style is lively, pertinent, and sharply focused, with an Asian-American perspective.

Rural Kentuckian, POB 32170, Louisville, KY 40232.
Editor: Gary Luhr. Phone: 502-451-2430. Reply date: 9/30/88. Monthly. Circulation: 330,000. POA. Buys FR for Kentucky. Replies to queries in 2 weeks. Lead time for seasonal articles: 4 months. Articles published 4-12 months after acceptance. Accepts CM, SQ and SS (if other submissions are outside Kentucky), PQ. Prefers features of 800-2000 words. Pays up to $250. SC: 9-by-12 SASE. WG: SASE. **Photos:** Photo editor: Gary Luhr. Uses BW prints, color slides. Pay for photos included in pay for ms. Pays $50/cover. Buys FR for Kentucky. Pays at same time as for mss; POP for cover. **Editorial Slant:** Kentucky-related recreation and travel. Avoid boosterism. Sample articles, 4/88: "Wildflowers of Kentucky," "Bybee Pottery."

Safari, 4800 West Gates Road, Tucson, AZ 85745.
Publications director: William Quimby. Phone: 602-620-1220. Reply date: 6/8/88. Bimonthly. Circulation: 10,000. POP. Accepts CM. Prefers features of 2000-2500 words. Pays $200. WG: SASE. **Photos:** Uses BW 5-by-7 or larger, 35mm transparencies and color prints. Pays $30/BW, $100/color, $150/cover. **Editorial Slant:** The official publication of Safari Club International. Hunting material from anywhere in the world if it focuses primarily on big game

rather than small game, birds, or fishing. Also ethnic and traditional hunts of particular regions. Sample articles, 5-6/88: "Ethiopia: The Bebeka Bull," "USA: Whitetails in the Dixie Highlands," "Pakistan: The Ghost of Chitral-gol," "USA: The Great Denver Lion Capture."

Sail, Charlestown Navy Yard, 100 First Avenue, Charlestown, MA 02129.
Editor: Patience Wales. Phone: 617-241-9500. Reply date: 10/28/88. Monthly. Circulation: 175,000. FL/year: 24 cruising features that focus on destinations. POA or POP, depending on article type. Buys FNASR. Replies to queries in 4-6 weeks. Lead time for seasonal articles: 4-6 months. Articles published 2 months to 3 years after acceptance. Accepts CM, PQ. Prefers features of 2000-2500 words. Departments or columns: 300-500 words. Pays $450-$800 for features. Pays expenses for established contributors. SC, WG: Write or phone. **Photos:** Design director: Elizabeth Pollock. Uses BW prints and negatives, color transparencies. Pays "standard page rate." Buys FNASR. Pays for photos 2 weeks after publication. Photos purchased without mss. **Editorial Slant:** For everyone who sails, whether aboard a one-design boat or an offshore racer, a daysailer or an auxiliary cruiser.

Salt Water Sportsman, 280 Summer Street, Boston, MA 02210.
Editor: Barry Gibson. Reply date: 9/30/88. Monthly. Circulation: 138,000. POA. Buys FNASR. Replies to queries in 2 weeks. Lead time for seasonal articles: 6 months. Accepts CM. Subsidized trips OK. Prefers features of 1200-1500 words. Departments or columns: 1200 words. Pays $350-$700. SC: SASE. WG: Write. **Photos:** Photo editor: Barry Gibson. Prefers 35mm Kodachrome 64. Pay for photos usually included in pay for articles. Buys FNASR. POA. Photos purchased without mss for covers. **Editorial Slant:** No articles that are strictly travel articles. All articles must have a fishing angle that would appeal to the knowledgeable angler. Has to have specific information on how and where to catch fish at a given destination. Fishing comes first and the destination is secondary.

San Francisco Focus, 680 Eighth Street, San Francisco, CA 94103.
Executive editor: Amy Rennert. Phone: 415-553-2800. Reply date: 11/24/88. Monthly. Circulation: 186,000. FL/year: 8 travel features, 30 short articles. POA. Buys FNASR. Pays kill fee for assigned articles. Replies to written queries in 3-4 weeks. Lead time

for seasonal articles: 3 months. Accepts CM, SS. Prefers features of 250-2000 words. Uses several writers for each feature. Pays $200-$1000. SC: $4.50. WG: SASE. **Photos:** Senior designer: Hazel Boissiere. Uses BW, 35mm color. Pays $50-$200/BW or color. Buys OTR. Pays 30 days from invoice. **Editorial Slant:** For upscale and highly literate residents of the San Francisco area.

San Francisco: The Magazine, 45 Belden Place, San Francisco, CA 94104.
Managing editor: Katharine Fong. Phone: 415-982-3232. Reply date: 11/24/88. Ten times/year. Circulation: 75,000. FL/year: 20. POP. Buys FR. Pays kill fee if agreed on beforehand. Replies to queries in 6 weeks to 2 months. Lead time for seasonal articles: 2 and a half to 3 months. Accepts CM (but prefers queries), SQ, SS, PPS (if published outside region). ES: Macintosh (modem). Subsidized trips OK. Prefers features of 1500-2000 words. Occasionally accepts departments or columns of 1200-1500 words. Pay varies greatly. Sometimes pays expenses. SC: $3. WG: SASE. **Photos:** Photo editor: Katharine Fong. Include with manuscript. Uses BW, color. Buys FR. POP. Photos purchased without mss. **Editorial Slant:** For affluent residents of the San Francisco area. Sample articles, 5/88: Bay Area gardens, "Magic Carpet to the Other India."

Saturday Evening Post, 1100 Waterway Boulevard, Indianapolis, IN 46202.
Travel editor: Rob Ehrgott. Phone: 317-636-8881. Reply date: 10/28/88. Nine times/year. Circulation: 600,000. FL/year: Approximately 24. POP. Usually buys AR. Kill fee varies. Replies to queries in 4-6 weeks. Lead time for seasonal articles: 3-6 months. Articles published within 6 months of acceptance. Accepts SQ, SS, PPS. Subsidized trips OK. Prefers features of 1000-1200 words. Departments or columns: 500-700 words. Pays 30-40 cents/word. Pays expenses. SC: $4. WG: Write. **Photos:** Photo editor: Rob Ehrgott. Uses color slides and transparencies. Pays $50/color. Buys OTR. POP. Photos purchased without mss. **Editorial Slant:** Positive and upbeat articles for a family audience.

Sea Kayaker, 1670 Duranleau Street, Vancouver, British Columbia, Canada V6H 3S4.
Managing editor: Beatrice Dowd. Phone: 604-263-1471. Reply date: 8/29/88. Quarterly. Circulation: 10,000-12,000. POP. Buys FNASR, SR. Accepts SQ and SS if so identified, PQ. Prefers features of 2000-

4000 words. Pays at least 5 cents/word (rates in U.S. currency). WG: SASE. **Photos:** Prefers BW prints; accepts color slides and color prints when necessary. Pays $15-$100/photo, $250/cover. Buys FR. POP. **Editorial Slant:** Focuses on sea kayaking and, to a much smaller extent, lake kayaking. Destination articles give straightforward descriptions of the paddling potential of specific areas. Sample articles, Summer 1988: "Nova Scotia, Land of Contrasts," "Summer in Greenland," "The Kayak Camper's Freshwater Needs."

Sea, The Magazine of Western Boating, POB 1579, Newport Beach, CA 92663.
Associate editor: Linda Yuskaitis. Phone: 714-646-3963. Reply date: 9/30/88. Monthly. Circulation: 60,000. FL/year: 12-24. POP. Buys FNASR or SR. Kill fee: Negotiable. Replies to queries in 4-6 weeks. Lead time for seasonal articles: 6 months. Articles published 3-6 months after acceptance. Accepts CM, SQ, SS, PPS, PQ. ES: WordStar. Subsidized trips OK. Prefers features of 800-3000 words. Departments or columns: 800-1500 words. Pays $100-$300 for features. Pays expenses. SC, WG: SASE. **Photos:** Photo editor: Linda Yuskaitis. Uses photos on recreational boating and related subjects. Pays $20-$35/BW, $25-$200/color, $250/cover. Buys FNASR. POP. Photos purchased without mss. **Editorial Slant:** Provides readers in 13 Western states with informative features on all aspects of boating, including short- and long-distance cruising.

Skies America, 9600 S.W. Oak Street, No. 310, Portland, OR 97223.
Editor: Terri Wallo. Phone: 503-244-2299. Reply date: 9/30/88. Publishes *Midway, Braniff, United Express, Horizon.* FL/year: 50; 80 percent freelance written. POP. Buys FR. Kill fee: 100 percent. Replies to queries in 2 weeks. Lead time for seasonal articles: 60 days. Articles published 30-60 days after acceptance. Accepts CM, SQ, SS, PPS. Prefers features of 1200-1500 words. Departments or columns: 800-1000 words. Pays $200-$500. Sometimes pays expenses. SC: $3 check. WG: SASE. **Photos:** Photo editor: Kelly Kerns. Pays $50/color, $100/cover. Buys OTR. POP. **Editorial Slant:** Publishes in-flight magazines for several regional and national airlines in the United States. Affluent readers. Uses stories featuring destination cities.

Skin Diver, 8490 Sunset Boulevard, Los Angeles, CA 90069.
Executive editor: Bonnie J. Cardone. Phone: 213-854-2960. Reply

date: 9/30/88. Monthly. Circulation: 216,092. FL/year: 70-80. POP. Buys OTR. Replies to queries in 6 weeks at most. Lead time for seasonal articles: 6-9 months. Accepts CM, PQ. ES: Diskette, modem. Pays $50 per published page. SC: $3. WG: Write. **Photos:** Uses BW, color transparencies. Pays $50/page/photos, $325/cover. Buys OTR and promotional rights. POP. **Editorial Slant:** Uses articles on adventure, travel, underwater photography, wrecks, treasure, conservation, local diving, marine life, shelling.

Sky, 12955 Biscayne Boulevard, North Miami, FL 33181.
Editor: Lidia De Leon. Reply date: 4/25/88. Buys FNASR. Kill fee: 100 percent. Replies to queries in 30-45 days. Prefers features of 1800-2000 words. Pays some expenses. Pays $300-$500. WG: SASE. **Photos:** Send photos to Lynn David Lerner, Art Director. Uses 35mm, 2¼-inch, or 4-by-5 color transparencies. **Editorial Slant:** In-flight magazine of Delta Airlines. Primary destination features are predetermined by Delta management 12 months in advance. Writers interested in submitting travel features should send a list of destinations they are equipped to handle, for consideration when specific area needs arise.

Small Boat Journal, POB 1066, Bennington, VT 05201.
Editor: Thomas Baker. Phone: 802-442-3101. Reply date: 9/30/88. Bimonthly. Circulation: 58,000. FL/year: 6-8. POA. Buys FR. Replies to queries in 4-5 weeks. Lead time for seasonal articles: 3-6 months. Articles published 6 months to 1 year after acceptance. Accepts CM. ES: IBM compatible (diskette). Prefers features of 1000-2000 words. Pays 15 cents/word. SC, WG: Write. **Photos:** Photo editors: Janet Thompson and Thomas Baker. Uses BW, 35mm slides. Pays $25/BW, $50-$100/color, $250-$300/cover. Buys OTR. POP. Photos purchased without mss. **Editorial Slant:** Devoted to the use and evaluation of boats under 30 feet long. Readers are sailors, powerboaters, rowers, kayakers, and canoeists.

Snow Country, 5510 Park Avenue, Trumbull, CT 06611.
Editor: John Fry. Phone: 203-373-7000. Reply date: 10/8/88. Monthly. Circulation: 250,000. FL/year: Over 24. POA. Buys FNASR. Kill fee: One-third. Replies to queries in 2 weeks. Lead time for seasonal articles: ms delivered 4 months beforehand. Articles published 3-4 months after acceptance. Accepts CM. ES: ATEX for assigned articles only. Prefers features of 750-1000 words. Departments or columns: 200 words. Pays expenses. SC: On newsstands.

WG: SASE. **Photos:** Photo editor: Nancy Graham. Uses slides. Pays $325/page/color, $750/cover. Buys FNASR. POP unless assigned. Photos purchased without mss. **Editorial Slant:** Off-season coverage of golf, tennis, hiking, sailboarding, and other summer recreation available at ski resorts. Separate editions for East and West coasts.

South Bay Accent, 4320 Stevens Creek Boulevard, Suite 230, San Jose, CA 95129.

Travel editor: Ludmilla Alexander. Phone: 408-244-5100. Reply date: 10/19/88. Bimonthly. Circulation: 40,000. FL/year: 6. POP. Buys FR, reprint rights if published outside of area. Replies to queries in 1 month. Lead time for seasonal articles: 4 months. Articles published 3 months after acceptance. Accepts SQ, PPS. Subsidized trips OK. Prefers features of 1700-1800 words. Departments or columns: 1500 words. Pays $100 for features, $60 for departments. SC and WG available. **Photos:** Query art director. Usually uses photos from tourist offices. **Editorial Slant:** Publishes news, service, and human interest stories geared to the affluent, active, and career-oriented professional living in Santa Clara County. Travel emphasis in February-March issue.

South Florida Magazine, 600 Brickell Avenue, No. 207, Miami, FL 33131.

Editor: Marilyn Moore. Phone: 305-374-5011. Reply date: 9/30/88. Thirteen times/year. Circulation: 43,000. FL/year: 8. POA. Buys FNASR. Kill fee: 50 percent. Replies to queries in 3-4 weeks. Lead time for seasonal articles: 2 months. Articles published 1 month after acceptance. Accepts CM, SQ, SS, PPS. ES: ASCII (300 baud modem). Subsidized trips OK. Prefers features of 2000-4000 words. Departments or columns: 1200-1500 words. Pays $100-$1000. Pays expenses. SC: $2.50. WG: SASE. **Photos:** Photo editor: Barbara Bose. Uses color. **Editorial Slant:** For residents of Palm Beach, Broward, Dade, and Monroe counties.

Southern Magazine, 201 East Markham Street, Little Rock, AR 72201.

Associate editor: Donovan Webster. Phone: 501-375-4114. Reply date: 9/30/88. Monthly. Circulation: 290,000. FL/year: 46-60. POA. Buys FNASR. Kill fee: 10 percent. Replies to queries in 6-10 weeks. Lead time for seasonal articles: At least 6 months. Accepts CM, SQ, SS. ES: Pure ASCII file accompanied by hard copy. Prefers features

of 1200-2000 words. Departments or columns: 800 words. Pays
$150-$1750. Pays expenses. SC: $4 to Circulation Department.
WG: Write. **Photos:** Photo editor: Jeff Stanton. Uses slides or
transparencies. Buys OTR. POA. Photos purchased without mss.
Editorial Slant: Explores all facets of the contemporary South. First-
person adventures on topics such as driving a swamp buggy or going
on a fox hunt. "Weekends" department uses articles based on anything from a festival to a personal adventure.

Southern Outdoors, POB 17915, Montgomery, AL 36141.
Editor: Dave Precht. Reply date: 6/13/88. Bimonthly. 90 percent
freelance written. POA. Buys AR. Replies to queries in 4 weeks.
Prefers features of 1000-1500 words. Pays 15 cents/word for stories
with photos. SC: $1. WG: SASE. **Photos:** Uses BW, color (Ko-
dachrome). Pays $25/BW, $50/color, $250/cover. Buys AR. **Edi-
torial Slant:** Covers fishing, hunting, shooting, camping, and boating
in the South.

Specialty Travel Index, 305 San Anselmo Avenue, No. 217, San
Anselmo, CA 94960.
Editor: C. Steen Hansen. Phone: 415-459-4900. Reply date: 9/30/
88. Biannual. Circulation: 45,000. FL/year: 10. POP. Buys OTR.
Replies to queries in 30 days. Lead time for seasonal articles: 3
months. Articles published 30-60 days after acceptance. Accepts
CM, SQ, SS, PPS, PQ. ES: MS-DOS, WordStar. Subsidized trips
OK. Prefers features of 1000-1200 words. Pays 15 cents/word. SC
and WG available. **Photos:** Photo editor: C. Steen Hansen. Uses
BW, color. **Editorial Slant:** Special interest and adventure travel
destinations and activities worldwide. No first person.

Sporting Classics, POB 1017, Highway 521S, Camden, SC 29020.
Editor: Chuck Wechsler. Phone: 803-425-1003. Reply date: 8/15/
88. Six times/year. Prefers features of 2500 words. Pays $300-$600
for article and photo package. Pays expenses if arranged beforehand.
Photos: Pays $50-$200/photo, $300-$500/cover. **Editorial Slant:**
Unusual articles and pictures that cover hunting and fishing opportunities around the globe. Sample articles, 7-8/88: "Trails on
the Tundra," hunting prairie chickens in South Dakota, fishing in
England.

Sports Afield, 250 West 55th Street, New York, NY 10019.
Editor-in-chief: Tom Paugh. Phone: 212-649-4000. Reply date: 6/

8/88. POA. Prefers features of 1500-2000 words. Pays at least $750 for features. **Photos:** Art director: Gary Gretter. Uses color transparencies (prefers 35mm Kodachrome 64). **Editorial Slant:** Entertaining and well-written outdoor articles, nature profiles, stories on personal adventures and new places to hunt and fish. Sample articles, 6/88: Fishing for shellcrackers and bluegills in Virginia, "Glimpses of Alaska," fishing on the Umpqua (Oregon), Hiwassee River trout.

Sports Illustrated, Time and Life Building, New York, NY 10020. Advance text editors: Victoria Boughton and Bob Brown. Phone: 212-522-1212. Reply date: 5/24/88. POA. Replies to queries in 4 weeks. Front-of-the-book stories are up to 2000 words. Departments or columns: 300-800 words. Pays $1250 for longer stories, at least $500 for shorts. **Editorial Slant:** "Escapes" section is on sport-related travel tips and advice such as unusual birding trips and pilgrimages to sporting shrines.

SR Dallas, 11551 Forest Central Drive, No. 305, Dallas, TX 75243. Editor: Frank Kelly. Phone: 214-341-9429. Reply date: 9/1/88. Monthly. POP. Pays kill fee for articles done on assignment. Buys FR, some SR if exclusive in Dallas-Fort Worth area. Lead time for seasonal articles: 6 weeks. Prefers features of 500-1200 words. Pays $75-$150. **Photos:** Pays $25/BW, $50/color. POP. **Editorial Slant:** Lifestyle publication for Dallas residents over 50 years of age. Sample articles, 7/88: Making money with travel photography, solo travel.

AR	all rights	OTR	one-time rights
ASMP	American Society of	POA	pays on acceptance
	Magazine	POB	post office box
	Photographers	POP	pays on publication
BW	black-and-white photos	PPS	previously published
CM	complete manuscript		submissions
ES	electronic submissions	PQ	phone queries
FL	freelance	SAE	self-addressed envelope
FL/year	number of freelance travel	SASE	self-addressed stamped envelope
	articles published per	SC	sample copy
	year	SQ	simultaneous queries
F(NAS)R	first (North American serial)	SR	second rights
	rights	SS	simultaneous submissions
ms(s)	manuscript(s)	WG	writer's guidelines
NA	North American		

Successful Meetings, 633 Third Avenue, New York, NY 10017. Senior editor: Maggie Thompson. Phone: 212-986-4800. Reply date: 1/23/88. Monthly. Circulation: 77,000. POA. Prefers features of 1500-10,000 words. Pays at least $350. **Editorial Slant:** For corporation and association meeting planners. "Site Selection" section uses articles that focus on meeting destinations: cities, states, regions, or countries. Highlight local history, culture, restaurants, entertainment, and sports, as well as the area's facilities: hotels, auditoriums, convention centers, and airports.

Sylvia Porter's Personal Finance, 380 Lexington Avenue, New York, NY 10017. Executive editor: Greg Daugherty. Phone: 212-557-9100. Reply date: 9/30/88. Ten times/year. Circulation: 500,000. FL/year: 10. POA. Buys AR. Kill fee: 20 percent. Replies to queries in 2 weeks. Lead time for seasonal articles: 4 months. Articles published 3 months after acceptance. Prefers features of 2000 words. Departments or columns: 200-1500 words. Pays 50 cents/word on average. Sometimes pays expenses. SC: 9-by-12 SASE. WG: SASE. **Photos:** Photos assigned by art department after ms is accepted. **Editorial Slant:** Articles on how to get the most for your travel dollar.

TakeOff, 4825 Everhart, Suite 7, Corpus Christi, TX 78411. Editor: Bob Parker. Reply date: 10/1/87. POP. Pays $50-$350. **Photos:** BW prints 4-by-5 or larger, color slides. Pays $10-$25/BW, $35-$50/cover. **Editorial Slant:** "The pilot's travel, recreation, and lifestyle magazine." Articles on travel and adventure, resorts, places to go, and things to see and do. Sample articles: Island-hopping through the Caribbean by light plane; winter sports facilities in the Lake Placid, New York, area; flying in to tour the Navajo reservation in Arizona.

Texas Highways, 11th and Brazos streets, Austin, TX 78701-2483. Editor: Frank Lively. Phone: 512-463-8581. Reply date: 9/30/88. Monthly. Circulation: Approximately 400,000. FL/year: 45. POA. Buys OTR. Kill fee: $100-$150. Replies to queries in 4 to 8 weeks. Lead time for seasonal articles: At least 1 year. Articles published 6 to 18 months after acceptance. Accepts CM, SQ, PPS. Subsidized trips OK. Prefers features of 1200-1500 words. Pays approximately 40 cents/word. SC, WG: Write or phone. **Photos:** Photo editor: Bill Reaves. Uses 35mm, 2¼-inch, or 4-by-5 transparencies. Pays $80/photo smaller than half page, $120/half-page photo, $170/full-page photo, $300/center spread or back cover, $400/front cover. Buys OTR. POP. Photos purchased without mss. **Editorial Slant:** Focuses on things to do or places to see in Texas. Include historical, cultural, and geographic aspects if appropriate.

Texas Monthly, POB 1569, Austin, TX 78767.
Editor: Gregory Curtis. Phone: 512-476-7085. Reply date: 4/24/88. Monthly. POA. Replies to queries in 6 to 8 weeks. Prefers features of 2500-5000 words. Departments or columns: Under 2500 words. **Photos:** Query art director. **Editorial Slant:** Stories must appeal to an educated Texas audience. Solidly researched reporting that uncovers issues of public concern, reveals offbeat and previously unreported topics, or uses a novel approach to familiar topics. Sample article: Stalking redfish on the Texas coast.

Tour & Travel News, 600 Community Drive, Manhasset, NY 11030.
Editor: Linda Ball. Phone: 516-562-5000. Reply date: 9/30/88. Weekly. Circulation: 60,000. FL/year: 100. POP. Buys FNASR. Replies to queries in about 3 weeks. Lead time for seasonal articles: 8 weeks. Articles published 1 to 4 weeks after acceptance. Accepts CM, ES. Subsidized trips OK. Prefers features of 1000 words. SC available. **Photos:** Photo editor: Linda Ball. Uses four-color slides. POA. Photos purchased without mss. **Editorial Slant:** Tabloid newspaper for the travel industry.

Tours & Resorts Magazine, 990 Grove Street, Evanston, IL 60201-4370.
Managing editor: Raymond Gudas. Phone: 312-491-6440. Reply date: 9/30/88. Bimonthly. Circulation: 250,000. FL/year: 60. POA. Buys OTR. Kill fee: $75-$100. Replies to queries in 4-6 weeks. Lead time for seasonal articles: 6 months. Articles published 4-6 months after acceptance. Accepts CM, ES. Prefers features of 1200-1500 words. Departments or columns: 800-1500 words. Pays $150-$500 for features, $125-$250 for departments. SC: SASE and $2.50. **Photos:** Photo editor: Raymond Gudas. Uses color slides and transparencies. Pays $25/color, $125/cover. Buys OTR. Pays after issue is printed. Photos purchased without mss. **Editorial Slant:** Primarily uses destination-oriented travel features and "anatomy-of-a-tour" stories showcasing organized tour operators.

Trailblazer, 15325 S.E. 30th Place, Bellevue, WA 98007.
Editor: Gregg Olsen. Phone: 206-644-1100. Reply date: 4/14/88.

POP. Replies to queries in 4-6 weeks. Prefers feature of 1000-3000 words. Pays 10 cents/word. SC: $2. **Photos:** Uses BW glossies, color slides 35mm or larger. Pays $15-$35/BW, $25-$100/color, $200/cover. **Editorial Slant:** Published by Thousand Trails, Inc., a developer and operator of membership campground resorts. Readers are active, outdoor-oriented adults who own RVs.

Trailer Boats Magazine, POB 5427, Carson, CA 90749-5427.
Editor: Jim Youngs. Phone: 213-537-6322. Reply date: 6/1/88. Replies to queries in 4 weeks. Pays $4.25/column inch for general travel stories, $100 for "Mini Cruise" articles with photos. **Photos:** Pays $7.50-$50/BW, $15-$75/color. **Editorial Slant:** For those who own or plan to buy a craft normally trailered behind the family vehicle. Camping and travel to freshwater or saltwater recreational areas attractive to trailer boaters are featured, as are true adventures involving small boats.

Trailer Life, 29901 Agoura Road, Agoura, CA 91301.
Editor: Bill Estes. Phone: 818-991-4980. Reply date: 4/4/88. Buys FNASR. Replies to queries in 6 weeks. Accepts SS. Prefers features of 1000-3000 words. Pays between $200 (for "Super Sites") and $350 (for full-length features accompanied by photos). **Photos:** Prefers 35mm Kodachrome 64; accepts Ektachrome Professional film. Pays $25-$100/BW, $50-$250/color, $200-$300/cover. Pays at same time as payment for articles. **Editorial Slant:** For RV travelers. Articles describing specific destinations and suggesting en route attractions and activities. All articles must include photos of RVs.

Travel & Leisure, 1120 Avenue of the Americas, New York, NY 10036.
Executive editor: Christopher Hunt. Phone: 212-382-5600. Reply date: 10/3/88. Monthly. Circulation: 1.1 million. FL/year: several hundred. POA. Buys first worldwide publication rights. Kill fee: 25 percent. Replies to queries in 1-4 weeks. Lead time for seasonal articles: 3 months to 1 year. Articles published 3 months to 1 year after acceptance. Accepts CM (rarely), SQ. Prefers features of 1000-2500 words. Departments or columns: 300-1500 words. Pays 50 cents to $1.50/word. Pays expenses. SC, WG: Write Reader Service Department. **Photos:** Photo editor: Hazel Hammond. Uses some BW, color transparencies. Pays $200-$600/BW or color, $1000/cover. Buys first worldwide publication rights. Pays guarantee on acceptance, page rate on publication. **Editorial Slant:** Readers ex-

pect to be able to make use of the information presented in any article. All places discussed should therefore be open to the public, and all information up to date and correct. Owned by American Express.

Travel Life, 505 Market Street, Knoxville, TN 37902.
Editor: Paula Spencer. Phone: 615-595-5000. Reply date: 2/16/88. Bimonthly. Circulation: 152,000. Prefers departments of 200-600 words. Pays 50 cents to $1/word. **Editorial Slant:** A workstyle and lifestyle magazine edited to both inform and entertain travel agents. Sample articles, 1-2/88: Ixtapa and Zihuatanejo, spring skiing in the American West.

Travel Marketing & Sales, 441 Lexington Avenue, No. 1209A, New York, NY 10017.
Editor: Angela Reale. Phone: 212-986-1025. Reply date: 10/18/88. Semimonthly. Circulation: 2,000. FL/year: Varies. POA. Buys FR. Replies to queries immediately. Articles published 2 weeks after acceptance. Accepts CM, SQ, PQ. ES: Fax. Subsidized trips OK. Prefers features of up to 500-1000 words. SC: Phone. **Photos:** Uses no photos. **Editorial Slant:** Newsletter is for industry executives and requires in-depth knowledge on the part of its writers. Marketing and promotional articles dealing with any aspect of travel. Case studies, interesting promotional campaigns, etc.

Travel People, 600 Community Drive, Manhasset, NY 11030.
Editor: Linda Ball. Phone: 516-562-5000. Reply date: 9/30/88. A supplement to *Tour & Travel News*.

Travel Smart, Dobbs Ferry, NY 10522.
Editor: H. Teison. Phone: 914-693-8300. Reply date: 9/30/88. Monthly. Circulation: 10,000. FL/year: 10. POP. Buys AR. Replies to queries in 1-2 weeks. Lead time for seasonal articles: 1 month. Articles published immediately after acceptance. Accepts CM, SQ, SS. Subsidized trips OK. Prefers features of 1000-2000 words. Departments or columns: 25-100 words. Pays up to $75. SC, WG: Write. **Photos:** Uses no photos. **Editorial Slant:** Interesting, unusual, and economical places for people to go, stay, eat. Articles must provide details.

Travel Smart for Business, Dobbs Ferry, NY 10522.
Editor: H. Teison. Phone: 914-693-8300. Reply date: 9/30/88. Monthly. Circulation: 1,000. FL/year: 10. POP. Buys AR. Replies

to queries in 1-2 weeks. Lead time for seasonal articles: 1 month. Articles published immediately after acceptance. Accepts CM, SQ, SS. Subsidized trips OK. Prefers features of 1000-2000 words. Departments or columns: 25-100 words. Pays up to $75. SC, WG: Write. **Photos:** Uses no photos. **Editorial Slant:** Articles must be specific. For example, an article on the business-class service of more than 20 airlines included the exact fares and nature of service for each airline. Assigns writers to do roundups of hotels and restaurants for "Insider" series.

Travel-Holiday, 28 West 23rd Street, New York, NY 10010.
Editor: Scott Shane. Phone: 212-633-4660. Reply date: 10/8/88. Monthly. Circulation: 800,000. FL/year: 150. POA. Buys FNASR. Kill fee: 25 percent on assigned articles. Replies to queries in 6-8 weeks. Lead time for seasonal articles: 6-8 months. Accepts CM. ES: Hayes modem (2400 baud). Subsidized trips OK. Prefers features of 1600-1800 words. Departments or columns: 1000-1300 words. Pays $350-$1000. SC: $1.25. WG: SASE. **Photos:** Photo editor: Chrissy Leontis. Uses 35mm and larger transparencies. Pays $50/ BW, at least $100/color, $500/cover. Buys OTR. POP. Photos purchased without mss. **Editorial Slant:** Feature articles dealing with foreign or domestic travel destinations, either off the beaten path or well known, but with a new twist or update. Short features on small towns or cities, as well as museums, markets, shopping, art galleries.

TravelAge East, 888 7th Avenue, New York, NY 10106.
Managing editor: Ed Sullivan. Phone: 212-977-8300. Reply date: 9/30/88. Weekly. Circulation: 34,000. FL/year: 100. POP. Buys FR. Replies to queries in 2 weeks. Lead time for seasonal articles: 2-3 months. Accepts CM, PQ. ES: WordPerfect. Subsidized trips OK. Prefers features of 800-1000 words. Pays at least $2/inch. Pays expenses. SC: Write. **Photos:** Uses no photos. **Editorial Slant:** Magazine is for travel professionals, not consumers. Destination stories never have a promotional tone.

TravelAge Europe, 888 7th Avenue, 29th Floor, New York, NY 10106.
Senior editor: Steve Noveck. Phone: 212-977-8330. Reply date: 9/30/88. Monthly. Circulation: 80,000. FL/year: Approximately 40. POP. Kill fee: Negotiable. Replies to queries in 1 week. Lead time for seasonal articles: 3-6 months. Accepts CM; SQ, SS, and PPS (as

long as they don't involve a competing trade publication); PQ. ES: IBM compatible. Subsidized trips OK. Prefers features of 1000-1250 words. Departments or columns: Approximately 500 words. Pays $6/inch. Pays expenses. SC: Contact senior editor. **Photos:** Uses BW, color slides or transparencies. Photos usually included in inch count for pay purposes, but this is negotiable. POP. **Editorial Slant:** Pieces should be oriented to travel trade in some way, but some general destination stories are acceptable.

TravelAge Midamerica, 320 North Michigan Avenue, No. 601, Chicago, IL 60601.
Managing editor: Karen Goodwin. Phone: 312-346-4952. Reply date: 9/30/88. Weekly. Circulation: 21,000. POP. Buys FR. Replies to queries in 2-3 months. Lead time for seasonal articles: 1 month. Accepts CM. Prefers features of 750-1200 words. Pays $2/inch. SC: Write. WG: SASE. **Photos:** Uses BW. **Editorial Slant:** Regional, news-oriented trade publication. Readers are travel agents who need information to help them sell to others.

TravelAge West, 100 Grant Avenue, San Francisco, CA 94108.
News editor: Robert Carlsen. Phone: 415-781-8353. Reply date: 6/23/88. Weekly. Tries to reply to queries within 2 weeks. Accepts CM. Destination articles up to 800 words. **Photos:** Uses BW. **Editorial Slant:** Travel trade newsmagazine primarily aimed at audience of travel agents. Does about 100 sections a year focusing on a particular area or subject. Schedule for the following year is available around October. Sample articles, 6/13/88: "Bargains Abound in Arizona's Off Season," "Travel Plans Promote Birding Programs to the Galapagos," "Classic Train Enthusiasts Make Tracks Through South America."

The Traveller, 45 Brompton Road, Knightsbridge, London SW3 1DE, England.
Editor: Caroline Sanders. Phone: 01-581-4130. Reply date: 6/8/88. Three times/year. POP. Prefers features of 1500-2000 words. Pays 50 pounds/1000 words. SC: 3 pounds to Membership Department of WEXAS at above address. **Photos:** Uses BW, color. Pays 14 pounds/BW, 16 pounds/color, 40 pounds/cover. **Editorial Slant:** Informative, illustrated articles on travel throughout the world, with special emphasis on travel off the beaten track and in developing countries.

Ultra, POB 792150, San Antonio, TX 78279-2150.
Managing editor: Blair Calvert Fitzsimons. Phone: 512-829-9230.
Reply date: 6/13/88. POP. Travel pieces of 1500 words. Pays $250-
$400. **Editorial Slant:** Articles on upscale travel destinations in the
United States, Latin America, and the Far East.

United Express.
See Skies America. In-flight magazine of United Express, the largest
regional airline in California.

USAir, 1301 Carolina Street, Greensboro, NC 27408.
Editor: Maggie Oman. Phone: 919-378-6065. Reply date: 9/30/
88. Monthly. Circulation: 335,000. POP. Buys FNASR. Kill fee:
Negotiable. Replies to queries in 3 weeks. Lead time for seasonal
articles: 3-4 months. Accepts CM (occasionally). Prefers features of
1500 words. Departments or columns: 1000-1200 words. Pays at
least $450 for features, at least $300 for departments. Pays expenses.
SC: $3. WG: SASE. **Editorial Slant:** In-flight magazine for pas-
sengers of USAir. Well-educated, informed business executives. No
puff pieces.

Vermont Life, 61 Elm Street, Montpelier, VT 05602.
Editor-in-chief: Tom Slayton. Phone: 802-828-3241. Reply date:
9/30/88. Quarterly. Circulation: 110,000. FL/year: 15-20. POA.
Buys FNASR. Kill fee: One-third. Usually replies to queries in 2
weeks. Lead time for seasonal articles: 1 year. Articles published 3-
6 months after acceptance. Accepts CM, SQ, SS. Prefers features of
under 2000 words. Departments or columns: Most under 1500
words. Pays $100-$500. SC: $4. WG available. **Photos:** Photo
editor: Tom Slayton. Uses color transparencies (Kodachrome preferred). Shots of Vermont. Pays $75-$200/BW, $75-$200/color,
$200/cover. Buys FNASR. POP. Photos purchased without mss.
Editorial Slant: The official state magazine. Interested in any article
or story idea that has to do with Vermont. Presents positive aspects
of life within the state's borders.

Vista, 999 Ponce Street, No. 600, Coral Gables, FL 33134.
Editor: Harry Caicedo. Phone: 305-442-2462. Reply date: 10/18/
88. Weekly. Circulation: 1.2 million. FL/year: 4-6. POA. Buys
first-time U.S. rights. Kill fee: 25 percent. Replies to queries in 1-
2 weeks. Lead time for seasonal articles: 2-3 months. Accepts CM,
SQ. Subsidized trips OK. Prefers features of 1200 words. Pays at

least 20 cents/word. Pays some expenses. SC, WG: Write. **Photos:** Photo editor: Harry Caicedo. Uses 35mm, 2¼-inch, or 4-by-5 color transparencies. Pays at least $75/BW, $150/color, $300/cover. Buys OTR. POP. **Editorial Slant:** The nation's only mass circulation Hispanic magazine. Distributed throughout the country by major newspapers in cities with high concentrations of Hispanic people. Sample articles in 1988: San Antonio, New York City nightlife, New Orleans. In English.

Vista USA, POB 161, Convent Station, NJ 07961.
Editor: Kathleen Caccavale. Reply date: 9/30/88. Quarterly. Circulation: 900,000. FL/year: Approximately 25 features, plus departments. POA. Buys FNASR. Kill fee: One-third. Replies to queries in 2-6 weeks. Lead time for seasonal articles: 18 months. Articles published at least 9 months after acceptance. Accepts CM, SQ, SS, PPS. Subsidized trips OK. Prefers features of 1500-2000 words. Departments or columns: 400-1000 words. Pays 35-50 cents/word. Pays expenses when appropriate. SC: 9-by-12 SASE with 5 first-class stamps. WG: SASE. **Photos:** Photo editor: Anthony Stroppa. Uses transparencies only, no prints. Pays $135-$250/color, $400/cover. Buys OTR. Pays for photos on approval or before publication. Photos purchased without mss. **Editorial Slant:** The magazine of the Exxon Travel Club. Material should relate to travel but should avoid hard-core travel information such as where to stay, where to dine. Emphasis should be on the flavor of an area, using a thematic approach that brings out what is unusual about it from the writer's point of view. Covers North America, including the United States, Canada, Mexico, and the Caribbean.

Volkswagen's World, 888 West Big Beaver Road, Troy, MI 48007.
Editor: Marlene Goldsmith. Phone: 313-362-6770. Reply date: 9/30/88. Three times/year. Circulation: 300,000. FL/year: 6. POA. Buys FNASR. Replies to queries in 2 weeks. Lead time for seasonal articles: 4 months. Articles published 3 months to 3 years after acceptance. Accepts SQ. ES: Macintosh, Microsoft Word, MacWrite (diskette). Subsidized trips OK. Prefers features of 750-1000 words. Pays $150/printed page; articles run at least 2 pages. SC, WG: Write. **Photos:** Photo editor: Marlene Goldsmith. Uses color only; prefers 35mm or large transparencies. Pay for photos included in pay for stories. Buys FNASR. POA. **Editorial Slant:** The magazine for Volkswagen owners in the United States. Travel stories should

have a specific slant, usually focusing on a particular person, a unique resort, or something of particular interest to VW owners.

The Walking Magazine, 711 Boylston Street, Boston, MA 02116. Senior editor: Doug Hardy. Phone: 617-236-1885. Reply date: 9/30/88. Bimonthly magazine and annual source book. Circulation: 525,000. FL/year: 20. POA. Buys FNASR. Kill fee: 20-30 percent. Replies to queries in 2-3 weeks. Lead time for seasonal articles: 8-10 weeks. Articles published at least 10 weeks after acceptance. Accepts CM, SQ, SS. ES: Fax. Subsidized trips OK. Prefers features of 1800 words. Departments or columns: 500-800 words. Pays between $750 (for first feature) and $2500. Departments: $350-$1200. Pays expenses. SC, WG: SASE. **Photos:** Photo editors: Carol Ross and Sonia Kaloosdian. Uses BW, 35mm color. Pays ASMP rates for photos: $150-$1000. Buys OTR. Pays for photos 30 days after receipt of invoice. Photos purchased without mss. **Editorial Slant:** Articles on places to walk when you're traveling. Sample articles: Walks in Nevada, Cape Cod, Kansas; "Casablanca: Searching for Bogart in the Old Walled City."

Washington Magazine, 200 West Thomas, 3rd Floor, Seattle, WA 98119. Managing editor: David Fuller. Phone: 206-285-9009. Reply date: 4/1/88. Bimonthly. POP for unsolicited articles, POA for assigned articles. Buys FR. Kill fee: 20 percent. Prefers features of 1500-2500 words. Departments or columns: 800-1200 words. Pays $350-$750 for features, $150-$250 for departments. May pay expenses if discussed in advance. SC: $2.50 and 10-by-13 SASE with $2 postage. WG: SASE. **Editorial Slant:** All facets of life in Washington state. Subjects include day or weekend travel, fairs and festivals, outdoors, wildlife, museums. Sample articles, 12/87: Winter travel roundup, Northwest ski report.

Webb Travelers, 1999 Shepard Road, St. Paul, MN 55116. Editor: Mary Lou Brooks. Phone: 612-690-7288. Reply date: 11/21/88. Quarterly. FL/year: 30-35. POP. Buys limited rights or AR. Kill fee: 25 percent. Replies to queries in 2-8 weeks. Lead time for seasonal articles: 6 months to 1 year. Articles published 2-4 months after acceptance. Accepts CM, SQ, PPS. Prefers features of 1200 words. Departments or columns: 500 words in "Healthwise." Pays $250-$350 for features, $150 for columns, $50-$150 for reprints. SC: SASE. WG: SASE. **Photos:** Photo editor: Julie Hally. Uses travel photos. Pays $125/quarter-page/color, $400/cover. Buys OTR. POP. Photos purchased without mss. **Editorial Slant:** Distributed to oil company travel club members. Emphasis on places to go by car in North America. Uses destination pieces.

The Western Boatman, 20700 Belshaw Avenue, Carson, CA 90746. Editor: Ralph Poole. Phone: 213-537-6322. Reply date: 9/30/88. Bimonthly. Circulation: 23,000. FL/year: 10-12. POP. Buys FNASR. Replies to queries in 6-8 weeks. Lead time for seasonal articles: 4-6 months. Articles published 2-6 months after acceptance. Accepts CM, PQ. ES: MS-DOS 2.0, WordPerfect. Subsidized trips OK. Prefers features of up to 1500 words. Departments or columns: 200-600 words. Pays $5/column inch. Pays some expenses if prearranged. SC, WG: Write or phone. **Photos:** Photo editor: Ralph Poole. Uses BW, color. Locales with pleasure boats in them, people having fun boating and fishing, waterfront scenes, historic sites. Pays $7-$50/BW, $15-$200/color, $300/cover. Buys FNASR. POP. Photos purchased without mss. **Editorial Slant:** Sports and adventure lifestyle magazine devoted to boats and boating in 13 Western states and off the Pacific coast of Canada and Mexico. Travel column covers restaurant reviews, special coves, seasonal waterfront celebrations.

Western Outdoors, 3197-E Airport Loop, Costa Mesa, CA 92626. Managing editor: Jack Brown. Phone: 714-546-4370. Reply date: 9/30/88. Ten times/year. Circulation: 161,000. POA. Buys FNASR. Replies to queries in 2-4 weeks. Lead time for seasonal articles: 6

AR	all rights	OTR	one-time rights
ASMP	American Society of	POA	pays on acceptance
	Magazine	POB	post office box
	Photographers	POP	pays on publication
BW	black-and-white photos	PPS	previously published
CM	complete manuscript		submissions
ES	electronic submissions	PQ	phone queries
FL	freelance	SAE	self-addressed envelope
FL/year	number of freelance travel	SASE	self-addressed stamped envelope
	articles published per	SC	sample copy
	year	SQ	simultaneous queries
F(NAS)R	first (North American serial)	SR	second rights
	rights	SS	simultaneous submissions
ms(s)	manuscript(s)	WG	writer's guidelines
NA	North American		

months. ES: By prior arrangement with editor. Subsidized trips OK. Prefers features of 1500-2000 words. Departments or columns: 750-1000 words. Pays at least $400. SC: $1.50. WG: SASE. Photos: Photo editor: Jack Brown. Pictures of fishing, hunting, wildlife (game). Pays $200-$250/cover. Buys FNASR. POP. Editorial Slant: Publishes a mix of instructional and destination articles dealing with fishing and hunting situations and locations exclusively in the West.

Western Sportsman, POB 737, Regina, Saskatchewan, Canada S4P 3A8.
Editor: Rick Bates. Reply date: 1/11/88. Bimonthly. FL/issue: 15-30. POP. Buys FNASR. Articles published 3-12 months after acceptance. Accepts CM. Prefers features of up to 2500 words. Departments or columns: 100-800 words. Pays up to $325 for article and photo package, $50 for shorts. SC: $3.50. WG: SASE. Photos: Uses BW, color (Kodachrome or Ektachrome, 8-by-10 Kodacolor prints). Pays $20-$25/BW, $75-$100/color, $175-$250/cover. POA. Photos purchased without mss. Editorial Slant: Articles describing an outdoor experience in Alberta or Saskatchewan, incorporating lots of how-to information.

Westways, POB 2890, Terminal Annex, Los Angeles, CA 90051-0890.
Executive editor: Mary Ann Fisher. Phone: 213-741-4760. Reply date: 11/23/88. Monthly. Circulation: 485,000. FL/year: Close to 90. POP. Buys FR. Kill fee: $75. Replies to queries in 2 weeks. Lead time for seasonal articles: 4 months. Articles published 4-6 months after acceptance. Accepts CM with photos as a complete package, SQ, SS. Subsidized trips OK. Prefers features of 1000-1500 words. Departments or columns: 500-600 words. Pays 30 cents/word. SC: $1. WG: SASE; publishes *Westways Writer*, a writer's newsletter available on request. Photos: Query executive editor. Uses BW (historical), 35mm slides. Pay varies for BW; pays $50/color. Buys OTR. Pays 2 weeks after publication. Photo essays acceptable. Editorial Slant: Articles pertaining to outdoor recreation and travel, Western history, modern activities in the West, and world travel. No first person.

Westworld, 4180 Lougheed Highway, Suite 401, Burnaby, British Columbia, Canada V5C 6A7.
Managing editor: Robin Roberts. Phone: 604-299-7311. Reply date: 8/22/88. Also publishes *Going Places* (Manitoba) and *Leisure Ways*

(Ontario). Combined circulation: Approximately 1 million. *Westworld* published four times/year, *Going Places* five times/year, and *Leisure Ways* six times/year. POP. Buys FNASR, SR. Kill fee: 50 percent. Accepts SQ if so stated. Articles of 500-2000 words. Pays 25 cents/word. **Photos:** Uses BW, color. Pays $25/BW, $35-$75/ color. **Editorial Slant:** Published for the CAA motor clubs of British Columbia, Alberta, Saskatchewan, Manitoba, and Ontario. Editorial focus on motoring and car-care tips, as well as domestic and international travel. Sample articles, Summer 1988: A trans-Canada trek, April Point Lodge, "Confessions of a Golden Gate Groupie," "Rediscover Vancouver Island."

Whole Life, POB 2058, Madison Square Station, New York, NY 10159.
Editor and publisher: Marc Medoff. Phone: 212-353-3395. Reply date: 10/12/88. Six times/year. Circulation: 60,000. FL/year: 30. POP. Buys AR. Replies to queries in 6-8 weeks. Lead time for seasonal articles: 4 months. Articles published 4-9 months after acceptance. Accepts SQ, SS. Subsidized trips OK. Prefers features of 750-3000 words. Pays $100-$500. Pays expenses. SC: $5. WG: $2. **Photos:** Photo editor: Marc Medoff. Uses BW. Pays $25-$75/ BW, $100-$300/cover. Buys AR. POP. Photos purchased without mss. **Editorial Slant:** "The journal for holistic health and natural living." Accepts freelance work for "Healthy Travel" column.

Wild West, 105 Loudoun Street, S.W., Leesburg, VA 22075.
Executive editor: C. Brian Kelly. Phone: 703-771-9400. Reply date: 9/30/88. See Empire Press.

WildBird, POB 6050, Mission Viejo, CA 92690.
Managing editor: Tim Gallagher. Phone: 714-855-8822. Reply date: 7/15/88. Pays after publication. Buys FNASR. Prefers features of 1000-2000 words. Departments or columns: 750 words. Pays at least $100 for features, $25 for departments. WG: SASE. **Photos:** Uses BW 5-by-7 or larger, 35mm or larger color transparencies (Kodachrome or Fujichrome). Pays $25/BW, $25-$50/color, $100/ cover. Buys FNASR. Pay usually included in article package. **Editorial Slant:** Dedicated to the appreciation of birds and to the promotion of birdwatching as an ecologically sound recreational pursuit. Sample article, 7-8/88: "Birders Guide to Hassayampa River Preserve."

Wildfowl, 1901 Bell, POB 35098, Des Moines, IA 50315.
Editor: Bob Wilbanks. Phone: 515-243-2472. Reply date: 9/30/
88. Bimonthly. Circulation: 28,000. Also publishes *Gun Dog* and
Wing & Shot. FL/year: 90 in all three titles. POA. Buys FR or OTR.
Kill fee: $50. Replies to queries in 1 week. Lead time for seasonal
articles: 90 days. Articles published 1 month to 1 year after acceptance. Accepts CM, SQ, SS, PQ. Prefers features, departments, and
columns of 1500-2000 words. Pays $300-$400. SC and WG available. **Photos:** Photo editor: Bob Wilbanks. Uses BW prints, color
transparencies. Pays $25/BW, $40-$80/color, $150/cover. Buys FR,
OTR. Pays for photos when selected. Photos purchased without
mss. **Editorial Slant:** For the duck and goose hunter. Sample articles, 6-7/88: Waterfowl shooting in Canada, shooting ducks in
South Dakota, "Northern New England's Hidden Hot Spots for
Ducks," the Sacramento Valley.

Wind Surf, POB 561, Dana Point, CA 92629.
Editorial director: Drew Kampion. Phone: 714-661-4888. Reply
date: 11/18/88. Monthly. Circulation: 50,000. FL/year: 20-30. POP.
Kill fee: 25 percent. Replies to queries in 30-60 days. Lead time
for seasonal articles: 2-3 months. Accepts CM, SQ, SS, PPS. ES:
Microsoft Word (5-1/4-inch diskette). Subsidized trips OK. Prefers
features of 1500-3000 words. Pays $200-$500. Sometimes pays
expenses. SC: Write to Yvonne Clarke. WG: SASE. **Photos:** Photo
editor: Brian Stamm. Uses Kodachrome or Fujichrome slides. Pay
depends on size published. POP. Photos purchased without mss.
Editorial Slant: First-person accounts of travel to boardsailing destinations across the United States and around the world. These
should be informative, involving, insightful, and, where possible,
humorous. Development of the characters who are doing the traveling is nearly as important as describing the destination and the
sailing.

Windy City Sports, POB 817, Wilmette, IL 60091.
Editor: Maryclaire Collins. Phone: 312-492-1080. Reply date: 9/
30/88. Monthly. Circulation: 100,000. FL/year: 12. Lead time for
seasonal articles: 3 months. Subsidized trips OK. Prefers features
of 1000 words. Pays $100. SC: $1. **Editorial Slant:** Regional tabloid
for Chicago. Published running and adventure sports travel in March
1989. Other topics: Racquet sports, skiing, scuba, walking, cycling,
tennis, hiking, camping. Has editorial schedule.

Wine Tidings, 5165 Sherbrooke Street West, No. 414, Montreal, Quebec, Canada H4A 1T6.
Editor: Barbara Leslie. Phone: 514-481-5892. Reply date: 6/13/88. Eight times/year. POP. Replies to queries in 4-5 weeks. Prefers features of 1000-1500 words. Departments or columns: 400-1000 words. Pays $100-$300 for features, $35-$150 for departments. WG: SASE. **Photos:** Uses BW, color prints or transparencies. Pays $20-$50/photo, $100-$250/cover. Photos purchased without mss. **Editorial Slant:** Should be directed at a Canadian audience with emphasis on wines available in Canada or readily available to Canadian tourists abroad. Accuracy of wine information is given primary consideration. Sample article, 4/88: Alberta Wine Boutique.

Wisconsin Trails, POB 5650, 6225 University Avenue, Madison, WI 53705.
Editor: Howard Mead. Phone: 608-231-2444. Reply date: 9/30/88. Bimonthly. Circulation: 50,000. POP. Buys OTR. Replies to queries in 3 months. Lead time for seasonal articles: 3-4 months. Accepts CM. Prefers features of 1000-1200 words. Pays $50-$300. WG: SASE. **Photos:** Photo editor: Nancy Mead. Uses BW prints, color transparencies. Pays $25-$50/BW, $50-$150/color. Buys OTR. Photos purchased without mss. **Editorial Slant:** Features Wisconsin people, places, events and activities.

Wisconsin Woman, 207 East Buffalo Street, Suite 419, Milwaukee, WI 53202.
Editor: Anne Siegel. Phone: 414-273-1234. Reply date: 10/12/88. Monthly. Circulation: 25,000. FL/year: 10-12. POP. Buys all Wisconsin rights. Replies to queries in 4-6 weeks. Lead time for seasonal articles: 4 months. Articles published 2 months after acceptance. Accepts CM, SQ, SS, PPS. Subsidized trips OK. Prefers features, departments, and columns of 1200-1500 words. Pays $100-$125. Pays mileage. SC: $2.50. WG: SASE. **Photos:** Uses color slides, prints. Pay for photos is included in pay for articles. Buys OTR. **Editorial Slant:** Wisconsin destinations preferred.

Woman's World, 177 North Dean Street, Englewood, NJ 07631.
Travel editor: Mary McHugh. Phone: 201-569-0006. Reply date: 9/30/88. Weekly. Circulation: 1.5 million. FL/year: 10. POA. Buys FNASR. Kill fee: 20 percent. Replies to queries in 6 weeks. Lead time for seasonal articles: 6 months. Articles published 1-2 months

after acceptance. Accepts CM, ES. Subsidized trips OK. Prefers features of 600 words. Pays $300. SC: On newsstands. WG: SASE. **Photos:** Photo editor: Nita Modha. Uses chromes. Photos purchased without mss. **Editorial Slant:** "In Real Life" stories deal with adventures. Sample article: "Escape from the Jungle."

The YACHT Magazine, POB 329, Newport, RI 02840.
Editor: James Robie Gilbert. Reply date: 5/23/88. Bimonthly. Replies to queries in 6-8 weeks. Prefers features of up to 2500 words. "In the Wind" department: Up to 1000 words. Pays $500-$1000 for features, $250 for "In the Wind." **Editorial Slant:** Explores the delights of yachting, with a particular emphasis on lifestyle. Sample article, 6/88: St. Tropez.

Yachting, POB 1200, 5 River Road, Cos Cob, CT 06807.
Managing editor: Cynthia Taylor. Phone: 203-629-8300. Reply date: 11/21/87. Prefers features of up to 2500 words. Pays $300-$1000. **Photos:** Uses 35mm Kodachrome 25. Pays $50-$250/BW, $250-$400/color, $1000/cover. **Editorial Slant:** Always looking for good cruising stories, preferably on an interesting boat and to an interesting destination.

Yankee Magazine, Main Street, Dublin, NH 03444.
Editor-in-chief: Judson Hale. Phone: 603-563-8111. Reply date: 4/14/88. POA. Buys AR, FR. Prefers features of 1500-2500 words. Pays $25-$750. **Photos:** Uses 35mm, 2¼-inch, or 4-by-5 color transparencies. **Editorial Slant:** Articles about New England and New Englanders past, present, or future; activities; controversies if of wide interest; history, particularly if there is a present-day tie-in.

Yellow Brick Road, 2445 Northcreek Lane, Fullerton, CA 92631.
Phone: 714-680-3326. Editor: Bobbi Zane. Reply date: 11/16/88. Monthly. Circulation: 1000. POP. Buys FR, SR. Replies to queries in 2-3 weeks. Lead time for seasonal articles: 2 months. Accepts CM, PPS, PQ. Prefers features of 1000-1200 words. Pays up to $50. SC available. **Photos:** Uses no photos. **Editorial Slant:** Needs articles on inns in the states west of the Rockies, particularly outside California. Inn reviews each month. Travel stories focusing on local travel where there are inns. Needs to have details in a sidebar.

MARGINAL MARKETS

Magazines are listed in this section for several reasons. Some of them may be new magazines that don't have established track records; others didn't respond to a request for writer's guidelines or had writer's guidelines that didn't give much information; others have indicated they don't want much freelance travel material. Some take fewer than 5 freelance travel articles per year or pay less than 5 cents per word.

After each listing is a code for the main reason the magazine is not included in Active Markets. These codes are:

LF Limited use of freelance travel articles
LI Limited information provided by magazine
LP Low pay

AAA Going Places, 1515 North Westshore Boulevard, Tampa, FL 33607.
Editor: Phyllis W. Zeno. Phone: 813-872-5923. Reply date: 4/1/88. Pays only $15 per printed magazine page, including photos. LP.

Above the Bridge, Star Route 550, Box 189C, Marquette, MI 49855.
Editor: Jacqueline Miller. Reply date: 1/10/88. Pays only 2 cents/word. LP.

Adventure Magazine, 5333 Mission Center Road, San Diego, CA 92108.
Editor: Natalie Best. Phone: 619-295-8202. Reply date: 9/10/87. Articles of 300-1000 words. Pays $50-$300. Uses BW negatives, transparencies, 35mm color slides. **Editorial Slant:** Topics include travel and vacation within the United States, travel hints, recipes for on-the-road cooking, RV travel stories, vacation stories about any American Adventure resorts, sightseeing near or around AA resorts. LI.

AIMPlus, 45 West 34th Street, No. 500, New York, NY 10001.
Travel editor: Janice Wald Henderson. Phone: 212-239-0855. Reply date: 6/8/88. Pays 60 days after acceptance. Replies to queries in 6 weeks. Buys FNASR. Prefers features of 800-1800 words. Pays $300-$600. **Editorial Slant:** A news, service, and general interest magazine for people with arthritis. Sample issue (1988) didn't have any travel articles. LF.

Airfair, 25 West 39th Street, New York, NY 10018.
Managing editor: Ratu Kamlani. Phone: 212-840-6714. Reply date: 4/18/88. Destination articles of 1500-2000 words. **Editorial Slant:** For airline employees, their parents, and retired airline employees. LI.

Albuquerque Singles Scene, 3507 Wyoming, N.E., Albuquerque, NM 87111.
Phone: 505-299-4401. Pays only 4 cents/published word. LP.

American Country, 105 Stoney Mountain Road, Hendersonville, NC 28739.
Editor: Alfred Meyer. Phone: 704-693-0211. Reply date: 6/8/88. No WG available. LI.

American Forests, POB 2000, Washington, DC 20013, or 1516 P Street, N.W., Washington, DC 20005.
Editor: Bill Rooney. Phone: 202-667-3300. Reply date: 6/8/88. **Editorial Slant:** Emphasizes the trends, issues, policies, management, and enjoyment of America's forest resources. LF.

American Heritage, 60 Fifth Avenue, New York, NY 10011.
Phone: 212-206-5500. Reply date: 4/14/88. POA. Prefers features of up to 6000 words. **Editorial Slant:** The subject is the American experience. Uses the past to illuminate the present. Featured travel in April 1987 and April 1988 issues. LI.

Animals, 350 South Huntington Avenue, Boston, MA 02130.
Editorial assistant: Suzanne Satagay. Phone: 617-541-5065. Reply date: 11/12/88. Bimonthly. Circulation: 70,000. FL/year: 4. POA. Buys FR. Kill fee: 15 percent. Usually replies to queries in 3 weeks. Lead time for seasonal articles: 2 months. Accepts CM, SQ, SS. ES: Fax. Subsidized trips OK. Prefers features of approximately 1500 words. Pays $250-$300. SC and WG available. **Photos:** Photo editor: Laura Ten Eyck. Uses 35mm color slides. Buys OTR. POA. Photos purchased without mss. **Editorial Slant:** National magazine published by the Massachusetts Society for the Prevention of Cruelty to Animals. Covers American and international wildlife, domestic animals, conservation. LF.

AOPA Pilot, 421 Aviation Way, Frederick, MD 21701.
Editor: Thomas Horne. Phone: 301-695-2350. Reply date: 8/20/88. Circulation: 265,000. POA. Buys FNASR. Accepts CM. Pays

$75-$250. **Photos:** Uses BW prints 5-by-7 or larger; color transparencies 35mm or larger. Pay for most photos included in pay for ms; some purchased alone for $25 and up. **Editorial Slant:** The official magazine of the Aircraft Owners and Pilots Association. LF.

Arkansas Times, Box 34010, Little Rock, AR 72203.
Editor: Mel White. Phone: 501-375-2985. Reply date: 9/18/88. Doesn't want to encourage travel submissions. Covers only in-state travel. LF.

Arthritis Today, 1314 Spring Street, N.W., Atlanta, GA 30309.
Editorial director: Cindy McDaniel. Phone: 404-872-7100. Reply date: 9/30/88. Bimonthly. Circulation: 700,000. FL/year: 3-4. POA. Buys OTR plus unlimited reprint rights in Arthritis Foundation publications. Kill fee: 25 percent. Replies to queries in 6-8 weeks. Lead time for seasonal articles: at least 4 months. Articles published 3-6 months after acceptance. Accepts CM, SQ, SS, PPS. Subsidized trips OK. Prefers features of 1500-2500 words. Departments or columns: 400-700 words. Pays $350-$700. Pays expenses. SC and WG available. **Photos:** Photo editor: Deb Gaston. Prefers 35mm color slides. Pays for photos on delivery. Photos purchased without mss. **Editorial Slant:** The magazine is a membership benefit of the Arthritis Foundation. Designed to help the person with arthritis live better today, emphasizing upbeat, informative articles that provide practical advice and inspiration. LF.

ASTA Agency Management, 666 Fifth Avenue, New York, NY 10103.
Editor: Patrick D. O. Arton. Phone: 212-765-5454. Reply date: 4/14/88. Monthly. **Editorial Slant:** Official publication of the American Society of Travel Agents. Focuses on the business of the travel industry. Special emphasis is devoted to the cruise industry. Especially interested in articles that analyze industry segments and developments, as well as those that report on trends in the travel industry and on particular companies. Sample articles, 3/88: "Conference Resorts Turn to Agents," "Off-Site Meetings in Offbeat Places," "New York City's Campaign for Agency Business," "Optimism Floods the Mediterranean with New Cruise Options." LI.

Atlanta Magazine, 1360 Peachtree Street, Atlanta, GA 30309.
Managing editor: Susan Percy. Phone: 404-872-3100. Reply date: 4/13/88. Runs only a couple of travel pieces a year, which are back-of-the-book service pieces. LF.

Baja Times, Box 5577, Chula Vista, CA, 92012-5577.
Editorial consultant: John Utley. Reply date: 6/3/88. Maximum pay
is $50. LP.

Baltimore, 16 South Calvert Street, Baltimore, MD 21202.
Editor: Stan Hevisler. Phone: 301-752-7375. Reply date: 9/30/88.
Monthly. Circulation: 60,000. FL/year: 3-4. POP. Buys FNASR.
Kill fee: One-third to one-half. Replies to queries in 2 weeks. Lead
time for seasonal articles: 2-3 months. Articles published 2-3 months
after acceptance. Accepts CM, SQ, PPS, ES. Prefers features of 1000-
3000 words. Departments or columns: 1000-1500 words. Pays $500-
$1500. Pays expenses. SC not available. WG: Write. **Photos:** Photo
editor: Mark Evans. Uses BW, color. Buys FNASR. POP. Photos
purchased without mss. LF.

Black Belt, POB 7728, Burbank, CA 91510-7728.
Assistant editor: Marian Stricker. Phone: 818-843-4444. Reply date:
1/25/88. Rarely uses travel pieces. LF.

Black Enterprise, 130 Fifth Avenue, New York, NY 10011.
Senior editor: Alfred Edmond. Phone: 212-242-8000. Reply date:
9/30/88. Monthly. Circulation: 230,000. FL/year: 9. Buys AR. Kill
fee: 25 percent. Replies to queries in 6-8 months. Lead time for
seasonal articles: 6 months. Articles published 4-6 months after
acceptance. Prefers features of 500 lines. Departments or columns:
100-200 lines. Pay varies. Pays expenses. **Photos:** Uses slides. Photos purchased without mss. **Editorial Slant:** Business-oriented consumer service magazine for Black professionals, corporate executives,
middle managers, entrepreneurs, and policy makers in the public
and private sectors. "Verve" is leisure and lifestyle section about
travel. LI.

Boating, One Park Avenue, New York, NY 10016.
Phone: 212-503-3979. Reply date: 2/1/88. Pays $350-$1000. **Photos:** Prefers Kodachrome 25. Pays $250/page, $500/cover. LI.

Bostonia, 10 Lenox Street, Brookline, MA 02146.
Managing editor: Lori Calabro. Phone: 617-353-3081. Reply date:
6/23/88. POA. Kill fee: 20 percent. Prefers features of 1500-5000
words. Departments or columns: 500-1500 words. **Editorial Slant:**
Brief items on people, architecture, art, trends, and happenings.
Features on topics of concern to educated professional Bostonians
and New Englanders. LI.

Bridal Guide, 441 Lexington Avenue, New York, NY 10017.
Executive editor: Lois Spritzer. Phone: 212-949-4040. Reply date: 5/22/88. Replies to queries in 8 weeks. SC: $2.50. **Editorial Slant:** Deals with honeymoon travel. LI.

British Heritage, POB 8200, Harrisburg, PA 17105.
Executive editor: Gail Huganir. Phone: 717-657-9555. Reply date: 4/14/88. SC: SAE and $3.50. **Editorial Slant:** Aims to present aspects of Britain's history and culture in an entertaining and informative manner. Sample articles: "Sup with Shakespeare," Chelsea Physic Garden, Australia's bicentennial. LI.

California Explorer, 238 Francisco Street, San Francisco, CA 94133.
Editor: Stuart Weiss. Phone: 415-362-6636. Reply date: 9/2/88. Pays $50-$100. **Editorial Slant:** All stories are destination stories and must have accurate info on the area: history, geology, flora and fauna, or whatever is interesting. LI.

California Magazine, 11601 Wilshire Boulevard, No. 1800, Los Angeles, CA 90025.
Phone: 213-479-6511. Reply date: 6/1/88. No WG. LI.

Camping & RV Magazine, POB 337, Iola, WI 54945.
Editor: Deb Lengkeek. Phone: 715-445-5000. Reply date: 8/1/88. Pays 3-5 cents/word. LP.

AR	all rights	OTR	one-time rights
ASMP	American Society of	POA	pays on acceptance
	Magazine	POB	post office box
	Photographers	POP	pays on publication
BW	black-and-white photos	PPS	previously published
CM	complete manuscript		submissions
ES	electronic submissions	PQ	phone queries
FL	freelance	SAE	self-addressed envelope
FL/year	number of freelance travel	SASE	self-addressed stamped envelope
	articles published per	SC	sample copy
	year	SQ	simultaneous queries
F(NAS)R	first (North American serial)	SR	second rights
	rights	SS	simultaneous submissions
ms(s)	manuscript(s)	WG	writer's guidelines
NA	North American		

Car Collector/Car Classics, POB 28571, Atlanta, GA 30328.
Editor: Donald Peterson. Phone: 404-998-4603. Reply date: 4/2/
88. Pays 5 cents/word. LI.

Caribbean Treasures, POB 1290, Keene, NH 03431.
Publisher: E. H. Close. Reply date: 6/16/88. WG do not give
information on pay. LI.

Catholic Forester, 425 West Shuman Boulevard, Naperville, IL 60566.
Editor: Barbara Cunningham. Reply date: 5/2/88. WG do not mention pay. LI.

Chesapeake Bay, 1819 Bay Ridge Avenue, Annapolis, MD 21403.
Editor: Betty Rigoli. Phone: 301-263-2662. Reply date: 1/7/88.
Monthly. POP. Buys FNASR. Pays $75-$85. **Editorial Slant:** All
material must be about the Chesapeake Bay—land or water. LF.

Chief Executive, 205 Lexington Avenue, New York, NY 10016.
Editor: J. P. Donlon. Phone: 212-213-3666. Reply date: 8/20/88.
Editorial Slant: Written by and for CEOs in U.S. and international
business. Includes unusual hobbies or avocations among top executives, such as CEOs traveling on safari. LF.

China Pacific Traveller, 11 Canton Road, Kowloon, Hong Kong.
Editor-in-chief: Derek Maitland. Sample articles: "Thailand—Going
for Gold," "Hainan Diary," Perth, Hong Kong. LI.

City Magazine, 5563 West 73rd Street, Indianapolis, IN 46268.
Editor: Nancy Comiskey. Phone: 317-298-7100. Reply date: 7/9/
88. Pay: $40-$325. **Editorial Slant:** "Directions" section covers
travel and is open to freelancers. LI.

Classic America, Box 2516, Westfield, NJ 07090.
Editor: Richard Aichele. Phone: 201-789-9219. Reply date: 1/22/
88. Quarterly. POP. Buys FNASR. Accepts CM. Prefers features
of 600-2000 words. Pays 8-20 cents/word. WG: SASE. **Photos:**
Uses BW, transparencies. **Editorial Slant:** Concentrates on the period of America's past from 1800 to 1935. Readers want to know
how and where aspects of that period can still be enjoyed. Sample
articles: "Cape May—Renaissance of a Victorian Seashore Resort,"
"Steamboating on the Delta Queen." LI.

Connecticut Magazine, POB 6480, Bridgeport, CT 06606.
Managing editor: Dale Salm. Reply date: 8/20/88. Pays within 1

month of publication. Kill fee: Up to 20 percent. Lead time for
seasonal articles: 3-4 months. Prefers features of 3000 words. Departments or columns: 1800 words. LI.

Country Inns Bed & Breakfast, POB 182, South Orange, NJ 07079.
Managing editor: Allison Kurtz Bernard. Phone: 201-762-7090.
Reply date: 4/22/88. Form letter response to questionnaire. LI.

Country Journal, POB 8200, Harrisburg, PA 17105-8200.
Managing editor: Paula Noonan. Phone: 717-540-8178. Reply date:
10/4/88. Not encouraging travel proposals from writers. LF.

Country Life, King's Reach, Stamford Street, London SE1 9LS, England.
Editor: Jenny Greene. Phone: 01-261-5000. Reply date: 5/26/88.
"Not interested in American contributions on travel, as our readers
tend to be interested in Europe." LF.

Country Magazine, POB 643, Milwaukee, WI 53201.
Publications manager: Bob Ottum. Phone: 414-423-0100. Reply
date: 5/22/88. WG do not mention travel. LI.

Country Times, 5-6 Church Street, Twickenham TW1 3NJ, Mid-
dlesex, England.
Deputy editor: Louise Abbott. Phone: 01-891-6070. Reply date:
8/29/88. No WG. Not looking for foreign travel pieces but does
cover Britain extensively. LI.

Coventry Journal, POB 124, Andover, CT 06232.
Editor: Bill Cisowski. Reply date: 10/3/88. Monthly. Circulation:
20,000. FL/year: 1-2. POA. Replies to queries in 1 month. Lead
time for seasonal articles: 3 months. Articles published 1-2 months
after acceptance. Accepts CM, SS, PPS. Prefers features of 1500
words. Pays $150 for feature articles. May pay expenses. SC: 50
cents. **Photos:** Photo editor: Bill Cisowski. Uses seasonal Connecticut photos. Pays $30/BW. Buys AR. POA. Photos purchased with-
out mss. LF.

Currents, 314 North 20th Street, Colorado Springs, CO 80904.
Editor: Eric Leaper. Phone: 719-473-2466. Reply date: 9/30/88.
Bimonthly. Circulation: 10,000. FL/year: 2-3. POP. Buys FR. Re-
plies to queries in 2-3 weeks. Lead time for seasonal articles: 2
months. Articles published immediately to 1 year after acceptance.
Accepts CM; SQ, SS (if so informed); PPS (rarely); PQ. Subsidized

trips OK. Prefers features of 750-2000 words. Departments or columns: 200-500 words. Pay varies. SC: $1 or 9-by-12 SASE and 5 cents. WG: SASE. **Photos:** Photo editor: Mary McCurdy. Uses BW action photos. Pays $30-$50/cover. Buys FR. POP. Photos purchased without mss. **Editorial Slant:** Uses mss and photos that have to do with whitewater rivers and river running done by people who do it on their own (without the help of commercial outfitters). LF.

Destinations, 1025 Connecticut Avenue, N.W., Washington, DC 20036.
Editor: Mark Beavers. Phone: 202-293-5890. Reply date: 1/8/88. **Editorial Slant:** "The International and Domestic Magazine of North American Bus Travel," published by the American Bus Association. Works on an assignment-only basis; interested writers should submit three clips along with a cover letter. Rarely accepts unsolicited mss, and sends WG only to writers working on assignments. LF.

Detroit Monthly, 1400 Woodbridge, Detroit, MI 48207.
Managing editor: Diane Brozek. Phone: 313-446-1638. Reply date: 1/8/88. No WG. **Editorial Slant:** Has a special winter travel section, usually published in January, and a summer travel section, around May. Occasionally runs other travel-type features such as a skiing getaway story in February. LI.

Diablo, 2520 Camino Diablo, No. 200, Walnut Creek, CA 94596.
Editor: Michael Connell Lester. Phone: 415-943-1111. Reply date: 6/21/88. Seldom runs travel stories. LF.

Dialogue, 3100 South Oak Park Avenue, Berwyn, IL 60402.
Acting editor: Bonnie Miller. Reply date: 6/1/88. Accepts submissions from vision-impaired writers. Top pay is $50. LI.

Discovery, Box 370, Colborne, Ontario, Canada K0K 1S0.
Editor: Mary Schmieder. Reply date: 6/8/88. Deals only with Canadian writers. Interested in receiving press releases from American travel organizations. Canada's only national lifestyle magazine for Canadians over 50. Generally carries two travel articles per issue. LF.

Domain, POB 1569, Austin, TX 78767-1569.
Editor: Catherine Chadwick. Phone: 512-476-7085. Reply date: 6/23/88. POA. Replies to queries in 6-8 weeks. Prefers features of 750-2000 words. Departments or columns: Under 2500 words.

Editorial Slant: Stories must appeal to an educated Texas audience. Likes solidly researched features that reveal the newest and best that Texas has to offer in travel. LI.

European Travel and Life, 122 East 42nd Street, No. 5007, New York, NY 10168.
Editor-in-chief: David Breul. Phone: 212-949-3500. Reply date: 5/22/88. No set WG. LI.

Family Circle, 110 Fifth Avenue, New York, NY 10011.
Travel editor: Kathy Sagan. Reply date: 6/8/88. Runs very little travel. LF.

Family Travel Times, c/o Travel With Your Children, 80 Eighth Avenue, New York, NY 10011.
Carol Eannarino. Phone: 212-206-0688. Reply date: 10/28/88. Ten times/year. Circulation: 20,000. FL/year: "A few." POP. Buys FNASR. Subsidized trips OK. Pays $50-$500, depending on project. SC: Write. **Photos:** Uses no photos. **Editorial Slant:** Writer must be a parent. LF.

Fiberarts, 50 College Street, Asheville, NC 28801.
Editor: Carol Laurence. Phone: 704-253-0468. Reply date: 5/9/88. Circulation: 21,000. POP. SC: $4. **Photos:** Pays $65-$250. LI.

Florida Keys, 505 Duval Street, Key West, FL 33040.
Editor and publisher: David Ethridge. Phone: 305-296-7300. Reply date: 5/22/88. POP. Pays $4-$5/column inch. **Photos:** Uses BW 5-by-7 prints, 35mm or 2¼-inch color transparencies. Pays $20/BW, $35/color. **Editorial Slant:** Uses material about the Florida Keys: history, natural history, people, lifestyles, environment, special events. LI.

Four Seasons, 55 Doncaster Avenue, No. 106, Thornhill, Ontario, Canada L3T 1L7.
Editorial coordinator: Lisa Furlonge. Phone: 416-881-6560. Reply date: 1/19/89. Six times/year. POP. Prefers features of 2000 words. WG: SASE. **Editorial Slant:** Distributed in Four Seasons Hotels in Canada and the United States. Travel features for affluent readers. LI.

Garden Design, 1733 Connecticut Avenue, N.W., Washington, DC 20009.
Editor: Karen D. Fishler. Phone: 202-466-7730. Reply date: 12/

3/88. Quarterly. Circulation: 30,000. FL/year: 4. Pays half on acceptance and half on publication. Buys FR or OTR. Kill fee: 30 percent. Replies to queries in 2-2½ months. Lead time for seasonal articles: 1 year. Articles published as much as 1 year after acceptance. Accepts CM. Subsidized trips OK. Prefers features of 1200-2000 words. Departments or columns: 1000 words. Pays $350 for features, $250 for departments. SC: $5. WG: SASE. **Photos:** Photo editor: Karen D. Fishler. Uses 35mm, 2¼-inch, and 4-by-5 transparencies. Pays $75-$200/color, $300/cover. Buys FR or OTR. POP. Photos purchased without mss. **Editorial Slant:** Published by the American Society of Landscape Architects for a sophisticated readership interested in the design, maintenance, and appreciation of fine gardens and residential landscapes. LF.

Garden Magazine, New York Botanical Garden, Bronx, NY 10458. Editor: Ann Botshon. Phone: 212-220-8657.
Reply date: 9/30/88. Bimonthly. Circulation: 36,000. FL/year: 2. POA. Replies to queries in 4-6 weeks. Lead time for seasonal articles: 1 year. Articles published 1-2 years after acceptance. Accepts CM, SQ, SS. Prefers features of 3000 words. Departments or columns: 500-1500 words. Pay varies. SC: $3. WG available. **Photos:** Photo editor: Ann Botshon. Pay varies according to size and use. Buys FR. Pays for photos on publication. Photos purchased without mss. **Editorial Slant:** Looking for articles about landscape design, environment, great botanical gardens. LF.

GEICO Direct, 1999 Shepard Road, St. Paul, MN 55116. Editor: Sharon Ross. Phone: 800-322-9322, ext. 288. Reply date: 9/30/88. Semiannual. Circulation: 200,000. FL/year: 2. POA. Buys FR and subsequent reprint rights. Kill fee: 10 percent. Replies to queries in 6 weeks. Lead time for seasonal articles: 1 year. Articles published 1 year after acceptance. Accepts PQ. Subsidized trips OK. Prefers features of 1200-1500 words. Departments or columns: 500 words. Pays $500 for major assigned stories. SC and WG available. **Photos:** Art director: John Baskerville (phone: 800-322-9322, ext. 275). Uses four-color transparencies. POA. Photos purchased without mss. **Editorial Slant:** Published by Government Employees Insurance Company and distributed to federal and military employees as well as general policyholders throughout the country. Articles are geared to automotive information and safety with respect to travel and home. LF.

The Geographical Magazine, One Kensington Gore, London SW7 2AR, England.
Editor: David Gwyn Jones. Phone: 01-584-4436. Reply date: 6/8/88. Monthly. Circulation: 500,000. **Editorial Slant:** Most readers are "very interested in today's world but do not have much academic experience." LI.

Golden Years, 233 East New Haven Avenue, POB 537, Melbourne, FL 32902-0537.
Editor-in-chief: Carol Brenner Hittner. Phone: 407-725-4888. Reply date: 5/20/88. Replies to queries in 12-14 weeks. Prefers articles of up to 500 words. Pays "65 cents per one-third-page column line." SC: $2 check or money order. WG: SASE. **Photos:** Uses BW glossies, 35mm slides, 4-by-5 transparencies. Pays $10/BW, $25/color. **Editorial Slant:** "The Magazine For Fantastic Floridians Over 50." LI.

Good Housekeeping, 959 Eighth Avenue, New York, NY 10019.
Articles editor: Joan Thursh. Reply date: 10/7/88. Monthly. POA. Buys AR, but writer retains the right to use material from the article as part of a book project. Kill fee: 25 percent. Replies to queries in 3 weeks. Prefers features of 2500 words. Departments or columns: 750-1000 words. Pays $1000-$1500 for features, $500-$750 for shorts. **Editorial Slant:** General interest women's magazine. LI.

Good Old Days, 306 East Parr Road, Berne, IN 46711.
Managing editor: Rebekah Montgomery. Phone: 219-589-8741. Reply date: 6/21/88. Pays 2 cents/word. LP.

Granta, 250 West 57th Street, No. 1203, New York, NY 10107.
Editor: Bill Buford. Phone: 212-246-1313. Reply date: 7/30/88. SC: $6.95 to Samples Department. British literary magazine that received over 5,000 unsolicited mss in its first year of publication in the United States. LF.

Grit, 208 West Third Street, Williamsport, PA 17701.
Reply date: 5/19/88. Weekly. **Editorial Slant:** Published for a general readership in small-town and rural America. Offers helpful, inspiring, uplifting articles and features that are both informative and entertaining. Emphasis is on people, even in articles about places and things. LI.

Gun Dog, 1901 Bell Avenue, Suite 4, POB 35098, Des Moines, IA 50315.
Editor: Bob Wilbanks. Phone: 515-243-2472. Reply date: 9/30/88. Bimonthly. Circulation: 60,000. FL/year: 3-4. POA. Buys FR, OTR. Pays kill fee. Replies to queries in 1-2 weeks. Subsidized trips OK. Prefers features of 2000 words. Pays $350 for features, $150 for fillers. Pays expenses for assignments. SC, WG: Write. **Photos:** Uses color transparencies. Pays $25/BW, $40-$80/color, $150/cover. Buys FR, OTR. POA. Photos purchased without mss. **Editorial Slant:** Published for upland bird and waterfowl hunters: gunners involved with the pointing, flushing, and retrieving breeds of bird dogs. LF.

Harper's Bazaar, 1700 Broadway, New York, NY 10019.
Features editor: Rusty Unger. Phone: 212-903-5000. Reply date: 6/13/88. **Editorial Slant:** For women late 20s and above, middle income and above, sophisticated, with at least two years of college. Publishes travel. No unsolicited mss. LF.

Highlander, Box 397, Barrington, IL 60011.
Editor: Angus J. Ray. Phone: 312-382-1035. Reply date: 9/30/88. The travel aspect of articles is secondary to coverage of Scottish history. LF.

Hometown Press, 2007 Gallatin Street, Suite 2, Huntsville, AL 35801.
Query Dr. J. C. Hindman. Phone: 206-539-3320. Reply date: 11/21/88. Bimonthly. Circulation: 10,000. FL/year: "2 maybe." POP. Replies to queries in 1 month. Lead time for seasonal articles: 3 months. Articles published 2 months after acceptance. Accepts SQ, PPS, PQ, ES. Prefers features of 1500 words. Departments or columns: Up to 750 words. SC: $3.75. WG: SASE. **Photos:** Art director: Chuck Craig. Uses BW, color. Pays after publication. Photos purchased without mss. **Editorial Slant:** About Alabama. LF.

Honolulu Magazine, 36 Merchant Street, Honolulu, HI 96813.
Editor: Brian Nicol. Phone: 808-524-7400. Reply date: 4/25/88. Monthly. POA. Pays $250-$400. **Photos:** Pays $15-$50. **Editorial Slant:** Historical events, lifestyle, trends related to Hawaii. LI.

House Beautiful, 1700 Broadway, New York, NY 10019.
Features director: Joanna Krotz. Phone: 212-903-5000. Reply date:

7/2/88. Primarily interested in service articles dealing strictly with the home. LF.

Hudson Valley, Box 429, 297 Main Mall, Poughkeepsie, NY 12602. Editor: Susan Agrest. Phone: 914-485-7844. Reply date: 8/23/88. Doesn't release WG unless firmly committed to working with a particular writer. Travel about the Hudson Valley. LF.

In Britain, Thames Tower, Black's Road, London W6 9EL, England. Editor: Bryn Frank. Phone: 01-846-9000. Reply date: 6/8/88. No WG. Published by the British Tourist Authority. LI.

Incentive, 633 Third Avenue, New York, NY 10017. Managing editor: Mary Riordan. Phone: 212-986-4800. Reply date: 4/2/88. Send two clips along with a letter that proposes a story idea. LI.

Indiana Horizons, 5563 West 73rd Street, Indianapolis, IN 46268. Phone: 317-298-7100. Reply date: 7/8/88. POP. Pays $40-$325. **Editorial Slant:** For Hoosiers over 50. Uses general interest and travel articles. LI.

Influence, 250 The Esplanade, 5th Floor, Toronto, Ontario, Canada M5A 1J2. Managing editor: Ernest Hillen. Phone: 416-365-9366. Reply date: 3/21/88. Sample article, 2/88: "At the Heart of Tibet." LI.

Inn Room, POB 3395, Escondido, CA 92025. Editor: Donna Abate. Phone: 619-489-5252. Reply date: 5/18/88. Not accepting any freelance articles or photos. Interested in hearing from public relations firms. LF.

Inside Chicago, 2501 West Petersen, Chicago, IL 60659. Managing editor: Barbara Young. Phone: 312-784-0800. Reply date: 6/8/88. Pays within 30 days of publication. Kill fee: 20 percent. **Editorial Slant:** Shorter pieces of 250-500 words about Chicago events. LI.

Island Life, Drawer X, Sanibel Island, FL 33957. Editor: Joan Hooper. Reply date: 10/8/88. Quarterly. Circulation: 20,000. FL/year: 10-12. POP. Buys SR. Usually replies to queries in 1-2 weeks. Lead time for seasonal articles: 6 months. Unsolicited articles published 1-2 years after acceptance. Accepts CM (with SASE), SQ, SS, PPS. Unsolicited mss without SASE are not returned. Subsidized trips OK. Prefers features of 800-1500 words. SC: $3. WG: SASE. **Photos:** Photo editor: Joan Hooper. Uses color submitted only with ms. Pay for photos included in pay for article. **Editorial Slant:** For affluent visitors to and residents of Southwest Florida. Articles on wildlife, historic sites, architecture, sports. LI.

Kaleidoscope, The Guide to Austin, POB 4368, Austin, TX 78704. Managing editor: Brenda Thompson. Phone: 512-339-9955. Reply date: 9/30/88. Four times/year. FL/year: 2-4. POP. Buys FR. Replies to queries in 1 week. Lead time for seasonal articles: 2 months. Accepts CM, SQ, SS, some PPS. Prefers features of 2000 words. Usually pays 10 cents/word. SC, WG: Write. **Photos:** Photo editor: Ann M. Gorbett. Photos used with stories only. **Editorial Slant:** Chamber of Commerce publication for newcomers to Austin. Travel pieces on places close to Austin, such as Georgetown and Wimberly. LF.

Mature Living, 127 9th Avenue North, MSN 140, Nashville, TN 37234.
Editor: Jack Gulledge. Reply date: 3/2/88. Maximum pay is 5 cents/word for all rights. Published by the Baptist Sunday School Board for senior adults 60 and over. LI.

Mature Outlook, 1716 Locust, Des Moines, IA, 50336. Editor: Marjorie Groves, Ph.D. Reply date: 10/28/88. Doesn't publish many travel articles. LF.

Medical Meetings, 63 Great Road, Maynard, MA 01754. Phone: 617-897-5552. Reply date: 2/25/88. Pays $300-$400 for articles of 1500-2000 words. LI.

Metropolitan Home, 750 Third Avenue, New York, NY 10017. Phone: 212-557-6600. Reply date: 6/8/88. Monthly. POA. Articles of 1000-1500 words. **Editorial Slant:** "Rules of the Road" section has smart tips on travel. LI.

Military Living R&R, POB 2347, Falls Church, VA 22042. Editor: Ann Crawford. Reply date: 3/3/88. Uses very little freelance material. LF.

Milwaukee Magazine, 312 East Buffalo, Milwaukee, WI 53202. Editor: J. Woodburn. Phone: 414-273-1101. Reply date: 9/30/88. Monthly. Circulation: 52,000. FL/year: 2. POP. Buys FR. Pays kill fee. Replies to queries in 4-6 weeks. Lead time for seasonal articles:

6 weeks. Articles published 6 weeks after acceptance. Accepts CM, PPS. Prefers features of 4000 words. Pays $400-$600. Pays expenses. SC: $3.25 to Circulation Department. WG: SASE to Assistant Editor. **Editorial Slant:** Uses travel pieces only about Wisconsin. LF.

Montreal, 1310 Greene Avenue, No. 920, Westmount, Quebec, Canada H3Z 2B5.
Associate editor: Ann Hamilton. Phone: 514-933-2555. Reply date: 6/13/88. **Editorial Slant:** Features of 1000-2500 words on anything pertaining to Montreal. LI.

Motor Boating & Sailing, 224 West 57th Street, New York, NY 10019.
Editor-in-chief: Peter Janssen. Phone: 212-649-3068. Reply date: 9/30/88. Monthly. Circulation: 148,000. FL/year: 2-3. POA. Buys OTR. Pays kill fee. Replies to queries in 1-3 months. Lead time for seasonal articles: 3 months. Accepts CM, SQ, SS. ES: Fax. Prefers features of 1500 words. Departments or columns: 500 words. Pays per agreement. Pays expenses per agreement. SC, WG: Write. **Photos:** Art director: Erin Kenney. Buys OTR. Pays for photos on publication. Photos purchased without mss. **Editorial Slant:** Covers powerboats and sailboats for people who own their own boats and are active in a yachting lifestyle. LF.

Mpls. St. Paul, 12 South Sixth Street, No. 1030, Minneapolis, MN 55402.

AR	all rights	OTR	one-time rights
ASMP	American Society of	POA	pays on acceptance
	Magazine	POB	post office box
	Photographers	POP	pays on publication
BW	black-and-white photos	PPS	previously published
CM	complete manuscript		submissions
ES	electronic submissions	PQ	phone queries
FL	freelance	SAE	self-addressed envelope
FL/year	number of freelance travel	SASE	self-addressed stamped envelope
	articles published per	SC	sample copy
	year	SQ	simultaneous queries
F(NAS)R	first (North American serial)	SR	second rights
	rights	SS	simultaneous submissions
ms(s)	manuscript(s)	WG	writer's guidelines
NA	North American		

Editor: Brian Anderson. Reply date: 8/3/88. Not encouraging queries or submissions. LF.

Ms., One Times Square, New York, NY 10036.
Editor-in-chief: Anne Summers. Phone: 212-719-9800. Reply date: 10/12/88. Travel department is known as "Ms. Adventures." LI.

New Body, 888 Seventh Avenue, New York, NY 10106.
Editor: Constance Boze. Reply date: 1/8/88. Eighty percent freelance written. Prefers features of 1000-2000 words. Pays $75-$200. **Editorial Slant:** Health and fitness magazine aimed at women ages 18-49. LI.

New Dominion, 2000 North 15th Street, No. 604, Arlington, VA 22201.
Editor-publisher: Walter Nicklin. Phone: 703-527-1199. Reply date: 4/29/88. Pays 15 cents/word. **Photos:** Pays $25-$40/photo, $200-$250/day. Buys OTR. **Editorial Slant:** For and about Northern Virginia. LI.

New England Living, 177 East Industrial Drive, Manchester, NH 03103-1899.
Phone: 603-668-7330. Reply date: 8/22/88. POA. **Photos:** Uses BW prints, 35mm or larger color transparencies and color prints. Magazine still under development. **Editorial Slant:** Stories on travel destinations around New England. Activity-oriented pieces also encouraged but not interested in personal accounts or travelogues. Each issue will focus on one New England bed and breakfast, inn, or hotel. LI.

New England Monthly, Box 446, Haydenville, MA 01039.
Phone: 413-268-7262. Reply date: 4/14/88. Prefers features of 2000-5000 words. Departments or columns: 1000-1800 words. Pays $350-$1400. **Editorial Slant:** Covers recreation and the outdoors in the New England states. LI.

New Woman, 215 Lexington Avenue, New York, NY 10016.
Executive editor: Stephanie von Hirschberg. Senior editor: Donna Jackson. Phone: 212-685-4790. Reply date: 6/8/88. Accepts CM. Prefers features of 1000-4000 words. Pays $500-$2000. Uses travel articles with a self-discovery angle. LI.

New York Magazine, 755 Second Avenue, New York, NY 10017.
Managing editor: Laurie Jones. Phone: 212-880-0700. Reply date:

5/23/88. Replies to queries in 3 weeks. Accepts CM. Prefers features of 1800-5000 words. Pay varies. **Editorial Slant:** Nonfiction relating to New York City, including profiles of New Yorkers, health and medicine, behavior and lifestyle, and service articles. LI.

Northwest, 34 East 51st Street, New York, NY 10022.
Editor: Bill McCoy. Reply date: 5/15/88. Monthly. Circulation: 350,000. Publishes 8 feature stories per issue on all topics. Replies to queries in 6 weeks. SC: $3 check or money order to Joseph McGurr. **Editorial Slant:** In-flight magazine of Northwest Airlines. Covers places to which Northwest flies. Sample article: "How to Find What's Hawaiian about Hawaii." LI.

Outdoor America, 1401 Wilson Boulevard, Level B, Arlington, VA 22209.
Editor: Kevin Kasowski. Phone: 703-528-1818. Reply date: 10/1/88. Quarterly. Circulation: 45,000. FL/year: 3-4. POP. Buys FR. Replies to queries in 8-10 weeks. Lead time for seasonal articles: 6 months. Accepts CM, SQ, PPS. No features. Prefers departments or columns of 600-1000 words. Pays 15 cents/word. SC: $1.50. WG: SASE. **Photos:** Photo editor: Kevin Kasowski. Uses BW, color transparencies. Pays $35-$70/BW, $50-$100/color, $200/cover. Buys OTR. POP. Photos purchased without mss. **Editorial Slant:** Conservation magazine published by the Izaak Walton League of America. "On the Road" department uses profiles of natural sites or regions of outstanding or unusual interest to conservationists. LF.

Pan Am Clipper, 34 East 51st Street, New York, NY 10022.
Phone: 212-888-5900. Reply date: 9/1/87. No WG. Most material is commissioned. SC: $3 to Phyllis Brown. LF.

Parentguide, 2 Park Avenue, New York, NY 10016.
Editor: Leslie Elgort. Phone: 212-213-8840. Reply date: 10/7/88. Monthly. Circulation: 205,000. FL/year: 8-10. POA. Replies to queries in 2-3 weeks. Lead time for seasonal articles: 2 months. Articles published 6 months after acceptance. Accepts CM, SQ, SS. Prefers features of 1000-1500 words. SC: SASE with $1.30 postage. WG: SASE. **Photos:** Photo editor: Leslie Elgort. Uses BW, covers. Shots of children. POA. Photos purchased without mss. **Editorial Slant:** Travel articles that are family-oriented. Also pieces about special getaways for parents who need a break from their kids. LI.

Parents, 685 Third Avenue, New York, NY 10017.
Phone: 212-878-8700. POA. Replies to queries in 3-4 weeks. Prefers features of 1500-3000 words. LI.

Pennsylvania Game News, POB 1567, Harrisburg, PA 17105-1567.
Editor: Bob Bell. Reply date: 5/22/88. POA. Replies to queries in 4 weeks. Pays 5-8 cents/word. **Photos:** Pays $10-$20/BW. **Editorial Slant:** Basic subjects are hunting and hunting-related activities. Material must have a Pennsylvania locale or be of such a nature that location is unimportant. LI.

Prevention, Rodale Press, 33 East Minor Street, Emmaus, PA 18098.
Assistant managing editor: Lewis Vaughn. Phone: 215-967-5171. Reply date: 9/12/88. Uses very little freelance material. LF.

Prime Times, 2819 First Avenue, #240, Seattle, WA 98121.
Publisher-editor: Anthony Thein. Reply date: 5/2/88. Uses very little freelance material. LF.

Private Pilot, POB 6050, Mission Viejo, CA 92690.
Editor: Mary Silitch. Phone: 714-855-8822. Reply date: 9/30/88. Monthly. Circulation: 125,000. FL/year: 3. POP. Buys FNASR. Replies to queries in 15-45 days. Lead time for seasonal articles: 6 months. Articles published 3-5 months after acceptance. Accepts CM, PPS. ES: IBM-compatible (modem). Prefers features of 1500-3000 words. Pays 10 cents/word. SC: $3. WG: SASE. **Photos:** Photo editor: Mary Silitch. Uses BW, color. Buys OTR. POP. **Editorial Slant:** Aviation writing of interest to private pilots and aircraft owners. LF.

The Robb Report, One Acton Place, Acton, MA 01720.
President: Samuel Phillips. Phone: 617-263-7749. Reply date: 6/13/88. Prefers features of 3000-3500 words. **Editorial Slant:** For affluent readers. Travel pieces are trend stories as well as destination pieces. LI.

The Rotarian, One Rotary Center, 1560 Sherman Avenue, Evanston, IL 60201.
Associate editor: Jo Nugent. Phone: 312-866-3000. Reply date: 10/12/88. Monthly. Circulation: 528,860. FL/year: 4-5. POA. Buys AR. Pays kill fee. Replies to queries in 2 weeks. Lead time for seasonal articles: 4 months. Accepts CM, SQ, SS, PPS, PQ (but prefers written). Prefers features of 1200-2000 words. Departments

or columns: 800 words. Pay "depends on value of each piece." SC, WG: 9-by-12 SASE. **Photos:** Photo editor: Judy Lee. Usually buys OTR. POA. Photos purchased without mss. LF.

Sacramento, Box 2424, Sacramento, CA 95812-2424.
Associate editor: Jan Haag. Phone: 916-446-7548. Reply date: 10/12/88. Monthly. Circulation: 26,000. FL/year: 2-3. POP. Buys FNASR. Replies to queries in 2-4 weeks. Lead time for seasonal articles: 4-6 months. Accepts SQ, SS, some PPS. Subsidized trips OK. Prefers features of 3000 words. Departments or columns: 1500 words. Pays $175-$250 for travel articles. Pays expenses of regular freelancers. SC: $4.50 to Circulation Manager. WG: SASE to Jan Haag. **Photos:** Design director: Chuck Daniel. Uses BW, color transparencies. Pays $25-$75/BW, $50-$150/color. Buys FNASR. POP. Photos purchased without mss. **Editorial Slant:** For the affluent and informed Sacramentan. Concentrate on the topical and the unusual. LF.

Sailing World, 111 East Avenue, Norwalk, CT 06851.
Editor: John Burnham. Phone: 203-853-9921. Reply date: 6/8/88. Formerly Yacht Racing and Cruising. POP. Pays $50/column of text. **Editorial Slant:** Cruising-oriented features, either instructional or narrative. LI.

Sailors' Gazette, 11265 Fourth Street East, Treasure Island, FL 33706.
Phone: 813-367-7643. Reply date: 9/30/88. Monthly. Circulation: 15,000. FL/year: 12. POP. Replies to queries in 30-60 days. Lead time for seasonal articles: 60 days. Articles published 30 days after acceptance. Accepts CM, SQ, SS, PPS. Prefers features of 800-1200 words. Departments or columns: 400-800 words. SC: $1. **Photos:** Photo editor: Susan Smith. Uses BW. Pays $10/cover. POP. Photos purchased without mss. LI.

San Diego Magazine, POB 85409, San Diego, CA 92138.
Associate editor: Virginia Butterfield. Phone: 619-225-8953. Reply date: 10/4/87. No WG. LI.

Scanorama, Box 19600, S-104, 32 Stockholm, Sweden.
Editor-in-chief: Karl Beijbom. Phone: 08-23-26-40. Reply date: 6/23/88. **Editorial Slant:** In-flight magazine of SAS airline. General interest magazine that contains articles on sports, culture, gastronomy, and business. LI.

Second Wind, 15 Ketchum Street, Westport, CT 06880.
Editor-in-chief: Paul Perry. Travel editor: Barbara Coats. Phone:
203-226-7463. Reply date: 10/88. Bimonthly. **Editorial Slant:** For
active, affluent people over 45. Sample articles, 10/88: "Vermont's
Horse-Country Holiday"; active cruises; short articles on skiing,
Brittany, Fiji, golf. LI.

Seventeen, 850 Third Avenue, New York, NY 10022.
Articles editor: Katherine Rich. Phone: 212-759-8100. Reply date:
5/24/88. POA. Replies to queries in 4 weeks. Lead time for seasonal
articles: 6 months. Prefers features of 1000-2500 words. Departments or columns: 1000 words. SC: On newsstands. WG: SASE.
Editorial Slant: Subjects of interest to teenagers. LI.

Sierra, 730 Polk Street, San Francisco, CA 94109.
Managing editor: Annie Stine. Phone: 415-923-5623. Reply date:
10/14/88. Publishes only outdoor adventure pieces with a conser-
vationist and environmental perspective. LF.

Silver Circle, 1001 Commerce Drive, Irwindale, CA 91706.
Editor: Jay Binkly. Reply date: 9/30/88. Quarterly. Circulation:
500,000. FL/year: 3-4. POA. Buys FR. Kill fee: 10 percent. Replies
to queries in 2-3 weeks. Lead time for seasonal articles: 6 months.
Articles published 3 months after acceptance. Accepts CM. Prefers
features of 1800 words. Pays $200-$800. SC, WG: 9-by-12 SASE.
Photos: Photo editor: Jay Binkly. Pays $40/color, $500/cover. Buys
FR. POP. **Editorial Slant:** Readers are mostly age 50 and over. No
destination pieces; wants service-oriented articles. LF.

Single Parent, 8807 Colesville Road, Silver Spring, MD 20910.
Editor: Donna Duvall. Phone: 301-588-9354, 800-638-8078. Top
pay is $75. LI.

Ski Guide, 287 MacPherson Avenue, Toronto, Ontario, Canada M4V
1A4.
Editor: Bob Weeks. Phone: 416-928-2909. Reply date: 7/24/88.
Annual. Circulation: 75,000. Accepts CM. **Editorial Slant:** Travel
features on popular and lesser-known ski holiday destinations. Covers
Canadian and foreign spots, including ski information, accommodations, attractions, prices, atmosphere, and how to get there. LI.

Ski Magazine, 380 Madison Avenue, New York, NY 10017.
Phone: 212-687-3000. Reply date: 12/1/87. Does not send WG to
people who wish to submit material on speculation. LF.

Skiing, 1515 Broadway, New York, NY 10036.
Phone: 212-719-6600. Reply date: 6/8/88. No WG. Not interested
in stories on first-time skiers. LF.

Snowmobile, 319 Barry Avenue South, No. 101, Wayzata, MN
55391.
Editor: Dick Hendricks. Reply date: 9/30/88. Four times/year: September, October, December, January. Circulation: 500,000. FL/
year: 3-4. POP. Buys FNASR. Replies to queries in 4 weeks. Lead
time for seasonal articles: 2 months. Articles published within 1
year of acceptance. Accepts CM, SQ, SS. Subsidized trips OK.
Prefers features of 1000 words or more. Departments or columns:
up to 500 words. Pays $250-$400 for features, $50-$150 for departments. SC: $3.50 check. WG: Write. **Photos:** Uses BW prints,
four-color transparencies. Pays $25/BW, $30-$50/color. Buys FNASR.
POP. **Editorial Slant:** Circulated throughout the United States and
Canada. Covers interesting places to snowmobile, snowmobiling
adventures, family or club snowmobiling activities, winter festivals
that include snowmobiling. LF.

Sons of Norway Viking, 1455 West Lake Street, Minneapolis, MN
55408.
Editor: Gaelyn Beal. Phone: 612-827-3611. Reply date: 9/30/88.
Monthly. Circulation: 72,000. FL/year: 1-2. POP. Buys FR. Replies
to queries in 4 months. Lead time for seasonal articles: 3 months.
Articles generally published within 6 months of acceptance. Accepts
CM, PPS, PQ. Prefers features of 1500-2800 words. Pays about
$150. SC and WG available. **Photos:** Photo editor: Gaelyn Beal.
Uses 35mm slides, vertical format for cover. Norwegian scenery.
Pays $20/BW or color, $100/cover. Buys OTR. POP. Photos purchased without mss only for cover. **Editorial Slant:** Interested only
in travel articles about Norway, not generic Scandinavia and not
tips for tourists. Wants in-depth articles about one significant destination: museum, city, or area of Norway, including some historical
background. Most readers have made several trips to Norway; many
have relatives there and are quite familiar with parts of the country.
LF.

Southern Boating, 1766 Bay Road, Miami Beach, FL 33139.
Editor: Skip Allen. Reply date: 1/12/88. POP. Prefers features of
1000-2500 words. Pays $50-$100, including art. **Editorial Slant:**
Publishes articles of interest to power and sailing yachters in Southern waters. Geographical area covers Southeastern coastal waters from

the Carolinas to Texas, including the Bahamas and the Caribbean. LI.

Southern RV, Box 811, Bradenton, FL 33506.
Editor: Ruth F. Silvertooth. Phone: 813-748-6408. Reply date: 7/2/88. Prefers feature of 800-1000 words. Pays 5 cents/word. **Photos:** Uses BW. Pays $5. **Editorial Slant:** Contents relate to RV travel, places of interest, camping areas, important events. LI.

Southern Travel, 5520 Park Avenue, Trumbull, CT 06611.
Editor: Shepherd Campbell. Reply date: 4/18/88. Prefers features of 2000-3000 words. Departments or columns: 1000 words. **Editorial Slant:** A service magazine for readers to use in planning trips and to refer to on the road for practical guidance. In 9/88 magazine was reportedly being sold, so editorial policy may change. LI.

Southwest Art, 5444 Westheimer, No. 1440, Houston, TX 77056.
Editor: Susan H. McGarry. Phone: 713-850-0990. Reply date: 9/30/88. Monthly. Circulation: 65,000. FL/year: 1-2. POA. Buys AR. Kill fee: One-third. Replies to queries in 1-6 months. Lead time for seasonal articles: 3-4 months. Articles published 1-6 months after acceptance. Accepts CM, SQ, SS, PQ. Prefers features of 2000 words. Departments or columns: 500-1200 words. SC, WG: Write Editorial Department. **Photos:** Photo editor: Susan H. McGarry. Uses BW glossies, 35mm, 2-1/4-inch, and 4-by-5 color transparencies. Buys OTR. Pays for photos in month of publication. **Editorial Slant:** For art collectors and art appreciators interested in the artists, events, and market trends in the traditional arts west of the Mississippi River. LF.

SporTreks, POB 623, Lebanon, NH 03766.
Publisher-editor: Lisa Rogak. Reply date: 9/30/88. Monthly. FL/year: 10. POP. Buys OTR. Replies to queries in 1 week. Lead time for seasonal articles: 2 months. Articles published 1 month after acceptance. Accepts CM, SQ, SS, PPS. Subsidized trips OK. Prefers features of 1500 words. Departments or columns: 750-1000 words. Pays $10-$50. SC: $5. **Photos:** Uses no photos. **Editorial Slant:** Newsletter that uses articles about keeping fit while traveling. LP.

Surfing, POB 3010, San Clemente, CA 92672.
Editor: David Gilovich. Phone: 714-492-7873. Reply date: 8/20/88. Prefers features of 2000 words. Departments or columns: 250-

500 words. Pays 10-25 cents/word. **Editorial Slant:** First-person travel stories and pieces on unique surfing locales. LI.

Taj, Indian Hotels Co. Ltd., Apollo Bunder, Bombay 400 039, India. Editor: Camellia Panjabi. Phone: 202-3366. Reply date: 2/29/88. **Editorial Slant:** Published by the Taj Group of Hotels, aimed at promoting tourism to India. Features stories that deal with people and their lifestyles, the arts, architecture, cuisine, and any other subject that will help promote an interest in and understanding of the country. LI.

Transitions Abroad, POB 344, Amherst, MA 01004. Phone: 413-256-0373. Reply date: 5/2/88. Pays $1-$1.50/column inch. For active international travelers of all ages. LI.

The Travel Agent Magazine, 825 Seventh Avenue, New York, NY 10019. Executive editor: Richard Kahn. Phone: 212-887-1919. Reply date: 4/25/88. Twice weekly. Prefers features of 500-1000 words. Pays $50. **Editorial Slant:** For and about travel agents. Articles on special interest travel and emerging travel markets such as women, singles, families, blue collar, youth, and disabled. Freelance stories focusing on destinations must have a strong travel agent slant and include information on packages, pricing, commission, policies, target markets, and marketing techniques. LI.

Traveling Times, 25115 West Avenue Stanford, Valencia, CA 91355-1227. Vice president: Pamela Garner. Phone: 805-295-1253. Reply date: 8/15/88. Uses very little freelance material. LF.

Travelore Report, 1512 Spruce Street, Philadelphia, PA 19102. Editor: Ted Barkus. Phone: 215-735-3838. Reply date: 4/3/88. Pays $25 for features. LP.

Tucson Lifestyle, 7000 East Tanque Verde Road, Tucson, AZ 85715. Editor: Sue Giles. Phone: 602-721-2929. Reply date: 9/30/88. Monthly. Circulation: 33,000. FL/year: 1-2. POA. Buys FR. Pays kill fee. Replies to queries in 6 weeks at most. Lead time for seasonal articles: 4 months. Accepts CM, SQ, PPS, PQ. Subsidized trips OK. Prefers features of 1500-2000 words. SC: $3.50. **Photos:** Photo editor: Judith Byron. Uses BW glossies, color. Pays $200-$300/ cover. Buys FR. Pays on receipt. Photos purchased without mss.

Editorial Slant: All stories should deal with Tucson or its residents, although magazine occasionally uses travel stories—with a local slant—about such locales as San Diego. LF.

Undercurrent, Box 1658, Sausalito, CA 94965.
Phone: 415-332-3684. Reply date: 6/4/88. **Editorial Slant:** First-person travel stories with information for serious divers. LI.

Vacations, 2411 Fountain View, Houston, TX 77057.
Editor: Shelby Hodge. Phone: 713-974-6903. Reply date: 4/25/88. **Editorial Slant:** No straight destination travel articles; consumer-oriented service publication. Emphasis on a good-value approach to travel. LI.

Valley Magazine, 16800 Devonshire Street, No. 275, Granada Hills, CA 91344.
Editor-in-chief: Jane Boeckmann. Phone: 818-368-3353. Reply date: 6/24/88. Monthly. Prefers features of 2000-4000 words. **Photos:** Uses BW (preferably 8-by-10 glossies), color transparencies. **Editorial Slant:** Articles of interest to San Fernando Valley residents and visitors. LI.

Vanity Fair, 350 Madison Avenue, New York, NY 10017.
Phone: 212-880-8800. Reply date: 7/3/88. No WG. Rarely publishes travel-related articles. LF.

WalkWays, 733 15th Street, N.W., No. 427, Washington, DC 20005.
Editor: Marsha Wallen. Phone: 202-737-9555. Reply date: 6/8/88. Bimonthly. Prefers features of 750 words. Pays 10 cents/word. SC: $1.50. **Photos:** Uses BW. Pays $10. **Editorial Slant:** Newsletter published by the WalkWays Center, a nonprofit membership organization. Travel stories should include resource materials: reservations, when to go, what to bring, maps. Sample articles: "Blindness No Bar to Nature Walk," "Walking in National Parks Holds Surprises for Sidewalk Strollers." LI.

Washington Motorist, 330 Sixth Avenue North, Seattle, WA 98109.
Editor: Janet Ray. Reply date: 4/13/88. Seldom uses freelance articles. LF.

Water Ski, POB 2456, Winter Park, FL 32790.
Editor: Terry Temple. Reply date: 8/22/88. Prefers features of 1500-

2500 words. Pays $75-$300. SC: $2.50. **Photos:** Pays $35-$200/ photo, $300/cover. LI.

The Water Skier, POB 191, Winter Haven, FL 33882.
Editor: Duke Cullimore. Reply date: 9/28/88. Buys few travel articles. LF.

Weight Watchers Magazine, 360 Lexington Avenue, New York, NY 10017.
Articles editor: Ruth Papazian. Phone: 212-370-0644. Reply date: 9/30/88. Monthly. Circulation: 1 million. FL/year: 1-2. POA. Buys FNASR. Kill fee: 25 percent for articles accepted then killed. Replies to queries in 6-8 weeks. Lead time for seasonal articles: 4 months. Articles usually published 2 months after acceptance. Accepts CM. Prefers features of 1200 words. Departments or columns: 750-850 words. Pays 35-50 cents/word. Pays expenses. SC: $1.75. WG: Write. **Photos:** Art director: Betty Alfenito. Uses four-color transparencies. Pays $700/cover. Buys OTR. POP. **Editorial Slant:** Special interest magazine, devoted to self-improvement through weight loss and related areas. LF.

Western People, Box 2500, Saskatoon, Saskatchewan, Canada S7K 2C4.
Phone: 306-665-3500. Reply date: 6/8/88. Weekly farm newspaper supplement. For and about people of the four western provinces. Emphasis is rural but not necessarily agricultural. LI.

AR	all rights	OTR	one-time rights
ASMP	American Society of	POA	pays on acceptance
	Magazine	POB	post office box
	Photographers	POP	pays on publication
BW	black-and-white photos	PPS	previously published
CM	complete manuscript		submissions
ES	electronic submissions	PQ	phone queries
FL	freelance	SAE	self-addressed envelope
FL/year	number of freelance travel	SASE	self-addressed stamped envelope
	articles published per	SC	sample copy
	year	SQ	simultaneous queries
F(NAS)R	first (North American serial)	SR	second rights
	rights	SS	simultaneous submissions
ms(s)	manuscript(s)	WG	writer's guidelines
NA	North American		

Western RV Traveler, 2019 Clement Avenue, Alameda, CA 94501. Phone: 415-865-7500. Reply date: 1/4/88. ES: Macintosh or compatible, Microsoft Word (diskette or modem). Pays $1.50/column inch. **Editorial Slant:** Stories are judged on how they serve the RV traveler. LI.

Wine & Spirits, POB 1548, Princeton, NJ 08542. Phone: 609-921-2196. Reply date: 6/8/88. Prefers travel features of 1000-1600 words. **Editorial Slant:** Discoveries of favorite restaurants, inns, spas, vineyards. Has limited coverage of travel and runs articles on only the most interesting out-of-the-way discoveries. LI.

Woman's Day, 1515 Broadway, New York, NY 10036. Articles editor: Rebecca Greer. Reply date: 9/30/88. Fifteen times/ year. Circulation: 7 million. FL/year: 1 or 2 general travel articles (not destination pieces), plus several articles for regional editions. POA. Kill fee: 25 percent. Replies to queries in 2-4 weeks. Lead time for seasonal articles: 4-6 months. Accepts CM. Regionals are 300-1000 words. Pays top rates. Pays expenses if agreed in advance. SC: At supermarkets. **Photos:** Art director: Brad Pallas. POP. **Editorial Slant:** Articles that will help women improve their lives in some way. LF.

Women's Sports & Fitness, POB 2456, Winter Park, FL 32790. Associate editor: Maria Madsen. Phone: 407-628-4802. Reply date: 9/30/88. Ten times/year. Circulation: 370,000. FL/year: 4. POP. Buys FNASR. Kill fee: 25 percent. Replies to queries in 1 month. Lead time for seasonal articles: 3 months. Articles published 2 months after acceptance. Accepts CM, SQ, SS, PPS. Subsidized trips OK. Prefers features of 2500-3000 words. Departments or columns: 400- 850 words. Pays $100-$750. Pays expenses. SC: $2. WG: SASE. **Photos:** Photo editor: Doug Dukane. Uses slides. **Editorial Slant:** National magazine for active women who are interested in health and fitness. LF.

Working Woman Magazine, 342 Madison Avenue, New York, NY 10173. Phone: 212-309-9800. Reply date: 6/13/88. POA. Replies to unsolicited material in 4 to 8 weeks. Prefers features of 2500 words. Departments or columns: 1500-2500 words. LI.

Working Woman Weekends, 342 Madison Avenue, New York, NY 10173.
Reply date: 11/21/87. POA. Departments of 75-600 words. **Editorial Slant:** Articles about weekend travel. LI.

Yacht Vacations Magazine, 830 N.E. Pop Tilton's Place, Jensen Beach, FL 34957.
Editor: Antonia Thomas. Phone: 407-334-0447. Reply date: 5/19/88. **Editorial Slant:** Emphasis on yacht charter vacations. Formerly known as Chartering. LI.

Yachtsman, Pier One, Alameda Marina, Alameda, CA 94501.
Phone: 415-865-7500. Reply date: 1/4/88. Pays during the month of publication. ES: Macintosh or compatible using Microsoft Word, diskette or modem. Pays $1.50/column inch. **Editorial Slant:** Stories are judged on how they serve the boater—sail or power. LI.

NOT IN THE MARKET

The following magazines do not publish travel articles, do not take freelance contributions, or do not pay.

Appalachia Bulletin, 5 Joy Street, Boston, MA 02108. Editor: Kelly Short. Phone: 617-523-0636. Reply date: 5/10/88. No pay.

Audubon, 950 Third Avenue, New York, NY 10022.
Executive editor: Gary Soucie. Phone: 212-832-3200. Reply date: 11/1/87. Not a travel story market.

Austin Magazine, POB 4368, Austin, TX, 78765.
Managing editor: Brenda Thompson. Reply date: 6/22/88. No travel articles.

Birmingham, POB 10127, Birmingham, AL 35202.
Editor: Joe O'Donnell. Phone: 205-323-5461. Reply date: 9/28/88. Doesn't do travel pieces.

Boston, 300 Massachusetts Avenue, Boston, MA 02115.
Editor: Janice Brand. Phone: 617-262-9700. Reply date: 10/1/88. Monthly. Circulation: 100,000. Doesn't use travel articles.

Caribbean Update, 52 Maple Avenue, Maplewood, NJ 07040.
Editor: Kal Wagenheim. Reply date: 5/23/88. Doesn't take freelance pieces.

Changing Times, 1729 H Street, N.W., Washington, DC 20006
Associate editor: Paul Plawin. Phone: 202-887-6485. Reply date:
5/17/88. Virtually all material is staff written.

Chicago, 414 North Orleans, Suite 800, Chicago, IL 60610.
Editor: Hillel Levin. Phone: 312-222-8999. Reply date: 4/22/88.
Does not use freelance travel writers.

City Living, 853 Howard Street, San Francisco, CA 94103.
Editor: Tom York. Reply date: 7/6/88. Doesn't run travel articles.

Dolls, 170 Fifth Avenue, 12th Floor, New York, NY 10010.
Editor: Krystyna Goddu. Reply date: 10/1/88. No travel articles.

Driving, AAA New Jersey Automobile Club, One Hanover Road,
Florham Park, NJ 07932.
Editor: Pamela Fischer. Reply date: 10/1/88. Doesn't use freelance.

Images, 50 Holly Street, Toronto, Ontario, Canada M4S 3B3.
Assistant editor: Leslie Jennings. Phone: 416-482-9399. Reply date:
10/1/88. Travel-related articles are written by staff writers.

International Family, 102 Greenwich Avenue, Greenwich, CT 06830.
Managing editor: Jennifer Fountain. Reply date: 1/3/88. Does not
pay. For international awareness and education. Particularly interested in items about learning a foreign language, geography, and
family travel.

Kiwanis, 3636 Woodview Trace, Indianapolis, IN 46268.
Executive editor: Chuck Jonak. Phone: 317-875-8755. Reply date:
10/7/88. All travel articles are staff written.

Lear's, 505 Park Avenue, 19th Floor, New York, NY 10022.
Executive editor: Audreen Ballard. Phone: 212-888-0007. Reply
date: 8/22/88. Does not consider travel articles.

London Hotel Magazine, Newcombe House, 45 Notting Hill Gate,
London W11 3LQ, England.
Editor: M. J. Shapiro. Phone: 01-243-8501. Reply date: 10/13/88.
All travel is written in house.

Maturity Magazine, 7376 142nd Street, Surrey, British Columbia,
Canada V3W 7T3.
Executive editorial assistant: L. A. Brendon. Phone: 604-590-4433.
Reply date: 8/22/88. Has its own travel staff.

Midwest Living, 1912 Grand, Des Moines, IA 50309.
Reply date: 10/1/88. Not looking at new queries.

Modern Maturity, 3200 East Carson, Lakewood, CA 90712.
Editor: Ian Ledgerwood. Reply date: 10/15/88. "Not interested at this time."

Moose Magazine, Supreme Lodge Building, Mooseheart, IL 60539.
Editor: Raymond Dickow. Reply date: 9/30/88. Monthly. Circulation: 1.3 million. No travel.

National Geographic World, 1145 17th Street, N.W., Washington, DC 20036.
Submissions editor: Eleanor Shannahan. Reply date: 6/1/88. Monthly. Does not accept freelance article submissions. **Photos:** Uses 35mm, 2¼-inch, and 4-by-5 color transparencies. Pays $200/page/photos, $400/cover. **Editorial Slant:** A picture magazine for young readers ages eight and older, covering a variety of subjects: science, nature, sports, adventure, unusual experiences. Sample articles, 6/88: Sailboarding, Arctic birds.

Playgirl, 801 Second Avenue, New York, NY 10017.
Travel editor: Alan Schwartz. Reply date: 10/28/88. All work is done in house.

Ranch and Coast, 12625 High Bluff Drive, San Diego, CA 92130-2053.
Editor: Mary Shepardson. Reply date: 5/25/88. Buys absolutely no freelance.

Review, 34 East 51st Street, New York, NY 10022.
Phone: 212-888-5900. Reply date: 5/10/88. In-flight magazine of Eastern Airlines. No WG. Uses only reprints.

Ruralite, Box 558, Forest Grove, OR 97116.
Associate editor: Walt Wentz. Reply date: 9/30/88. Publishes zero to one travel articles per year.

Savvy Woman, 3 Park Avenue, New York, NY 10016.
Senior editor: Susan Pelzer. Reply date: 5/19/88. No freelance openings in the travel column.

7 Days, 36 Cooper Square, New York, NY 10003.
Assistant to editor: Kiki Jamieson. Phone: 212-353-9250. Reply date: 9/30/88. Doesn't use travel writing.

Shape, 21100 Erwin Street, Woodland Hills, CA 91367.
Acquisitions editor: Jennifer Koch. Phone: 818-715-0600. Reply
date: 9/20/88. All articles are written by staffers.

South Carolina Wildlife, POB 167, Columbia, SC 29202.
Managing editor: Linda Renshaw. Phone: 803-734-3972. Reply
date: 10/28/88. Does not publish travel articles.

Southern California Guide, 11385 Exposition Boulevard, No. 102,
Los Angeles, CA 90064.
Editor: Valerie Summers. Phone: 213-391-8255. Does not accept
freelance material or publish material submitted by public relations
firms.

Southern Living, POB 523, Birmingham, AL 35201.
Managing editor: Bill McDougald. Phone: 205-877-6000. Reply
date: 7/5/88. Does not accept unsolicited material.

Speaking of Travel, POB 880, Hermosa Beach, CA 90254.
Editor: Les Barry. Phone: 213-376-2913. Reply date: 5/10/88. Does
not pay.

Travel Fit, Box 6718, FDR Station, New York, NY 10150.
Reply date: 6/25/88. Does not solicit articles.

Travelhost, 8080 North Central, 14th Floor, Dallas, TX 75206.
Administrative assistant: Mary Sandford. Phone: 214-691-1163.
Reply date: 4/19/88. Does not publish articles written by freelance
writers.

Wine Country, 985 Lincoln Avenue, Benicia, CA 94510.
Editor: Shirley Ray. Reply date: 9/29/88. No longer accepting freelance work.

WNC Business Journal, POB 8204, Asheville, NC 28804.
Editor: Marilyn Nason. Reply date: 10/14/88. Publishes 4 travel
articles per year. Pays in copies.

RETURN TO SENDER

The following magazines have ceased publication or mail has been
returned. Dates in parentheses indicate when I learned of their demise
or when mail was returned.

Airport (England) (11/88)
Association and Society Manager (8/88)
Attenzione (5/88)
Buffalo Spree (6/88)
Charlotte (6/88)
Colorado Outdoors Journal (8/88)
Echelon (9/88)
Go (New Orleans) (1/88)
Grandparenting! (1/88)
Health & Racquet Club Members (7/88)
Images of Hampton Roads (5/88)
Instant Travel Communications (10/88; service is dormant)
International Assignment (5/88)
M/r (5/88)
Maine Life (11/88)
Medical Insights (1/88)
Men's Look (5/88)
New Orleans (9/88)
Oasis (2/88)
Pace (4/88; airline merged with USAir)
Recreation & Camping Texas (9/88)
Sawasdee (5/88)
Travel and Learning Abroad (1/88)
West Michigan (6/88)

3

Newspaper Markets

INFORMATION for these listings was gathered from questionnaires sent out in April and August 1988, with follow-up phone calls in winter 1988-89. Newspapers are listed alphabetically by state and then by city.

ACTIVE MARKETS

UNITED STATES

Alaska

Anchorage Daily News, POB 149001, Anchorage, AK 99514-9001.
Travel editor: Jim Macknicki. Phone: 907-257-4356. Reply date: 9/12/88. FL/year: 25. Prefers articles of 1500 words. Pays $150 with color slides. **Photos:** Uses BW, color. Does not publish press releases.

Arizona

Arizona Daily Star, POB 26807, Tucson, AZ 85726-6807.
Travel editor: Jacquie Villa. Phone: 602-573-4124. Reply date: 4/11/88. FL/year: Approximately 30. Prefers articles of 900-1200 words. Pays $65. **Photos:** Uses color slides. Accepts press releases.

California

Bakersfield Californian, POB 440, Bakersfield, CA 93302.
Travel editor: Pete Tittl. Phone: 805-395-7370. Reply date: 11/6/88. As of November 1988, paper was planning to increase frequency of its travel section from monthly to weekly. Pays $50-$100. **Photos:** Color slides are an asset. Ten percent of readers read the *Los*

Angeles Times, so SS to the *Times* are not acceptable. SS to *Fresno Bee* acceptable. Also has a "Travel Bookshelf" section and a "Travel Tips" section that covers bargains and discounts.

Los Angeles Herald-Examiner, 1111 South Broadway, Los Angeles, CA 90015.
Travel editor: Jim Burns. Phone: 213-744-8473. Reply date: 4/6/88. FL/year: Over 100. Prefers articles of 1200 words. Pays $150 for lead, $75 for inside. **Photos:** Uses BW inside, four-color on cover. Uses press releases when rewritten and verified.

Los Angeles Times, Times Mirror Square, Los Angeles, CA 90053.
Travel editor: Jerry Hulse. Phone: 213-972-7000. Reply date: 8/23/88. FL/year: Many. Prefers articles of 1500 words. Pays at least $150. **Photos:** Uses BW, color on cover. Doesn't publish press releases verbatim but sometimes condenses them.

Riverside Press-Enterprise, 3512 14th Street, Riverside, CA 92501.
Sunday editor: Bob Hirt. Phone: 714-684-1200. Reply date: 4/1/88. FL/year: 36-40. Prefers articles of 1000-1500 words. Pays $35-$50. **Photos:** Pays $10/BW, $35-$50/color. Accepts press releases.

San Francisco Examiner, POB 7260, San Francisco, CA 94120.
Travel editor: Donald W. George. Phone: 415-777-7931. Reply date: 5/24/88. FL/year: Over 100. Prefers articles of 1500 words plus or minus. Pays at least $100. **Photos:** Uses BW. Uses press releases.

San Jose Mercury News, 750 Ridder Park Drive, San Jose, CA 95190.
Assistant special sections editor: Carolyn Snyder. Phone: 408-920-5441. Reply date: 4/11/88. FL/year: Varies. Prefers articles of 25-35 column inches. Pay depends on use of article. **Photos:** Uses BW, color. Does not accept press releases.

Marin Independent Journal, POB 330, San Rafael, CA 94915.
Travel editor: Ron Franscell. Phone: 415-883-8600. Reply date: 4/6/88. Articles must be approved in advance by editor. Prefers articles of 1000-1200 words. Pays $40. **Photos:** Uses BW, color. Pays $25/photo. Accepts press releases. Articles should appeal to California travelers, preferably those in the San Francisco Bay Area.

Santa Barbara News-Press, POB NN, De La Guerra Plaza, Santa Barbara, CA 93102.
Assistant features editor: Linda Bowen. Phone: 805-966-3911. Re-

ply date: 4/7/88. FL/year: Over 50. Prefers articles of 25-30 column inches. Pays $25. **Photos:** Uses BW, color. Pays $10/photo. Accepts press releases for information only.

Colorado

Denver Post, 650 15th Street, Denver, CO 80202.
Travel editor: Mary Ellen Botter. Phone: 303-820-1599. Reply date: 10/27/88. FL/year: Approximately 100. Prefers articles of 30-40 column inches. Pays $100. **Photos:** Uses color. Pays $25/photo taken by author. Considers press releases for "Travel Notes" column.

Connecticut

Waterbury Republican, POB 2090, Waterbury, CT 06722-2090.
Copy editor, travel: Mark Azzara. Phone: 203-574-3636. Reply date: 5/18/88. FL/year: 52. Prefers articles of at least 5 pages, double spaced. Pays $250 on average for article and artwork. **Photos:** Uses color slides and prints. Artwork *must* accompany story. Looks at press releases and summarizes interesting ones monthly.

District of Columbia

Washington Post, 1150 15th Street, N.W., Washington, DC 20071.
Travel editor: Linda Halsey. Phone: 202-334-7591. Reply date: 4/4/88. FL/year: Varies. Prefers articles of 1500-2000 words, plus sidebar for pertinent practical information. Pays $250-$400. **Photos:** Uses BW. Address press releases to "The Fearless Traveler." Buys first North American publication rights with no multiple submissions. Tries to reply within 3 weeks. Likes articles with a strong sense of place, color, anecdote, and history.

Florida

Fort Lauderdale News/Sun Sentinel, 101 North New River Drive, Fort Lauderdale, FL 33301.
Travel editor: Jean Allen. Phone: 305-761-4000. Reply date: 4/22/88. FL/year: Approximately 100. Prefers articles of about 1500 words, plus sidebar. Pays $150-$200. **Photos:** Uses BW, color. Uses rewritten press releases.

Sunshine Magazine, Fort Lauderdale News/Sun-Sentinel, 101 North New River Drive, Fort Lauderdale, FL 33301.
Editor: John Parkyn. Phone: 305-761-4000. Reply date: 4/18/88. Mainly interested in stories on destinations within the general orbit

of South Florida: other parts of Florida, the Bahamas, the Caribbean, and occasionally Central or South America.

Gainesville Sun, PO Drawer A, Gainesville, FL 32602.
Travel editor: Diane C. Chun. Phone: 904-378-1411. Reply date: 6/23/88. FL/year: Approximately 30. Prefers articles of 1000 words or less. Pays up to $50 for article and photos. **Photos:** Uses BW, color. Rewrites most press releases to conform to *Sun* style if used. Prefers no first-person articles, unless that's the best way to tell the story. If no photos are submitted, give addresses of potential photo sources, such as tourism bureaus.

Miami Herald, One Herald Plaza, Miami, FL 33101.
Travel editor: Jay Clarke. Phone: 305-376-3655. Reply date: 4/18/88. FL/year: 100-125. Article length varies. Pays at least $75. **Photos:** Uses BW, color. Does not accept press releases.

Orlando Sentinel, POB 2833, Orlando, FL 32802.
Travel editor: Mike Etzkin. Phone: 407-420-5486. Reply date: 4/18/88. FL/year: Approximately 100. Prefers articles of about 1000 words. Pays $100-$125, more if art is included. **Photos:** Uses some BW, color. Accepts press releases.

St. Petersburg Times, POB 1121, St. Petersburg, FL 33731-1121.
Travel editor: Robert N. Jenkins. Phone: 813-893-8111. Reply date: 4/7/88. FL/year: "Lots." Prefers articles of 1000-1200 words. Pay varies. **Photos:** Uses BW, color. "Hate" press releases.

AR	all rights	OTR	one-time rights
ASMP	American Society of	POA	pays on acceptance
	Magazine	POB	post office box
	Photographers	POP	pays on publication
BW	black-and-white photos	PPS	previously published
CM	complete manuscript		submissions
ES	electronic submissions	PQ	phone queries
FL	freelance	SAE	self-addressed envelope
FL/year	number of freelance travel	SASE	self-addressed stamped envelope
	articles published per	SC	sample copy
	year	SQ	simultaneous queries
F(NAS)R	first (North American serial)	SR	second rights
	rights	SS	simultaneous submissions
ms(s)	manuscript(s)	WG	writer's guidelines
NA	North American		

Sarasota Herald-Tribune, POB 1719, Sarasota, FL 34230.
Travel editor: Joan Cullers. Phone: 813-957-5211. Reply date: 10/24/88. FL/year: 52. Prefers articles of 1500 words and over. Pays $50 for article and color illustration. **Photos:** Uses color slides. "Glad to see" press releases but "rarely use any."

Illinois

Chicago Tribune, 435 North Michigan Avenue, Chicago, IL 60611.
Executive travel editor: Larry Townsend. Phone: 312-222-3232. Reply date: 10/28/88. FL/year: Over 500. Prefers articles of 900-1200 words. Pays $100-$350 depending on where played. **Photos:** Uses BW, color. Never uses press releases. Writers must be using word processor.

Peoria Journal Star, One News Plaza, Peoria, IL 61643.
Travel editor: Fred Filip. Phone: 309-686-3000. Reply date: 8/27/88. FL/year: 15-20. Prefers articles of 20 column inches. Pays about $30. **Photos:** Uses BW. Publishes rewritten press releases.

Indiana

South Bend Tribune, 225 West Colfax Avenue, South Bend, IN 46626.
Travel editor: Frederick Karst. Phone: 219-233-6161. Reply date: 4/11/88. FL/year: Approximately 50. Prefers articles of 800-1200 words. Pays $25-$75. **Photos:** Uses BW. Happy to receive press releases but rarely uses them as feature stories.

Kentucky

Louisville Courier Journal, 525 West Broadway, Louisville, KY 40202.
Travel editor: Elmer Hall. Phone: 502-582-7151. Reply date: 5/9/88. FL/year: Approximately 30. Prefers articles of 1000-1500 words. Pays $60-$75. **Photos:** Uses BW. Does not accept press releases for publication.

Louisiana

Baton Rouge Advocate, 525 Lafayette, Baton Rouge, LA 70802.
Travel editor: Cynthia Campbell. Phone: 504-383-1111. Reply date: 10/28/88. FL/year: 24-30. Prefers articles of 800-1200 words. Pays $75 on average. **Photos:** Uses BW 8-by-10. Rewrites press releases or pulls information from them; does not use releases verbatim.

Maine

Maine Sunday Telegram, POB 1460, Portland, ME 04104.
Travel editor: Betsy Gattis. Phone: 207-775-5811. Reply date: 4/3/88. FL/year: 35-40. Prefers articles of 1000-1200 words. Pays $35-$50. **Photos:** Uses BW. Accepts press releases.

Maine Say, 25 Silver Street, Waterville, ME 04941.
Travel editor: Kimberlee Barnett. Phone: 207-873-3341. Reply date: 4/4/88. FL/year: "No limit." Prefers articles of 3-4 double-spaced pages. Pays at least $20. **Photos:** Uses BW. Accepts press releases.

Maryland

Baltimore Sun, POB 1377, Baltimore, MD 21278-0001.
Travel editor: Tim Warren. Phone: 301-332-6156. Reply date: 11/28/88. FL/year: 12-24. Prefers articles of 1200-1600 words. Pays $125-$175. **Photos:** Uses 35mm color. Pays $25/photo.

Massachusetts

Boston Globe, 135 Morrissey Boulevard, Boston, MA 02107.
Travel editor: Bill Davis. Phone: 617-929-2944. Reply date: 4/5/88. FL/year: 250-300. Prefers articles of 1000-1500 words. Pays $150 for articles, extra for photos. **Photos:** Prefers BW prints. Accepts press releases.

Boston Herald, One Herald Square, Boston, MA 02106.
Travel editor: Stephen Morgan. Phone: 617-426-3000. Reply date: 4/7/88. FL/year: Approximately 150. Prefers articles of 1200 words. Pays $75-$100. **Photos:** Uses BW. Doesn't run press releases as stories.

Christian Science Monitor, One Norway Street, Boston, MA 02115.
Feature editor: David Holmstrom. Phone: 617-450-2000. Reply date: 4/11/88. FL/year: 35. Prefers articles of 850-1250 words. Pays $125-$150. **Photos:** Prefers BW, can convert slides if photos are clear. Uses press releases for tips and information.

Valley Advocate, 87 School Street, Hatfield, MA 01038.
Travel editor: Kitty Axelson. Reply date: 4/14/88. FL/year: Approximately 25. Prefers articles of 700-2400 words. Pays $15-$25. **Photos:** Uses BW. Rarely accepts press releases. Readers are well

educated, liberal, ages 20-50, generally interested in health and fitness, culture, and increasing understanding.

Springfield Union-News, 1860 Main Street, Springfield, MA 01103.
Travel editor: Romola Rigali. Phone: 413-788-1294. Reply date: 10/24/88. FL/year: 20-25. Article length varies. Pay varies. **Photos:** Uses BW, color. Publishes few press releases.

Worcester Telegram, 20 Franklin Street, Worcester, MA 01613.
Travel editor: Diana Scott. Phone: 508-793-9434. Reply date: 11/28/88. FL/year: 150-200. Prefers articles of 25-35 column inches. Pays $40. **Photos:** Uses BW, color.

Michigan

Detroit News, 615 Lafayette Boulevard, Detroit, MI 48231.
Travel editor: Susan Pollack. Phone: 313-222-2300. Reply date: 8/23/88. FL/year: Approximately 50. Prefers articles of 750-1250 words. Pay varies. **Photos:** Uses some BW, mainly color. Doesn't publish press releases.

Grand Rapids Press, 155 Michigan Street, N.W., Grand Rapids, MI 49503.
Travel editor: Jane Haradine. Phone: 616-459-1587. Reply date: 4/7/88. FL/year: 75-100. Prefers articles of 30 column inches, or 4-5 double-spaced pages. Pays $40-$75 for article. **Photos:** Uses BW, color. Pays $25 for first two photos, $20 for next two, and so forth. Uses press releases for background or "Travel Notes." Prefers receiving story and art at same time.

Minnesota

Minneapolis Star Tribune, 425 Portland Avenue, Minneapolis, MN 55488.
Travel editor: Catherine Watson. Phone: 612-372-4282. Reply date: 4/14/88. FL/year: 40. Prefers articles of 6-8 double-spaced pages, including an "If You Go" sidebar. Pays $100 for article and sidebar. **Photos:** Uses 2-3 BW with each article. Does not accept press releases. Query first, preferably by phone. Uses stories on Midwest destinations only.

St. Paul Pioneer Press, 345 Cedar Street, St. Paul, MN 55101.
Travel editor: Richard Leiby. Phone: 612-222-5011. Reply date: 4/12/88. FL/year: 20-30. Prefers articles of 1250-1750 words. Pays

up to $200. **Photos:** Uses BW; prefers color prints, slides OK. Does not accept press releases.

New Jersey

The Record, 150 River Street, Hackensack, NJ 07601.
Travel editor: Judi Dash. Phone: 201-646-4181. Reply date: 8/20/88. FL/year: "No limit." Prefers articles of 1000-1500 words. Pays $100. **Photos:** Uses BW, color slides, color photos. Pays $25/photo. Doesn't publish press releases. Stories should have practical information in sidebar: how to get there, the cost, and who to call for more information.

Sunday Press, Devins Lane, Pleasantville, NJ 08232.
Travel editor: Paul Merkoski. Phone: 609-645-1234. Reply date: 4/12/88. FL/year: Approximately 30. Pays $25 for articles, $35 for articles with photos. **Photos:** Uses BW, color (which will run BW), no slides. Accepts press releases. "A good picture often sells a story because it encourages creative page design."

Trenton Times, 500 Perry Street, Trenton, NJ 08618.
Travel editor: Susan Sprague. Phone: 609-396-3232. Reply date: 4/4/88. FL/year: "No set amount." Prefers articles of 24-45 column inches. Pays $50-$100. **Photos:** Uses BW, color. Canned photos from tourism boards are fine. Accepts press releases. Tries to run a color feature every week.

New York

Buffalo News, One News Plaza, Buffalo, NY 14240.
Assistant features editor: Joseph Roland. Phone: 716-849-4505. Reply date: 4/14/88. FL/year: 100-150. Uses articles of any length. Pay varies. **Photos:** Uses BW, color. Accepts press releases.

Newsday, 235 Pinelawn Road, Melville, NY 11747.
Travel editor: Steve Schatt. Phone: 516-454-2980. Reply date: 11/27/88. FL/year: 175. Prefers articles of 600-1400 words. Pays $100-$300. **Photos:** Uses BW, color.

Middletown Times Herald, 40 Mulberry Street, Middletown, NY 10940.
Travel editor: Moe Mitterling. Phone: 914-343-2181. Reply date: 4/5/88. FL/year: 25-30. Prefers articles of 800-1000 words. Pays $50. **Photos:** Uses BW. Doesn't accept press releases.

New York Daily News, 220 East 42nd Street, New York, NY 10017. Travel editor: Harry Ryan. Phone: 212-210-1699. Reply date: 4/21/88. FL/year: 60-75. Prefers articles of 900-1000 words plus small sidebar with facts. Pays $125-$150. **Photos:** Uses BW. Pays $25/photo. Accepts press releases.

New York Post, 210 South Street, New York, NY 10002. Travel editor: Paul Jackson. Phone: 212-815-8633. Reply date: 4/21/88. FL/year: Approximately 100. Prefers articles of 350-500 words. Pays $125-$200. **Photos:** Uses BW. Accepts press releases.

Ohio

Akron Beacon Journal, 44 East Exchange Street, Akron, OH 44328. Assistant features editor/travel: John Olesky. Phone: 216-375-8160. Reply date: 4/8/88. Prefers articles of 800-1000 words. Pays $100 for originals, $50 for reprints. **Photos:** Uses BW. Shots of recognizable landmarks. Uses press releases as possible tips. Emphasizes United States, Canada, Mexico, and Caribbean.

Cleveland Plain Dealer, 1801 Superior Avenue, Cleveland, OH 44114. Travel editor: David Molyneaux. Phone: 216-344-4560. Reply date: 4/14/88. FL/year: 100. Prefers articles of 1000-1200 words. Pays at least $75. **Photos:** Uses BW. Doesn't accept press releases. Prefers professional writers.

Columbus Dispatch, 34 South Third Street, Columbus, OH 43215. Travel editor: Lisa Reuter-May. Phone: 614-461-5000. Reply date: 4/29/88. FL/year: Approximately 24. Query first. Prefers articles of 1000-1500 words. Pays $40-$100. **Photos:** Uses BW. Accepts press releases. Prefers phone queries. Do not send stories and art you want returned unless both have been requested by travel editor.

Dayton Daily News, 37 South Ludlow Street, Dayton, OH 45402. Travel editor: Scott Bateman. Phone: 513-225-2088. Reply date: 4/18/88. FL/year: NA. Prefers articles of 500-1000 words. Pays $75-$100. **Photos:** Uses BW. Doesn't accept press releases.

Oregon

Sunday Oregonian, 1320 S.W. Broadway, Portland, OR 97201. Editor, Northwest: Jack Hart. Phone: 503-221-8327. Reply date: 4/3/88. FL/year: 20-30. Prefers articles of 1200-1500 words. Pays $200-$400. **Photos:** Uses mainly slides. Doesn't accept press releases. Only Northwest travel destinations.

Pennsylvania

Philadelphia Inquirer, 400 North Broad Street, Philadelphia, PA 19101.
Travel editor: Mike Shoup. Phone: 215-854-2000. Reply date: 4/14/88. FL/year: 50-100. Prefers articles of 800-1200 words for inside, 1200-2500 words for cover. Pays up to $150 for inside articles, up to $200 for cover articles. **Photos:** Uses BW. Doesn't accept press releases. No articles based on subsidized trips.

Tennessee

Knoxville News Sentinel, POB 59038, Knoxville, TN 37950-9038.
Travel editor: Christine Anderson. Phone: 615-523-3131. Reply date: 4/29/88. FL/year: "No set number." Prefers articles of 20 column inches. **Photos:** Uses BW. Accepts press releases.

Texas

Dallas Morning News, Communications Center, Dallas, TX 75265.
Travel editor: Karen Jordan. Phone: 214-977-8222 (no PQ). Reply date: 10/25/88. FL/year: 100. Prefers articles of under 1200 words. Pay varies. **Photos:** Uses BW, color slides, color prints with negatives. Looks at all press releases. Gleans information and background from some for follow-up stories and notes columns; others are filed for background and reference later. Prefers to see finished story and art.

Dallas Times Herald, 1101 Pacific, Dallas, TX 75202.
Travel editor: Robin Fowler. Phone: 214-720-6104. Reply date: 11/4/88. FL/year: 50. Prefers articles of 1000-1500 words. Pays $100-$250. **Photos:** Uses BW, color. Doesn't publish press releases. Queries only. Most freelance work is assigned.

Houston Post, POB 4747, Houston, TX 77210.
Travel editor: Middy Randerson. Phone: 713-840-6702. Reply date: 8/17/88. FL/year: 25. Prefers articles of 1200-1800 words. Pays $100. **Photos:** Uses color slides. Doesn't publish press releases.

San Antonio Express-News, POB 2171, San Antonio, TX 78297-2171.
Travel editor: Julie Cooper. Phone: 512-225-7411. Reply date: 4/11/88. FL/year: "Lots." Prefers articles of 800-1500 words. Pays $50. **Photos:** Uses BW, color slides. Pays $15/BW, $30/color. Accepts press releases.

Utah

Ogden Standard-Examiner, 455 23rd Street, Ogden, UT 84401.
Midweek editor: Marilyn Bennett. Phone: 801-394-7711. Reply
date: 4/5/88. FL/year: "Variable." Prefers articles of 15-25 column
inches. Pays $35. **Photos:** Uses color slides. Accepts press releases.

Salt Lake City Tribune, 143 South Main Street, Salt Lake City, UT
84110.
Travel editor: Thomas McCarthy. Phone: 801-237-2078. Reply date:
9/28/88. FL/year: 75. Prefers articles of 1000 words. Pays $30-
$100. **Photos:** Uses BW, color. Sometimes publishes press releases.

Virginia

Richmond Times-Dispatch, 333 East Grace Street, Richmond, VA
23219.
Travel editor: Jack Norton. Phone: 804-649-6405. Reply date: 4/
19/88. FL/year: 50-150. Prefers articles of 500-1200 words. Pays
$75-$150 for article and photos. **Photos:** Uses color. Doesn't accept
press releases.

Fairfax Journal, 6885 Commercial Drive, Springfield, VA 22151.
Tempo editor: Robert Menacker. Phone: 703-750-8069. Reply date:
8/17/88. FL/year: 25. Prefers articles of 1000 words. Pays $50.
Photos: Uses color. Doesn't publish press releases.

Washington

Seattle Times, Box 70, Seattle, WA 98111.
Travel editor: John Macdonald. Phone: 206-464-2244. Reply date:
10/28/88. FL/year: 20-30. Prefers articles of 800-1000 words. Pays
$100-$500. **Photos:** Uses BW, color. Press releases OK. Doesn't
use articles based on free or reduced-rate travel.

Tacoma News Tribune, Box 11000, Tacoma, WA 98411.
Travel editor: Bill Smull. Phone: 206-597-6022. Reply date: 10/
24/88. FL/year: 30-50. Prefers articles of 600-800 words. Pays $50
for cover stories, $35 for inside stories. **Photos:** Uses BW, color.
Pays $15/BW, $35/color. Seldom uses press releases.

Wisconsin

Appleton Post-Crescent, 306 West Washington, Appleton, WI 54911.
Travel editor: Myrna Collins. Phone: 414-733-4411. Reply date:

4/8/88. FL/year: Approximately 30. Prefers articles of up to 1000 words. Pays $20. **Photos:** Uses BW, color. Pays $10/BW, $30/color. Accepts press releases. No blatantly commercial stories. Prefer no first-person writing.

Milwaukee Journal, POB 661, Milwaukee, WI 53201.
Travel editor: Eleanor Coleman. Phone: 414-224-2342. Reply date: 11/28/88. FL/year: Varies. Prefers articles of 1000-1200 words. Pays $50-$175. **Photos:** Uses BW, color. Pays $15-$25/BW, $50/color.

Milwaukee Sentinel, Box 371, Milwaukee, WI 53201.
Travel editor: Rick Rommell. Phone: 414-224-2186. Reply date: 4/12/88. FL/year: 20-30. Prefers articles of 1200 words. Pays $75. **Photos:** Uses BW. Pays $10/photo. Occasionally uses press releases in tips column.

CANADA

Pay is expressed in Canadian dollars unless otherwise noted. When submitting work to Canadian papers, use metric measurements and Canadian spellings, and give prices in Canadian dollars.

British Columbia

Vancouver Sun, 2250 Granville Street, Vancouver, British Columbia, Canada V6H 3G2.
Travel editor: Bart Jackson. Reply date: 10/24/88. FL/year: Over 100. Prefers articles of 400-1200 words. Pays $75-$135. **Photos:** Uses BW, color slides. Doesn't publish press releases.

Nova Scotia

Halifax Herald Ltd., 1650 Argyle Street, POB 610, Halifax, Nova Scotia, Canada B3J 2T2.
Travel editor: Dennis Wood. Phone: 902-426-2811. Reply date: 5/15/88. FL/year: "No limit." Prefers articles of 800-1000 words. Pays $35. **Photos:** Uses BW, color. Pays $10/photo. Accepts press releases.

Ontario

Hamilton Spectator, 44 Frid Street, Hamilton, Ontario, Canada L8N 3G3.
Book/travel editor: Kate Taylor. Phone: 416-526-3450. Reply date:

5/19/88. FL/year: Approximately 100. Prefers articles of 750-1250 words. Pays $75-$125. **Photos:** Uses color slides.

Kitchener-Waterloo Record, 225 Fairway Road, Kitchener, Ontario, Canada N2G 4E5.
Travel editor: Jon Fear. Phone: 519-894-2231. Reply date: 11/6/88. FL/year: Approximately 50. Prefers articles of 1500 words. Pays up to $150 for articles and photos. **Photos:** Uses color. Doesn't publish press releases.

London Free Press, POB 2280, London, Ontario, Canada N6A 4G1.
Travel editor: David Scott. Phone: 519-679-0230. Reply date: 6/4/88. FL/year: Up to 60. Prefers articles of 800 words. Pays $75. **Photos:** Uses BW, color. Requires slides or negatives, which will be returned.

Ottawa Citizen, 1101 Baxter Road, Ottawa, Ontario, Canada K2C 3M4.
Travel editor: Ken Gray. Phone: 613-829-9100. Reply date: 1/9/89. FL/year: 30-35. Pays $75-$200. **Photos:** Uses color. Accepts press releases.

Toronto Star, One Yonge Street, Toronto, Ontario, Canada M5E 1E6.
Travel editor: George Bryant. Phone: 416-869-4877. Reply date: 10/24/88. FL/year: Approximately 200. Prefers articles of 1000 words. Pays $140-$160. **Photos:** Uses mostly BW.

Windsor Star, 167 Ferry Street, Windsor, Ontario, Canada N9A 4M5.
Travel editor: Lisa Monforton. Phone: 519-255-5711. Reply date: 11/7/88. FL/year: "Many." Article length depends on subject. Pays $50. **Photos:** Uses BW, color. Pays $15/BW, $25/color. Publishes press releases, usually rewritten.

Quebec

Montreal Gazette, 250 rue St. Antoine West, Montreal, Quebec, Canada H2Y 3R7.
Travel editor: Ashok Chandwani. Phone: 514-282-2222. Reply date: 5/15/88. FL/year: 50-100. Prefers articles of 800-1500 words. Pays at least $150. **Photos:** Uses BW, color. Prefers color negatives but accepts slides. Accepts press releases on merit. Doesn't buy from

freelancers who accept freebies or subsidies. ES: Preferred (diskette or modem).

Montreal La Presse, 7 rue St. Jacques, Montreal, Quebec, Canada H2Y 1K9.
Travel editor: Francois Trepanier. Phone: 514-285-7070. Reply date: 11/8/88. Articles must be written in French. Prefers short articles. Pays $250-$350. **Photos:** Uses BW, color. Rewrites press releases.

MARGINAL MARKETS

These newspapers take 20 or fewer freelance articles per year.

UNITED STATES ━━━━━━━━━━━━━━━━━━━━━━━

Alabama

Birmingham News, POB 2553, Birmingham, AL 35202.
Travel editor: Garland Reeves. Phone: 205-325-2446. Reply date: 4/21/88. FL/year: 10. Prefers articles of 20-30 column inches. Pays $90 for articles with color photos, $100 for same when article is transmitted electronically. **Photos:** Uses BW, color. Accepts press releases. Primarily interested in articles on the Southeast.

Montgomery Advertiser, 200 Washington Avenue, Montgomery, AL 36104.

AR	all rights	OTR	one-time rights
ASMP	American Society of	POA	pays on acceptance
	Magazine	POB	post office box
	Photographers	POP	pays on publication
BW	black-and-white photos	PPS	previously published
CM	complete manuscript		submissions
ES	electronic submissions	PQ	phone queries
FL	freelance	SAE	self-addressed envelope
FL/year	number of freelance travel	SASE	self-addressed stamped envelope
	articles published per	SC	sample copy
	year	SQ	simultaneous queries
F(NAS)R	first (North American serial)	SR	second rights
	rights	SS	simultaneous submissions
ms(s)	manuscript(s)	WG	writer's guidelines
NA	North American		

Weekend editor: David Rountree. Phone: 205-262-1611. Reply date: 8/29/88. FL/year: "A couple." Prefers articles of 12-15 column inches. Pays $25, "more or less." **Photos:** Uses BW. Rewrites press releases if they're of regional interest. Most interested in regional stories with good BW art.

Alaska

Anchorage Times, 820 Fourth Avenue, Anchorage, AK 99501.
Query travel editor. Phone: 907-263-9000. Reply date: 1/9/89. FL/year: 2-4. Prefers articles of 40 column inches or more. Pays $25. **Photos:** Uses BW, color slides. Prefers press releases from tourist bureaus. "We are always looking for well-written travel features with personal, informative touch. We usually use articles written by residents of Alaska who have taken a trip."

Arizona

Arizona Republic, POB 1950, Phoenix, AZ 85001.
Travel editor: Tom Bauer. Phone: 602-271-8977. Reply date: 10/24/88. FL/year: 10-15. Prefers articles of 25-35 column inches, with tips in sidebars. Pays $150-$400. **Photos:** Uses color. Seldom uses press releases but will sometimes rewrite and publish them. Looking for stories that are unusual or something they can't write themselves. No Grand Canyon or Mexico stories.

Phoenix Gazette, POB 1950, Phoenix, AZ 85001.
Tempo editor: Lilah Lohr. Phone: 602-271-8651. Reply date: 3/31/88. Very rarely uses freelancers. Accepts press releases.

California

Contra Costa Times, 2640 Shadelands Drive, Walnut Creek, CA 94598.
Travel editor: John Dengel. Phone: 415-935-2525. Reply date: 4/22/88. FL/year: "Not many." Gets most stories from wire services. Prefers articles of 600-800 words. Pays $50 "tops, page one with color or BW to jump to." **Photos:** Uses BW, color. Deluged with press releases.

Fresno Bee, 1626 E Street, Fresno, CA 93786.
Travel editor: Don Mayhew. Phone: 209-441-6350. Reply date: 4/2/88. FL/year: 12. Prefers articles of up to 1000 words. Pays $100-

$200. **Photos:** Uses BW, color (prefers first-generation slides). Accepts press releases.

Los Angeles Daily News, POB 4200, Woodland Hills, CA 91365. Travel editor: Carol Martinez. Phone: 818-713-3682. Reply date: 4/4/88. FL/year: 10-12. Prefers articles of 1200 words. Pays $50-$125. **Photos:** Uses color slides or prints. Uses press releases as a source of information.

San Diego Tribune, 350 Camino de la Reina, San Diego, CA 92108. Travel editor: Evelyn Kieran. Phone: 619-299-3131. Reply date: 8/22/88. FL/year: "Very few." Prefers articles of 900 words. Pays $100. **Photos:** Uses BW, color. Does not publish press releases.

Stockton Record, POB 900, Stockton, CA 95201.
Features editor: Janet Krietemeyer. Phone: 209-943-6397. Reply date: 10/21/88. FL/year: 10. Prefers articles of 1000-2500 words. Pays $75-$150. **Photos:** Uses BW. Doesn't publish press releases. Interested mostly in Northern California stories.

The Tribune, POB 24424, Oakland, CA 94623-1304.
Travel editor: Bari Brenner. Phone: 415-645-2250. Reply date: 1/9/89. FL/year: Few. Prefers articles of 1200 words. Pays up to $50. **Photos:** Uses mostly BW; illustrates one article per month with color.

Colorado

Colorado Springs Gazette, 30 South Prospect, Colorado Springs, CO 80906.
Travel editor: Linda Duval. Phone: 719-632-5511. Reply date: 4/7/88. FL/year: Few. Prefers articles of "moderate" length. Pays $40. **Photos:** Uses color. Pays $25/photo. Seldom uses press releases.

Connecticut

Hartford Courant, 285 Broad Street, Hartford, CT 06115.
Assistant features editor: Nancy LaRoche. Phone: 203-241-3868. Reply date: 4/7/88. FL/year: 5-6. Prefers articles of 1500 words with "Travel Tips" sidebar. Pays $150. **Photos:** Uses 35mm color. Doesn't accept press releases. Destination stories preferred.

New Haven Register, 40 Sargent Drive, New Haven, CT 06511.
Travel editor: Hayne Bayless. Phone: 203-562-1121. Reply date: 8/20/88. FL/year: "A few." Prefers articles of up to 30 column

inches. Pays $50-$100. **Photos:** Uses some BW, a lot of color. Doesn't publish press releases.

Delaware

Wilmington News-Journal, 831 Orange Street, Wilmington, DE 19899.
Features editor: Larry Nagengast. Phone: 302-573-2192. Reply date: 8/22/88. Occasionally uses freelancers. Prefers articles of 20 column inches. Pays $75. **Photos:** Uses BW, color. Uses press releases as reference material.

District of Columbia

USA Today, Box 500, Washington, DC 20044.
Travel editor: Ron Schoolmeester. Phone: 703-276-3400. Reply date: 8/17/88. FL/year: "Limited." Length and pay negotiable. **Photos:** On assignment only. Doesn't publish press releases.

Florida

Fort Myers News-Press, 2442 Anderson Avenue, Fort Myers, FL 33901. Travel editor: Karen Feldman Smith. Phone: 813-335-0200 (no PQ). Reply date: 4/14/88. FL/year: 15-20. Prefers articles of 1000-1200 words. Pays $50. **Photos:** Uses color. Pays $10/photo. Uses some press releases for travel briefs. Provides "excellent clips."

Georgia

Atlanta Journal Constitution, POB 4689, Atlanta, GA 30302. Travel editor: Colin Bessonette. Phone: 404-526-5479. Reply date: 8/22/88. FL/year: Over 50 in 1988, but will review policy in 1989. Prefers articles of 1200-1500 words. Pay depends on length, placement, quality. **Photos:** Uses BW inside, color on front page. Accepts and rewrites a few press releases as travel tips. Doesn't encourage unsolicited freelance material since stories can be assigned to staff writers.

Illinois

Arlington Heights Herald, POB 280, Arlington Heights, IL 60006. Travel editor: Eileen Brown. Phone: 312-870-3600. Reply date: 8/20/88. FL/year: 3-4. Prefers articles of 30-40 column inches. Pays $75-$125. **Photos:** Uses BW, color. Doesn't publish press releases.

Chicago Sun-Times, 401 North Wabash Avenue, Chicago, IL 60611.
Travel editor: Jack Schnedler. Phone: 312-321-2181. Reply date:
4/14/88. FL/year: Buys very little unsolicited material. "The shorter,
the better" for article length. Pays $100-$150. **Photos:** Uses mostly
BW. Doesn't publish press releases.

Indiana

Evansville Courier, 201 N.W. Second Street, Evansville, IN 47703.
Features editor: Joycelyn Winnecke. Phone: 812-424-7711. Reply
date: 4/18/88. FL/year: Approximately 10. Prefers articles of 25
column inches. Pays $25. **Photos:** Uses BW. Accepts press releases.

Fort Wayne Journal-Gazette, 600 West Main Street, Fort Wayne,
IN 46802.
Travel editor: Harriet Howard Heithaus. Phone: 219-461-8333.
Reply date: 8/22/88. FL/year: 1-2. Prefers articles of 3-4 double-
spaced pages. Pay negotiable. **Photos:** Uses BW, color. Uses press
releases for background and further contacts.

Maine

Bangor Daily News, 491 Main Street, Bangor, ME 04401.
Travel editor: Joan H. Smith. Phone: 207-942-4881. Reply date:
8/15/88. FL/year: 12-15. Prefers articles of 2 double-spaced pages.
Pays $30. **Photos:** Uses BW. Pays $5. Does not publish press
releases. Don't duplicate articles that might run on the wires. Regional, offbeat, or highly consumer-oriented pieces are more likely
to be used.

Massachusetts

New Bedford Standard Times, 555 Pleasant Street, New Bedford,
MA 02742.
Travel editor: Bradford Hathaway. Phone: 617-997-7411. Reply
date: 10/26/88. FL/year: Few. Query first. **Photos:** Uses BW. Does
not publish press releases.

Michigan

Flint Journal, 200 East First Street, Flint, MI 48502.
Travel editor: Gary H. Piatek. Phone: 313-766-6302. Reply date:
10/28/88. FL/year: 6-10. Pays $60-$100. **Photos:** Uses BW, color.
Rarely uses press releases.

Saginaw News, 203 South Washington Avenue, Saginaw, MI 48605. Feature editor: Kenneth Tabacsko. Phone: 517-776-9705. Reply date: 4/4/88. FL/year: 10-20. Length varies. Pays $40-$60. **Photos:** Uses BW. Accepts press releases.

Missouri

St. Louis Post-Dispatch, 900 North Tucker Boulevard, St. Louis, MO 63101.
Travel editor: Joan Dames. Phone: 314-622-7311. Reply date: 4/5/88. FL/year: "Only a few." Prefers articles of 1500 words. Pays $50 for articles and color photos. **Photos:** Uses color. Uses press releases for background.

Nebraska

Omaha World-Herald, World-Herald Square, Omaha, NE 68102. Sunday Magazine editor: David Hendee. Phone: 402-444-1000. Reply date: 10/23/88. FL/year: 12. Prefers articles of 400-1000 words. Pays $40-$100. **Photos:** Uses BW, color slides and prints. Doesn't publish press releases. Prefers stories that have a link to Nebraska and surrounding states or that would appeal to Midlanders. Plans issues as far as three months in advance. Special travel sections in March and October.

New Jersey

Cherry Hill Courier Post, POB 5300, Cherry Hill, NJ 08034. Travel editor: Stewart Ettinger. Phone 609-486-2439. Reply date: 1/9/89. FL/year: 12. Prefers articles of 15-20 column inches, plus sidebars. Pays $35 for stories, extra for sidebars and original artwork. **Photos:** Uses BW. Accepts press releases for background only.

Morristown Daily Record, POB 217, Morristown, NJ 07054. Phone: 201-428-8900. Reply date: 8/20/88. FL/year: 2-3. Prefers articles of 15-20 column inches. Pays $50-$70. **Photos:** Uses BW, color. Doesn't publish press releases.

New Mexico

Albuquerque Journal, PO Drawer J, Albuquerque, NM 87103. Assistant features editor: Roger Ruvolo. Phone: 505-823-3927. Reply date: 4/8/88. FL/year: Up to 12. Prefers articles of 1200 words. Pays $150 for articles with three good color slides. **Photos:** Uses color. Shots of vistas or with human element.

New York

Rochester Democrat, 55 Exchange Street, Rochester, NY 14614.
Travel editor: Michael Johansson. Phone: 716-232-7100. Reply date:
10/24/88. FL/year: 15-20. Prefers articles of about 20 column inches.
Pays $70-$75. **Photos:** Uses BW. Doesn't publish press releases.

Staten Island Advance, 950 Fingerboard Road, Staten Island, NY
10305.
Travel editor: Robert Raymond. Phone: 718-981-1234. Reply date:
10/24/88. FL/year: Some. Prefers articles of 900 words. Pays $40.
Photos: Uses BW. No press releases.

North Carolina

Charlotte Observer, 600 South Tryon Street, Charlotte, NC 28232.
Travel editor: Sandy Hill. Phone: 704-379-6483. Reply date: 4/14/
88. FL/year: Few. Prefers articles of under 30 inches. Pay depends
on story. **Photos:** Uses BW, color. Uses press releases for information.

Greensboro News & Record, POB 20848, Greensboro, NC 27420.
Travel editor: Allen Johnson. Phone: 919-373-7054. Reply date:
4/9/88. FL/year: Approximately 5. Prefers articles of 20 column
inches. Pays $35-$50. **Photos:** Uses BW. Accepts some press releases.

Winston-Salem Journal, 418 North Marshall Street, Winston-Salem,
NC 27102.
Travel editor: Dick Creed. Phone: 919-727-7302. Reply date: 8/
22/88. FL/year: Very few. Prefers articles of 20-30 column inches.
Pay negotiable. **Photos:** Uses BW. Seldom publishes press releases.

North Dakota

Fargo Forum, 105 Fifth Street North, Fargo, ND 58102.
Travel editor: Syb Gullickson. Phone: 701-235-7311. Reply date:
8/22/88. Accepts stories only from writers in the area. Prefers articles
of 35-40 column inches. Pays $100 for cover stories. **Photos:** Uses
BW. Pays $25/photo. Rewrites press releases as tips for travelers.

Ohio

Youngstown Vindicator, POB 780, Youngstown, OH 44501-0780.
Special projects editor: Tricia McChesney. Phone: 216-747-1471.
Reply date: 9/28/88. FL/year: Few.

Oregon

Salem Statesman-Journal, 280 Church Street, N.E., Salem, OR 97301.
Travel editor: Mark Cook. Phone: 503-399-6767. Reply date: 4/25/88. FL/year: 4. Prefers articles of 700 words. Pays $25-$40. **Photos:** Uses BW. Pays $15/photo. Accepts press releases. No first-person stories.

Pennsylvania

Sunday Patriot News, 812 King Boulevard, Harrisburg, PA 17105.
Travel editor: James Beidler. Phone: 717-255-8100. Reply date: 4/7/88. FL/year: 4-6. Prefers articles of 1000-1500 words. Pays $25. **Photos:** Uses BW. Accepts press releases.

National News Bureau, 2019 Chancellor Street, Philadelphia, PA 19103.
Editor: Harry Jay Katz. Phone: 215-569-0700. Reply date: 4/6/88. FL/year: "15-ish." This is a syndicate. Prefers articles of 750-1000 words. Pay varies. **Photos:** Uses BW. Accepts press releases.

Delaware County Daily Times, 500 Mildred Avenue, Primos, PA 19018.
Travel editor: Trish Cofiell. Phone: 215-622-8819. Reply date: 8/20/88. FL/year: "Several." Pays $40. **Photos:** Uses BW inside, color outside. Publishes press releases.

Puerto Rico

El Nuevo Dia, POB 297, San Juan, PR 00902.
Travel editor: Jose Diaz de Villegas. Phone: 809-721-7070. Reply date: 4/18/88. Occasionally uses freelancers. Prefers articles of over 1200 words. Pays $150. **Photos:** Uses BW, color slides and prints. Uses press releases as background information. Paper is in Spanish.

Texas

Austin American Statesman, 166 East Riverside Drive, Austin, TX 78704.
Travel editor: Alison Smith. Phone: 512-445-3500. Reply date: 10/24/88. FL/year: 12. Prefers articles of 30-40 column inches with sidebar. Pay varies. **Photos:** Uses BW. Uses some press releases on tours originating locally.

El Paso Times, 401 Mills, El Paso, TX 79999.
Newsfeatures editor: Jose Cantu-Weber. Phone: 915-546-6154. Reply date: 10/24/88. Few articles used, and those are usually on the Southwest and Mexico. Prefers articles of 18-25 column inches. Pays $25. **Photos:** Uses BW. Looks at press releases.

Virginia

Newport News Press, 7505 Warwick Boulevard, Newport News, VA 23607.
Travel editor: Ruth Schechter. Phone: 804-247-4600. Reply date: 10/28/88. FL/year: 15-20, mostly locally written. Prefers articles of 25-40 column inches. Pays $45-$100. **Photos:** Uses BW, color. Uses generic interest press releases, not specific announcements.

Richmond News Leader, 333 East Grace Street, Richmond, VA 23219.
Travel editor: Katherine Calos. Phone: 804-649-6435. Reply date: 4/4/88. FL/year: Few. Prefers articles of 1000-1500 words. Pay varies. **Photos:** Uses BW, color. Looks at press releases.

Roanoke Times/World-News, 201 West Campbell Avenue, Roanoke, VA 24010.
Travel editor: Ray Reed. Phone: 703-981-3346. Reply date: 10/24/88. FL/year: 5. Prefers articles of 1200-1500 words. Pays $40. **Photos:** Uses BW. Ignores press releases.

Washington

Everett Herald, Box 930, Everett, WA 98206.
Travel editor: Mike Murray. Phone: 206-339-3439. Reply date: 4/7/88. FL/year: Varies. Prefers articles of 750-800 words. Pays $55. **Photos:** Uses BW, color. Pays $25/photo. Accepts press releases.

Seattle Post-Intelligencer, 101 Elliott Avenue West, Seattle, WA 98119.
Travel editor: John Engstrom. Phone: 206-448-8330. Reply date: 5/9/88. FL/year: 15-20. Prefers articles of 1000 words, plus short sidebars. Pays $75-$125. **Photos:** Uses BW. Pays $25/photo taken by author, $10/stock photo. Accepts press releases. Very consumer and bargain oriented. Lots of useful nuts and bolts: tips, prices, addresses, opinions, beyond-the-guidebook discoveries.

Spokane Spokesman-Review, 999 West Riverside, Spokane, WA 99201.
Travel editor: Kathryn J. DeLong. Phone: 509-459-3481. Reply date: 4/27/88. FL/year: Approximately 12. No extremely long stories. Pays $25-$100. **Photos:** Uses BW, color. Accepts press releases.

Vancouver Columbian, POB 180, Vancouver, WA 98666.
Travel editor: Anne Voegtlin. Phone: 206-694-3391. Reply date: 4/7/88. FL/year: 3-6. Prefers articles of 500-1000 words. Pays $15-$75. **Photos:** Uses BW, color. Pays extra for photos. Uses press releases as story ideas or for background on stories.

Wisconsin

Wisconsin State Journal, 1901 Fish Hatchery Road, Madison, WI 53708.
Travel editor: Genie Campbell. Phone: 608-252-6180. Reply date: 10/28/88. FL/year: 10. Prefers articles of 25 inches. Pays $50-$75. **Photos:** Uses BW. Publishes very few press releases.

CANADA ━━━━━

British Columbia

Vancouver Province, 2250 Granville Street, Vancouver, British Columbia, Canada V6H 3G2.
Travel editor: Joseph Kula. Phone: 604-732-2050. Reply date: 5/15/88. FL/year: 12. Prefers articles of up to 750 words, short sidebars. Pays around $100 for a main feature, more with sidebars and photos. **Photos:** Uses BW, color. Very infrequently uses press releases. Keep stories bright, put yourself in the picture. Show people in photos. Carries stories on California during the late fall, winter, and early spring.

Ontario

Toronto Globe and Mail, 444 Front Street West, Toronto, Ontario, Canada M5V 2S9.
Travel editor: Peter Harris. Reply date: 5/9/88. Mr. Harris had some trenchant comments for freelancers: "We do consider freelance submissions (with BW photos much preferred), but I must emphasize that we are in a constant state of siege by an army of freelancers who write, phone, fax, or telex us with queries, or send us as many as ten different manuscripts in one envelope (now I know how Custer

felt—they just keep coming). In short, we are swamped with free-lance stuff, and the number accepted is a very small percentage of the total number of submissions."

Toronto Sun, 333 King Street East, Toronto, Ontario, Canada M5A 3X5.
Travel editor: Linda Fox. Reply date: 5/15/88. FL/year: "Perhaps 3." Prefers articles of 800 words. Pays US$60. **Photos:** Uses color only. Accepts press releases.

NOT IN THE MARKET

These newspapers do not use freelancers or do not pay. Some may take press releases.

UNITED STATES

Alabama

Birmingham Post-Herald, POB 2553, Birmingham, AL 35202.
Travel editor: Suzanne Dent. Phone: 205-325-2306. Reply date: 4/4/88. Accepts press releases.

Huntsville Times, 2317 Memorial Parkway, S.W., Huntsville, AL 35807.
Travel editor: Vicki Davis. Phone: 205-532-4413. Reply date: 4/4/88. Accepts press releases.

AR	all rights	OTR	one-time rights
ASMP	American Society of Magazine Photographers	POA	pays on acceptance
		POB	post office box
		POP	pays on publication
BW	black-and-white photos	PPS	previously published
CM	complete manuscript		submissions
ES	electronic submissions	PQ	phone queries
FL	freelance	SAE	self-addressed envelope
FL/year	number of freelance travel articles published per year	SASE	self-addressed stamped envelope
		SC	sample copy
		SQ	simultaneous queries
F(NAS)R	first (North American serial) rights	SR	second rights
		SS	simultaneous submissions
ms(s)	manuscript(s)	WG	writer's guidelines
NA	North American		

Mobile Press-Register, 304 Government Street, Mobile, AL 36630.
Sunday editor: Gordon Tatum. Phone: 205-433-1551. Reply date:
4/14/88.

Arkansas

Arkansas Gazette, 112 West Third Street, Little Rock, AR 72203.
Travel editor: Bill Lewis. Phone: 501-371-3728. Reply date: 4/2/
88. Accepts press releases.

California

Modesto Bee, 1325 H Street, Modesto, CA 95352.
Travel editor: Walt Williams. Phone: 209-578-2311. Reply date:
4/6/88.

Monterey Peninsula Herald, POB 271, Monterey, CA 93942.
Travel editor: Dennis Sharp. Phone: 408-646-4366. Reply date: 8/
17/88. Publishes press releases selectively.

Palo Alto Weekly, POB 1610, Palo Alto, CA 94302.
Assistant editor: Carol Blitzer. Phone: 415-326-8210. Reply date:
4/14/88. "Sorry. We no longer solicit or accept freelance travel
pieces."

Peninsula Times Tribune, 245 Lytton Avenue, Palo Alto, CA 94301.
Travel editor: Karen Smith. Phone: 415-853-5208. Reply date: 8/
16/88. Publishes press releases.

Sacramento Bee, POB 15779, Sacramento, CA 95852.
Travel editor: Janet Fullwood. Phone: 916-321-1000. Reply date:
4/2/88. No press releases.

Sacramento Union, 301 Capitol Mall, Sacramento, CA 95812.
Travel editor: Jackie Peterson. Phone: 916-442-7811. Reply date:
4/4/88. Accepts press releases if they are newsworthy.

San Bernardino Sun, 399 D Street, San Bernardino, CA 92401.
Assistant travel editor: John Weeks. Phone: 714-889-9666. Reply
date: 4/1/88. "A short, well-written press release on a general interest subject, accompanied by color slide(s), stands an excellent
chance in our travel section."

Connecticut

Bridgeport Post, 410 State Street, Bridgeport, CT 06604.
Travel editor: Charles Walsh. Phone: 203-333-0161. Reply date:
8/20/88.

District of Columbia

Washington Times, 3600 New York Avenue, N.W., Washington, DC 20002.
Travel editor: Denny Townsend. Phone: 202-636-3000. Reply date: 4/7/88. Accepts press releases.

Florida

Lakeland Ledger, 401 South Missouri Avenue, Lakeland, FL 33802.
Travel editor: Lynne Croft. Phone: 813-687-7000. Reply date: 5/19/88.

Pensacola News-Journal, One News-Journal Plaza, Pensacola, FL 32501.
Features editor: Lloyd Goodman. Phone: 904-435-8550. Reply date: 4/8/88. Accepts press releases.

Tampa Tribune, 202 South Parker Street, Tampa, FL 33606; POB 191, Tampa, FL 33601.
Travel editor: Dorothy Smiljanich. Phone: 813-272-7650. Reply date: 8/29/88.

Georgia

Augusta Chronicle, 725 Broad Street, Augusta, GA 30913.
Travel editor: Kim Hays. Phone: 404-724-0851. Reply date: 8/17/88.

Macon Telegraph and News, POB 4167, Macon, GA 31213.
Travel editor: Tethel Brown. Phone: 912-744-4345. Reply date: 4/7/88. Accepts press releases.

Hawaii

Honolulu Advertiser, 605 Kapiolani Boulevard, Honolulu, HI 96813.
Travel editor: Ronn Ronck. Phone: 808-525-8034. Reply date: 4/5/88. No press releases.

Honolulu Star-Bulletin, 605 Kapiolani Boulevard, Honolulu, HI 96813.
Phone: 808-525-8660. Reply date: 10/8/88. Paper has no travel section.

Illinois

Rockford Register Star, 99 East State Street, Rockford, IL 61104.
Travel editor: Co Leber. Phone: 815-987-1200. Reply date: 4/7/88. Accepts press releases.

Indiana

Hammond Times, 417 Fayette Street, Hammond, IN 46320.
News editor: Rick Barter. Phone: 219-933-3228. Reply date: 10/24/88.

Indianapolis Star, 307 North Pennsylvania Street, Indianapolis, IN 46204.
Travel editor: Cecil Richmond. Phone: 317-633-9396. Reply date: 9/8/88.

Iowa

Quad City Times, 124 East Second Street, Davenport, IA 52801.
Travel editor: Shirley Davis. Phone: 319-383-2200. Reply date: 4/4/88. Accepts press releases on specific areas and events usually closer than 100 miles to Davenport.

Waterloo Courier, 501 Commercial Street, Waterloo, IA 50704.
Travel editor: Carolyn Cole. Phone: 319-291-1400. Reply date: 8/22/88. Publishes press releases.

Kansas

Topeka Capital-Journal, 616 Jefferson, Topeka, KS 66607.
Travel editor: R. J. Peterson. Phone: 913-295-1286. Reply date: 4/7/88. Uses BW photos with press releases. Open to suggestions for places staff writers can travel to cover.

Kentucky

Lexington Herald-Leader, Main and Midland, Lexington, KY 40507.
Arts/entertainment editor: Jim Durham. Phone: 606-231-3261. Reply date: 8/22/88. No press releases.

Massachusetts

Lowell Sun, 15 Kearney Square, Lowell, MA 01853.
Travel editor: Suzanne Dion. Phone: 617-458-7100. Reply date: 4/4/88.

Michigan

Ann Arbor News, 340 East Huron Street, Ann Arbor, MI 48106.
Travel editor: Andy Chappelle. Phone: 313-994-6989. Reply date: 4/1/88. Accepts press releases.

Detroit Free Press, 321 West Lafayette Boulevard, Detroit, MI 48231.
Travel editor: Rick Sylvain. Phone: 313-222-6521. Reply date: 8/
17/88.

Kalamazoo Gazette, 401 South Burdick Street, Kalamazoo, MI 49007.
Travel editor: Larry Pratt. Phone: 616-345-3511. Reply date: 4/4/
88. Accepts press releases.

Lansing State Journal, 102 East Lenawee, Lansing, MI 48919.
Travel editor: Jack Bolt. Phone: 517-377-1073. Reply date: 4/11/
88. FL/year: 1-2. Prefers articles of 12-15 column inches. No pay.
Photos: Uses BW. Accepts press releases.

Macomb Daily, 67 Cass Avenue, Mount Clemens, MI 48046.
Features editor: Ken Kish. Phone: 313-469-4510. Reply date: 4/
7/88. Accepts press releases.

Oakland Press, 48 West Huron, Pontiac, MI 48056.
Features editor: Holly Gilbert. Phone: 313-332-8181. Reply date:
4/4/88. Accepts press releases.

Nebraska

Lincoln Journal-Star, POB 81689, Lincoln, NE 68501.
Travel editor: Margaret Ehlers. Phone: 402-473-7219. Reply date:
4/7/88. Policy under review.

Nevada

Las Vegas Review Journal, POB 70, Las Vegas, NV 89125.
Travel editor: Cathy Tobin. Phone: 702-383-0292. Reply date: 8/
22/88. Publishes press releases if useful to readers.

Las Vegas Sun, 121 South Highland, Las Vegas, NV 89127.
Travel editor: Jim Barrows. Phone: 702-385-3111. Reply date: 4/
11/88. Rarely uses freelancers. Prefers articles of 1200 words. No
pay. **Photos:** Uses BW. Uses press releases.

Reno Gazette-Journal, 955 Kuenzli Street, Reno, NV 89520.
Travel editor: Allan U. Risdon. Phone: 702-788-6314. Reply date:
4/5/88.

New Jersey

Bridgewater Courier News, 1201 Route 22, Bridgewater, NJ 08807.
Features editor: Connie Ballard. Phone: 201-722-8800. Reply date:
8/23/88. No press releases.

Jersey Journal, 30 Journal Square, Jersey City, NJ 07306.
Features editor: Margaret Schmidt. Phone: 201-653-1000. Reply
date: 8/20/88. Doesn't publish press releases but often uses them
as jumping-off points, particularly for food articles.

Newark Star-Ledger, Star-Ledger Plaza, Newark, NJ 07101.
Travel editor: Joel Sleed. Phone: 201-877-4040. Reply date: 4/7/
88. Accepts press releases.

Passaic Herald News, 988 Main Street, Passaic, NJ 07055.
Travel editor: Rosalie Longo. Phone: 201-365-3133. Reply date:
4/8/88.

New York

Press and Sun-Bulletin, POB 1270, Binghamton, NY 13902.
Travel editor: Barb Van Atta. Phone: 607-798-1171. Reply date:
4/4/88. Accepts freelance travel articles but doesn't pay. Accepts
press releases. "Desperate for art, maps, items for briefs about the
Northeast."

New York Times, 229 West 43rd Street, New York, NY 10036.
Travel editor: Nora Kerr. Reply date: 11/28/88. Not interested in
submissions from freelance travel writers.

Schenectady Gazette, 332 State Street, Schenectady, NY 12301.
Travel editor: Gail Shufelt. Phone: 518-374-4141. Reply date: 11/
4/88.

Syracuse Herald American, Box 4915, Clinton Square, Syracuse,
NY 13221.
Travel editor: Nivart Apikian. Phone: 315-470-2236. Reply date:
4/4/88.

White Plains Reporter, One Gannett Avenue, White Plains, NY
10604.
Travel editor: Carol Capobianco. Phone: 914-694-9300. Reply date:
4/5/88. Accepts press releases.

North Carolina

Asheville Citizen, 14 O. Henry Avenue, Asheville, NC 28802.
Sunday editor: Russ Williams. Phone: 704-252-5611. Reply date:
10/24/88.

Ohio

Cincinnati Enquirer, 617 Vine Street, Cincinnati, OH 45202.
Travel editor: Sara Pearce. Reply date: 4/4/88. Accepts press releases.

Toledo Blade, 541 Superior Street, Toledo, OH 43660.
Travel editor: Fred Nofziger. Phone: 419-245-6123. Reply date: 4/
12/88. Accepts press releases.

Oklahoma

Oklahoman, POB 25125, Oklahoma City, OK 73125.
Travel editor: Gail Driskill. Phone: 405-232-3311. Reply date: 4/
7/88.

Tulsa Tribune, POB 1770, Tulsa, OK 74102.
Travel editor: Jenk Jones, Jr. Phone: 918-581-8400. Reply date:
4/1/88.

Oregon

Eugene Register-Guard, 975 High Street, Eugene, OR 97440.
Travel editor: Dean Rea. Phone: 503-485-1234. Reply date: 4/5/
88.

Pennsylvania

The Morning Call, Box 1260, Allentown, PA 18105.
Travel writer: Randy Kraft. Phone: 215-820-6557. Reply date: 4/
11/88. Accepts press releases.

Scranton Times, Box 3311, Scranton, PA 18505.
Travel editor: Ed Rogers. Phone: 717-348-9120. Reply date: 4/5/
88. Accepts press releases.

South Carolina

Charleston News-Courier, 134 Columbus Street, Charleston, SC 29402.
Travel editor: Elizabeth Moye. Phone: 803-577-7111. Reply date:
8/22/88. Accepts press releases.

Tennessee

Nashville Banner, 1100 Broadway, Nashville, TN 37203.
Lifestyles editor: Pat Embry. Phone: 615-529-8286. Reply date: 4/
14/88.

Nashville Tennessean, 1100 Broadway, Nashville, TN 37202.
Travel editor: Gene Wyatt. Phone: 615-259-8058. Reply date: 9/1/88.

Texas

Corpus Christi Caller-Times, 820 Lower North Broadway, Corpus Christi, TX 78469.
Travel editor: Gretchen Ray. Phone: 512-884-2011. Reply date: 4/7/88. May start taking freelance in 1989.

Fort Worth Star Telegram, 400 West Seventh Street, Fort Worth, TX 76102.
Travel editor: Jerry Flemmons. Phone: 817-390-7669. Reply date: 4/3/88.

Lubbock Avalanche Journal, POB 491, Lubbock, TX 79408.
Travel editor: Ted Simon. Phone: 806-762-8844. Reply date: 4/7/88.

San Antonio Light, POB 161, San Antonio, TX 78291.
Travel editor: Joel Solis. Phone: 512-271-2767. Reply date: 11/12/88. Publishes some press releases.

Waco Tribune-Herald, 900 Franklin, Waco, TX 76701.
Lifestyle editor: Teresa Johnson. Phone: 817-757-5720. Reply date: 4/5/88. Accepts press releases.

Vermont

Burlington Free Press, 191 College Street, Burlington, VT 05402.
Features editor: Stephen Mease. Phone: 802-863-3441. Reply date: 10/28/88. Uses photos with press releases.

West Virginia

Charleston Daily Mail, 1001 Virginia Street East, Charleston, WV 25301.
Travel editor: Crystal Dempsey. Phone: 304-348-4809. Reply date: 4/18/88. Accepts press releases.

CANADA

Quebec

Le Journal de Montreal, 4545 Frontenac, Montreal, Quebec, Canada
H2H 2R7.
Travel editor: Yves Rochon. Phone: 514-521-4545. Reply date: 10/
24/88. Publishes press releases. Paper is in French.

4

Book Markets

INFORMATION for the book publisher market listings was gathered from questionnaires sent out in June 1988, with follow-up phone calls in November 1988.

ACTIVE MARKETS

AARP Books, 1900 East Lake Avenue, Glenview, IL 60025. Editor-in-chief: A. Jean Lesher. Phone: 312-729-3000. Reply date: 6/88. Publishes only 1 or 2 travel books/year. Royalty: 10 percent of net receipts is the beginning rate. Prefers a query letter first, containing the idea, the author's credentials to write on the subject, and the projected length. "If we like the idea, we will ask for a full proposal." Practical books for readers ages 50 and above. Sample titles: *Travel Easy, On the Road in an RV, Motorcoach Adventures* (1989). Interested in something on water vacations and learning vacations.

Alaska Northwest, 130 Second Avenue South, Edmonds, WA 98020. Director, Book Division: Maureen Zimmerman. Phone: 206-774-4111, 800-533-7381. Reply date: 6/88. Averages 6 books/year. Royalty varies. Send query or sample chapters with outline. Publishes *The Milepost, The Alaska Wilderness Milepost*, and *Northwest Mileposts* travel guides. Also publishes the magazine *Northwest Living!* (see listing in chapter 2 for details). Sample titles: *Alaska: A Pictorial Geography, Anchorage and the Cook Inlet Basin, A Tourist Guide to Mount McKinley*.

Appalachian Mountain Club, 5 Joy Street, Boston, MA 02108. Editorial director: Susan Cummings. Phone: 617-523-0636. **Reply**

date: 7/88. Averages 8 books/year. Royalty: 10 percent of list. Proposal should include brief description of book, table of contents, sample chapter(s), author's biographical statement, market assessment. Subject areas: Wilderness travel, mountaineering, outdoor recreation, nature (nonfiction only). Sample title: *Guide to Backcountry Skiing in New England.*

Backcountry Publications, POB 175, Woodstock, VT 05091. Vice president: Carl Taylor. Phone: 802-457-1049. Reply date: 4/88. Averages 8-10 books/year. Royalty varies. Proposal should include an outline, sample chapter, rationale why your guide is different and marketable. Publishes outdoor recreation guides for hiking, bicycle touring, and canoeing. These are not travel guides in the traditional sense, but the bicycle touring books especially contain a great deal of information on historic and natural sights, as well as shops, restaurants, and lodgings. Merged with the Countryman Press. Sample titles: *Vermont: An Explorer's Guide, New York State's Special Places, Fifty Hikes in New Jersey.*

Barron's, 250 Wireless Boulevard, Hauppauge, NY 11788. Acquisitions editor: Grace Freedson. Phone: 516-434-3311. Reply date: 6/88. Publishes 5-10 items/year, mostly travel books focusing on language materials, dictionaries, and audio tapes designed for both the business traveler and the tourist. Royalty varies. Sample titles: *Talking Business* (Japanese, Korean, French, Spanish, Italian, and German), *Now You're Talking* (audio cassette and book for tour-

AR	all rights	OTR	one-time rights
ASMP	American Society of	POA	pays on acceptance
	Magazine	POB	post office box
	Photographers	POP	pays on publication
BW	black-and-white photos	PPS	previously published
CM	complete manuscript		submissions
ES	electronic submissions	PQ	phone queries
FL	freelance	SAE	self-addressed envelope
FL/year	number of freelance travel	SASE	self-addressed stamped envelope
	articles published per	SC	sample copy
	year	SQ	simultaneous queries
F(NAS)R	first (North American serial)	SR	second rights
	rights	SS	simultaneous submissions
ms(s)	manuscript(s)	WG	writer's guidelines
NA	North American		

ists, in seven languages), *Getting By* (book with two audio cassettes, in 13 languages).

Bear Flag Books, POB 840, Arroyo Grande, CA 93420-0840. General manager: Karen Reinecke. Phone: 805-473-1947. Reply date: 10/88. Averages 6 books/year. Royalty varies. Submit outline or manuscript accompanied by SASE and be prepared to assist in marketing and promotion. Features titles on California travel, history, and nature. Prefers books over 100 pages, illustrated with line drawings or BW photographs or both. Uses color slides for covers. Considers reprints of out-of-print titles. Sample titles: *Back Roads of the Central Coast, Nature Walks on the San Luis Coast.*

Beautiful America, POB 646, Wilsonville, OR 97070. President: Beverly Paul. Phone: 503-682-0173. Reply date: 5/88. Averages 12 books/year. Royalty varies. Prefers brief outline as proposal; do not send a complete manuscript. Publishes books that contribute both knowledge and beauty to the American literary scene. Sample titles: *The Oregon Trail: A Photographic Journey, West Coast Victorians, Public and Private Gardens of the Northwest.*

Binford and Mort, 1202 N.W. 17th Avenue, Portland, OR 97209. Editor: James S. Roberts. Phone: 503-221-0866. Reply date: 6/88. Averages 5-12 books/year. Royalties: 10 percent on average. Submit query letter, several chapters, and SASE. Nonfiction material on the Pacific Northwest. Sample titles: *Bend in Central Oregon; Early Portland: Stumptown Triumphant; Early State Atlases: California (Northern Edition), California (Southern Edition), Idaho, Oregon, Washington.*

Chelsea Green, POB 283, Chelsea, VT 05038. Publishers: Ian and Margo Baldwin. Consulting editor: Patricia Graves. Phone: 802-685-3108. Reply date: 6/88. Publishes 3-4 travel books/year, starting in 1989. Royalty: 8-12.5 percent of net. Advance: Up to $1500. Prefers a query letter first, describing the project and the author's intentions, along with table of contents and introductory chapter. Interested in off-beat travel, essays on travel. Has series on cemeteries of the great cities of the world and on the permanent collections of the world's great art museums. Series on spas and health resorts introduced in spring 1989. Sample titles: *New York's Great Art Museums, Europe's Best Spas, Permanent Californians: A Biographical Guide to California's Cemeteries, Hidden Peru.*

Chicago Review Press, 814 North Franklin, Chicago, IL 60610. Editors: Linda Matthews and Amy Teschner. Phone: 312-337-0747. Reply date: 6/88. Averages 2 books/year. Royalty: 10-12.5 percent. Advance: Little or none. Prefers query letter with sample chapter and SASE. Publishes specialty travel books, usually for the adventurous traveler who chooses less common destinations and likes to travel independently. Also likes detailed guides to individual places that receive only general treatment in bigger guides. Sample titles: *A Hitchhikers' Guide to Africa and Arabia, The Liberated Traveller, Volunteer Vacations, Nino Lo Bello's Guide to the Vacation.*

China Books, 2929 24th Street, San Francisco, CA 94110. Manager, Book Division: Nancy Ippolito. Phone: 415-282-2994. Reply date: 10/88. Averages 4 books/year. Royalty: 8-10 percent. Prefers outline and 2 sample chapters plus samples of photography if appropriate. Books about mainland China. Sample titles: *Magnificent China, Shopping in China.*

Chronicle Books, 275 Fifth Street, San Francisco, CA 94103. Senior editor: William LeBlond. Phone: 415-777-7240. Reply date: 7/88. Publishes approximately 10 travel books/year. Royalty: Standard trade book rates. Send query letter, including an outline and perhaps 1-2 sample chapters. Multiple submissions are acceptable, as are computer printouts. Send duplicate illustrations if applicable. Books are almost always guidebooks, not accounts of travel. Sample titles: *The Historic Hotels of Scotland, The Missions of California, Combing the Coast.*

Cordillera Press, Inc., POB 3699, Evergreen, CO 80439. Publisher: Walter R. Borneman. Phone: 303-670-3010. Reply date: 11/88. Averages 6-7 books/year. Royalty varies. Prefers a query letter of 2-3 pages with specific details. "The guidebooks we are able to market most effectively are those which target a specific audience in a specific area, e.g., backpackers and mountaineers in the San Juan Mountains of southwestern Colorado. While we have published some guides that are strictly route descriptions, we find that it is easier to market books that have a historical aspect as well. We publish guidebooks related to outdoor sports in North America, e.g., hiking, climbing, backpacking and watersports." Sample titles: *The San Juan Mountains: A Hiking and Climbing Guide, The Outdoor Athlete: Total Training for Outdoor Performance, Arizona's Mountains: A Hiking and Climbing Guide.*

The Countryman Press, Woodstock, VT 05091.
Vice president: Carl Taylor. Phone: 802-457-1049. Reply date: 6/88. Publishes 1-2 travel books/year. Royalty varies. Needs to see a well-fleshed-out proposal, preferably including a sample chapter. Generally, books deal with the Northeastern United States. Sample titles: *New England's Special Places, Vermont: An Explorer's Guide, Walks and Rambles on the Delmarva Peninsula.*

Falcon Press, POB 1718, Helena, MT 59624.
Publisher: Bill Schneider. Phone: 406-442-6597. Reply date: 6/88. Averages 10 books/year. Royalty: 10-15 percent, on a sliding scale that increases with number of units sold. Pay for photos and maps included in royalty. Prefers query letter of 2-3 pages that describes the slant the book will take, similar books on the market, the marketing potential, and, as applicable, the author's writing and photography skills. Author can include writing samples. Always looking for people to write recreational guidebooks. Likes to cover an entire state instead of a smaller region. Plans on covering many more states in its "Hikers Guide" series. Sample titles: *The Hikers Guide to California, The Rockhound's Guide to Montana.*

Fodor's Travel Guides, 201 East 50th Street, New York, NY 10022.
Assistant editor: Kathy Ewald. Reply date: 6/88. Has 140 titles in print. No royalty; all writing is done for a flat fee or on a work-for-hire basis. Contributors are professional writers living in the locale covered by the guide or with special expertise in that particular area. Prefers a letter with resume, some information on author's knowledge of area, plus samples of writing. "Send something that you're proud of and that is not travel related but shows a talent for descriptive writing." Largest publisher of travel guides in the country. Updates guides annually. Over a 3-year period all 140 guides are rewritten from scratch. Sample titles: *North Africa, Caribbean, Texas, San Francisco.*

Globe Pequot Press, 138 West Main Street, Chester, CT 06412.
Managing editor: Bruce Markot. Phone: 203-526-9571, 800-243-0495. Reply date: 7/88. Publishes 30 travel books/year. Royalty: Schedules usually begin at 7.5 percent of net. Submit outline, sample chapters, and author credentials. Discourages submission of CM. A national "regional" publisher, this press's numerous series include "Recommended Country Inns," "Bed & Breakfast in . . .," "Off the Beaten Path" (unusual things to see and do in individual states),

"Short Nature Walks," and "Short Bike Rides." Each of the books in these series focuses on a single state or region, is written by an author from the area, and is updated regularly. Globe Pequot's current list of more than 250 titles includes regional books for every part of the United States, as well as an extensive selection of international guidebooks, including those on Canada and the Caribbean. Sample titles: *Recommended Country Inns of New England, Michigan Off the Beaten Path, Bed & Breakfast in California, and Short Bike Rides on Long Island.*

Golden West Publishers, 4113 North Longview, Phoenix, AZ 85014. Editor: Hal Mitchell. Phone: 602-265-4392. Reply date: 6/88. Publishes 2-3 travel books/year. Royalty: 6-10 percent. Query before sending ms. Publishes only trade paperbacks and travel books about Arizona and the Southwest. *The Other Mexico, Ghost Towns and Historical Haunts in Arizona, Prehistoric Arizona.*

Gulf Publishing, POB 2608, Houston, TX 77252-2608. Editor-in-chief: William Lowe, Jr. Phone: 713-529-4301. Reply date: 11/88. Averages 5 books/year. Royalty: In general, 10-12.5 percent of gross. Prefers query letter with sample chapter, table of contents, and synopsis of what is covered and how it will be covered. "We're the largest for-profit publisher of regional travel guides in Texas. Our regional books continue to sell very well. We're now expanding to cover new states with our popular 'Camper's Guide' series and our 'Mariner's Atlas' series." Sample titles: *Backroads of Texas; Historic Homes of Texas;* "Camper's Guide" series includes Texas, Minnesota, Florida, California.

The Harvard Common Press, 535 Albany Street, Boston, MA 02118. President: Bruce Shaw. Phone: 617-423-5803. Reply date: 11/88. Publishes 4 travel books/year. Royalty: 5 percent of list for paper, 8 percent of list for cloth. Submit outline and sample chapter with SASE. Sample titles: *Going Places: The Guide to Travel Guides, Travel Writer's Markets, Best Places to Stay in Hawaii* (part of the "Best Places to Stay" series).

Hippocrene Books, 171 Madison Avenue, New York, NY 10016. President: George Blagowidow. Phone: 212-685-4371. Reply date: 7/88. Lists 48 travel books in 1989 catalog. Royalty: 7.5 percent of list for paper, 10 percent of list for cloth. Prefers formal book proposal with sample chapters plus a letter explaining the project.

Publishes international guidebooks, special interest guides (travel with children, travel for single women), as well as regional guides (on the Berkshires and Long Island). Is starting a series of travel books providing cultural and historical background on various destinations, such as *An American's Guide to the Soviet Union,* by Professor Brinkle. Sample titles: *Netherlands Antilles, The Traveler's Guide, Travel Passes Worldwide.*

Hunter Publishing, Inc., 239 South Beach Road, Hobe Sound, FL 33455.
Publisher: Michael Hunter. Phone: 407-546-7986. Reply date: 6/88. Publishes 45 books/season. Royalty varies. Query first with outline and description of the project. Focuses on guides, maps, and language courses for travelers. Seeking practical guides to destinations that are growing in popularity but that are not served by many existing guides, such as the Caribbean, India, Canada, Mexico. Specialized approaches welcome: walking or gourmet tours. Sample titles: *Insider's Guide to Hawaii, Visitor's Guide to Austria, Rio Alive.*

Intercultural Press, 130 North Road, Vershire, VT 05079.
Editor-in-chief: David S. Hoopes. Phone: 802-685-4448. Reply date: 6/88. Averages 6 books/year. Royalty: From 5 percent for trade paperbacks, on a sliding scale that increases with number of units sold. Prefers a query letter but will accept an extensive prospectus. Interested in cross-cultural communication, culture shock theory, educational exchange, and travel emphasizing in-depth cross-cultural experience and learning. Titles: *Communicating with China, Living in the U.S.A., Survival Kit for Overseas Living.*

International Resources, POB 840, Arroyo Grande, CA 93420-0840.
General manager: Karen Reinecke. Phone: 805-473-1947. Reply date: 10/88. Averages 3 books/year. Royalty varies. Submit outlines or mss accompanied by SASE and be prepared to assist in marketing and promotion. Interested in travel off the beaten path and to unusual destinations. Looks for color and BW illustrations. This is a new market. Sample title: *An Uncommon Guide to Easter Island.*

John Muir Publications, POB 613, Santa Fe, NM 87504.
Vice president: Steven Cary. Phone: 505-982-4078. Reply date: 5/88. Will publish 35 travel titles in 1989. Royalty varies and depends on the author's proven writing skills, topic of the book, and publisher's analysis of its sales potential. Advances negotiable. Prefers

a well-developed outline of the book, summary of author's knowledge and experience, analysis of existing books, and author's interpretation of existing market. Recently published books on gypsying over 40 and all-suite hotels. Interested in books for people over 40, people with young children, South and Central America. All must have an unusual angle. Sample titles: *Buddhist America, Healing Centers, Catholic Retreat Centers, 22 Days in Mexico.*

Liberty Publishing Company, Inc., 440 South Federal Highway, Suite B-3, Deerfield Beach, FL 33441.
Acquisitions editor: Suzanne Little. Phone: 305-360-9000. Reply date: 7/88. Publishes 2-3 travel books/year. Royalty: 6-12 percent of net. Proposed books must be at least 75 percent complete. Submit outline or detailed table of contents, 2-3 sample chapters, and a cover letter. Reports in 10-12 weeks. Publishes general interest titles but will bring out other regional books. Sample titles: *Weekends for Two* (Mid-Atlantic region), *One-Day Celestial Navigation.*

MarLor Press, 4304 Brigadoon Drive, St. Paul, MN 55126.
Editorial director: Marlin Bree. Phone: 612-484-4600. Reply date: 6/88. Averages 6 books/year. Royalty varies and is based on net. Prefers a query letter with a marketing statement that describes the concept of the book and what is unique about it as compared to others on the market. Publishes guidebooks and books on affordable travel. Looking for books that contain useful information on saving time, energy, and money. Does not publish first-person accounts, anecdotes, or reminiscences. Sample titles: *New York for the Independent Traveler, Best Low Cost Things to See and Do, Kid's Trip Diary, Guide to Budget Motels, Holiday Memory Book and Record.*

Meadowbrook Press, 18318 Minnetonka Boulevard, Deephaven, MN 55391.
Acquisitions editor: Wendy Ann Williams. Phone: 612-473-5400. Reply date: 6/88. Averages 3-4 books/year. Pays $2000 advance against 7.5 percent royalty, or purchases book for $1500-$3000. Submit detailed proposal. Books on free attractions, travel tips, budget motels. Sample titles: *Best European Travel Tips, The Traveler's Guide to European Customs and Manners, Asian Customs and Manners.*

Melior Publications, North 10 Post Street, Suite 550, POB 1905, Spokane, WA 99210-1905.
Vice president: Barbara Greene Chamberlain. Phone: 509-455-9617.

Reply date: 9/88. Has not previously published any travel books and any move into that market will depend on the quality of the submissions received. Royalty: 7-12.5 percent. Query or submit outline and 2-5 chapters. Include information on your background and clips of published work. Prefers photocopied submissions. WG: SASE. Interested in seeing travel books with strong regional appeal and a historical angle of some kind—tied to sites that are on the National Register of Historic Places, for example.

Menasha Ridge Press, 2905 Kirkcaldy Lane, Birmingham, AL 35243.
Publisher: R. W. Sehlinger. Phone: 205-991-0373, 800-247-9437. Reply date: 11/88. Averages 10 books/year. Advance: $1000. Royalty varies and is based on receipts. Submit summary of background, experience, and credentials along with a proposal that shows how your book is different from others on the market, detailed table of contents, summary of each chapter, and a sample chapter, usually the first. No WG. Publishes how-to and guidebooks, restaurant guides, books on travel and outdoor recreation. Sample titles: *The Unofficial Guide to Walt Disney World, Caribbean Ports of Call, Canoe Trails of the Deep South.*

Mills and Sanderson, 442 Marrett Road, Suite 5, Lexington, MA 02173.
Publisher: Georgia Mills. Phone: 617-861-0992. Reply date: 6/88. Averages 3 books/year. Royalty: 12.5 percent of net. WG: Write. Prefers a query letter first. If interested in book idea, will ask for proposal with chapter-by-chapter outline plus sample chapters. Do not send mss. Sample titles: *Adventure Traveling,* covering unique vacation topics from mountain adventures to big game safaris to ghost hunting trips; *Smart Travel,* on getting your money's worth; second edition of *The Cruise Answer Book*; *Sicilian Walks.*

Moon Publications, 722 Wall Street, Chico, CA 95928.
Editor: Deke Castleman. Phone: 916-345-5473. Reply date: 6/88. Averages 10 travel guides/year. Royalty: Descending rate according to invoice net. Prefers a query letter first. Recently published books include those on specific areas: Alaska, Arizona, California, China, Egypt, Philippines. Looking for proposals for travel guides to the Pacific Basin, Latin America, and Western states (Colorado, Montana, Wyoming, Idaho). Sample titles: *Washington Handbook, British Columbia Handbook, South Korea Handbook.*

Mountain Press Publishing, POB 2399, Missoula, MT 59806. Publisher: David Flaccus. Phone: 406-728-1900. Reply date: 6/88. Averages 12-15 books/year. Royalty: 12 percent. Pays advance and travel expenses. Prefers a query letter describing the book. Needs writers with a geological or historical background. Trying to expand "Roadside Geology" and "Roadside History" series on U.S. states. Sample titles: *Roadside Geology of Arizona; Roadside Geology of Virginia; Time, Rocks, and the Rockies.*

Mountaineers, 306 Second Avenue West, Seattle, WA 98119. Director: Donna De Shazo. Phone: 206-285-2665, 800-553-4453. Reply date: 6/88. Publishes 10-12 books/year. Royalty varies. Prefers outline of book with sample chapters but will look at CM. WG: Phone. Publishes nonfiction books on the outdoors, field guides, adventure narratives, and guidebooks to specific areas, self-propelled sports, independent travel, natural history. Sample titles: *Guide to Trekking in Nepal, Paddling Hawaii, Walking in Switzerland, Europe by Bike, A Pocket Doctor.*

Mustang Publishing, POB 9327, New Haven, CT 06533. President: Rollin A. Riggs. Phone: 203-624-5485. Reply date: 6/88. Averages 6-8 books/year. Royalty: On average, 6-8 percent on cover price for trade paperbacks. Submit query letter, a few sample chapters, and SASE for reply. "In general, we're looking for travel books that target the 18- to 35-year-old traveler." Sample titles: *Europe for Free, Europe: Where the Fun Is, Hawaii for Free, The Nepal Trekkers Handbook, Let's Blow Through Europe.*

Passport Books, 4255 West Touhy Avenue, Lincolnwood, IL 60646-1975. Editor: Michael Ross. Phone: 312-679-5500. Reply date: 6/88. Averages 10-12 books/year. Royalty varies. Prefers a query letter with synopsis and outline of the book. Publishes books on international travel and language books for the traveler. Sample titles: *Brazil on Your Own;* "At Its Best" series (Holland, Spain, Italy, Germany, etc.), 10 titles on China, "Everything Under the Sun" series.

Pelican Publishing Company, 1101 Monroe Street, POB 189, Gretna, LA 70054. Assistant editor: Dean Shapiro. Phone: 504-368-1175. Reply date: 6/88. Averages 30 titles/year, with about 500 titles currently in print: cloth and trade paperback originals (90 percent) and reprints (10 percent), including cloth, trade paperback, and mass market. Royalty varies. Submit a query letter with SASE. Publishes guidebooks, not travelogues or personal accounts. Open to any area, region, or continent of the world and all things related to travel. Sample titles: *Stern's Guide to the Cruise Vacation, The Maverick Guide to Australia, Adventuring on the Eurail Express.*

Pilot Books, 103 Cooper Street, Babylon, NY 11702.
Publisher: Samuel Small. Phone: 516-422-2225. Reply date: 4/88. Averages 25 books/year. Royalty: 10-15 percent, on a sliding scale that increases with number of units sold. Requires introduction, sample chapter, and outline. Books on discount travel opportunities, specialized senior citizen travel guides. Sample titles: *National Directory of Budget Motels, The Travel & Vacation Discount Guide, The Senior Citizen's Guide to Budget Travel in the United States and Canada.*

Prentice Hall, Gulf & Western Building, One Gulf & Western Plaza, New York, NY 10023.
Managing editor: Jennifer Aldrich. Phone: 212-373-8865. Reply date: 6/88. Has close to 400 titles in print. Royalty and work-for-hire agreements vary and are based on salability of the title, experience with the author, etc. Submit complete and detailed outline and a few sample chapters. Interested in reviewing proposals for guides to adventure travel or with a historical bent. Publishes Baedeker, Frommer, American Express, Mobil, Insight, and others.

Pruett Publishing Company, 2928 Pearl Street, Boulder, CO 80301. Managing editor: Gerald Keenan. Phone: 303-449-4919. Reply date: 4/88. Averages 25-30 books/year. Royalty: 10-12.5 percent. Submit query and synopsis. Reports within 30 days. Outdoor recreational guides, books for the railroad enthusiast, and regional (Western) history. Sample titles: *On Foot in the Grand Canyon, Border Towns of the Southwest, Small People in Colorado Places.*

Riverdale Company, 5506 Kenilworth Avenue, Suite 102, Riverdale, MD 20737.
Editor: Mary Power. Phone: 301-864-2029. Reply date: 7/88. Publishers of *The Travelers Almanac, North America; Planning Your Vacation Around the Weather.*

Sandlapper Publishing, Inc., POB 1932, Orangeburg, SC 29116-1932.

Publisher: Frank Handal. Book editor: Nancy M. Drake. Phone: 803-531-1658. Reply date: 7/88. Royalty: 10-15 percent of net. Prefers a chapter-by-chapter synopsis. WG: Phone or write. Publishes history, biography, travel about South Carolina and the Southeast. Sample titles: *Azaleas and Stucco: A Walking Guide to the College of Charleston, Fishing the Southeast Coast, Contemplative Fishing Guide to the Grand Strand.*

Sierra Club Books, 730 Polk Street, San Francisco, CA 94109.
Senior editor: James Cohee. Phone: 415-776-2211. Reply date: 6/88. Publishes 2-4 travel books/year. Royalty: 7.5 percent of cover price. Prefers an outline, sample chapters, and a resume. Outdoor adventure, recreational opportunities, points of interest, cultural events, local color and history, flora, fauna, natural history, and geography. All books should emphasize getting out into the natural world. Sample titles: *Adventuring in the San Francisco Bay Area, The Best Ski Touring in America.*

Stewart, Tabori & Chang, 740 Broadway, New York, NY 10003-9518.
Contact: Maureen Graney. Phone: 212-460-5000. Reply date: 10/1/88. Publishes 1 volume in "Outdoor Traveler's Guide" series per year and has authors lined up for Caribbean and Canada. Offers an advance and royalty. "We will ask each candidate to send us a resume, references, and appropriate clips, and to explain in a detailed letter how he or she would approach the subject and handle material.

AR	all rights	OTR	one-time rights
ASMP	American Society of	POA	pays on acceptance
	Magazine	POB	post office box
	Photographers	POP	pays on publication
BW	black-and-white photos	PPS	previously published
CM	complete manuscript		submissions
ES	electronic submissions	PQ	phone queries
FL	freelance	SAE	self-addressed envelope
FL/year	number of freelance travel	SASE	self-addressed stamped envelope
	articles published per	SC	sample copy
	year	SQ	simultaneous queries
F(NAS)R	first (North American serial)	SR	second rights
	rights	SS	simultaneous submissions
ms(s)	manuscript(s)	WG	writer's guidelines
NA	North American		

We may eventually ask interested writers to write a sample chapter." "Outdoor Traveler's Guides" are a new series of illustrated guides to the natural history and outdoor activities of selected non-U.S. travel destinations, such as Canada, the Alps, Scandinavia, East Africa, the British Isles, India, the Himalayas, and the Andes. Text will cover geology, wildlife, vegetation, and sea life. Each book will have about 75,000 words, including 40 short text vignettes about plants and animals. Sample titles: *The Outdoor Traveler's Guide to Australia, The Outdoor Traveler's Guide to the Caribbean, The Bahamas* (fall 1989).

Stoneydale Press, 205 Main Street, Drawer B, Stevensville, MT 59870. Publisher: Dale Burk. Phone: 406-777-2729. Reply date: 6/88. Averages 2-3 books/year. Royalty: 12 percent of receipts on first printing, 15 percent of receipts on all subsequent printings. Prefers a full book proposal with outline, sample chapters, and market analysis. All books are related to hunting or fishing, with travel tied in with those activities. Sample titles: *Successful Big Game Hunting, Montana Hunting Guide, Elk Hunting in the Northern Rockies.*

Texas Monthly Press, POB 1569, Austin, TX 78767-1569. Publications coordinator: Angela Shelf Medearis. Phone: 512-476-7085. Reply date: 7/88. Publishes at least 2 travel books per year and constantly revises the ones currently in print. Royalty negotiable. Prefers query letter with synopsis of book and SASE. Publishes guides to cities, states, and Mexico. Sample titles: *Historic Galveston; Authentic Texas Cafes;* guides to the Hill Country, Houston, Austin, New Mexico, and Mexico.

TL Enterprises, 29901 Agoura Road, Agoura, CA 91301. General manager, Book Division: Rena Copperman. Phone: 818-991-4980. Reply date: 5/88. Will publish 6 titles in 1989. Royalty: 5-7.5 percent of receipts. Submit 2 complete copies of ms. "RVing America's Backroads" series will cover 2 states per book and include historical, geographical, botanical, zoological, and travel information. Sample titles: *An RV's Annual: The Best of "Trailer Life" and "MotorHome," RVing America's Backroads: California, RVing America's Backroads: Idaho and Montana.*

Travel Keys, POB 160691, Sacramento, CA 95816. Publisher: Peter B. Manston. Phone: 916-452-5200. Reply date: 6/88. Publishes 4-6 books/year, mostly done in house. Hires for research or work for hire. No formal WG. Publishes mostly but not entirely material on Europe. Sample titles: *Flea Markets of Britain, Travel Key Europe.*

Ulysses Press, Sather Gate Station, Box 4000-H, Berkeley, CA 94704. Publisher: Ray Riegert. Phone: 415-644-0915. Reply date: 6/88. Averages 6 books/year. Pays on work-for-hire basis. "Ideally, book proposals should include a chapter outline and two sample chapters and follow the structure and format established in the existing 'Hidden' titles. Send SASE. Publishes a series of 'Hidden' guides. These are lengthy (400-page) guidebooks that include standard information like hotel and restaurant reviews, shopping and night-life listings, and sightseeing descriptions. But they go a step further, with information on off-the-beaten-track destinations, campgrounds, hiking trails, and adventure travel facilities." Sample titles: *Hidden Hawaii, Hidden Mexico, Hidden San Francisco and Northern California.*

Umbrella Books, POB 1460, Friday Harbor, WA 98250-1460. President: Jerome K. Miller. Phone: 206-378-5128. Reply date: 6/88. Averages 6 books/year. Royalty varies. Send a proposal containing working title, brief description, outline with chapter summaries, information about computer. Include resume and sample of previous publications. Specializes in tour guides for the Pacific Northwest, including popular vacation destinations, outdoor activities, historic buildings, artifacts, flora and fauna. Sample title: *The Umbrella Guide to Friday Harbor & San Juan Island.*

Wilderness Press, 2440 Bancroft Way, Berkeley, CA 94704-1676. Editorial director: Thomas Winnett. Phone: 415-843-8080. Reply date: 4/88. Averages 4-6 books/year. Royalty: 8 percent to authors who have not published in the field before, 10 percent to those who have. Considers book proposals, outlines, sample chapters, and CM. Authors must personally cover all the places they write about. Specializes in guides to hiking in wilderness areas, national parks, and national forests, but has also published guides to urban parks, hot springs, and ski tours. Sample titles: *Sierra North, Bicycling Across America.*

Woodbine House, 10400 Connecticut Avenue, Suite 512, Kensington, MD 20985. Editor: Susan Stokes. Phone: 301-949-3590, 800-843-7323. Reply date: 7/88. "This year we published one travel book (on the national seashores). The previous year we also published one travel book (on Arlington National Cemetery)." Royalty varies, but averages 10 percent for the first 5000 units, more thereafter. Submit the following information: title of book, approximate length, number of chapters, chapter titles, approximate length per chapter, short description of each chapter, short author profile, where book can be marketed, other works on the subject, estimated completion date. Nonfiction only, all kinds. 250 page minimum. "We are interested in acquiring new travel books for next year—of every type except books of strictly regional appeal or personal accounts." Sample titles: *National Seashores: Complete Guide to America's Scenic Coastal Parks, Arlington Cemetery: Shrine to America's Heroes.*

A World of Travel, 106 South Front Street, Suite 2E, Philadelphia, PA 19106.
Acquisitions editor: Ms. E. Markham. Phone: 215-592-0356, 800-777-0400. Reply date: 6/88. Formerly Fisher's World. Publishes 10 books/year. Royalty: Sliding scale that increases with number of units sold. Pays expenses. Query on article or guidebook ideas with published clips. WG: SASE. Free book catalog on request. Guides also include 3-4 articles of 1500-1800 words written by authors other than main author. Articles are on unusual situations experienced by the authors themselves, covering music, sports, fashion, art, food, wine, and historic or native sites. Future books will include Egypt, Turkey, Brazil, Hungary, Moscow, Austria, Belgium and Luxembourg, Denmark, Israel, India, China, Southeast Asia, Scandinavia. Sample titles: *Madrid and North Spain, Rome and Central Italy, Jamaica and Western Caribbean, Atlanta and the Old South.*

DISTRIBUTORS

Carousel Press, POB 6061, Albany, CA 94706.
Editor: Carole Terwilliger Meyers. Phone: 415-527-5849. Reply date: 6/88. Has a catalog of books on family travel: destination guides with family information, general travel including information of use to families. If you are the author or publisher of an appropriate book, submit a review copy with publicity materials. Reprints of published family-oriented travel articles also considered.

Faber and Faber, 50 Cross Street, Winchester, MA 01890.
Reply date: 7/88. Attach ideas for marketing and specify the in-

tended audience for your work. List past publication credits. Distributes travel titles, but doesn't publish any at this time.

Seven Hills Books, 49 Central Avenue, Suite 300, Cincinnati, OH 45202.
President: Ion Itescu. Reply date: 4/88. Distributors of mostly foreign presses. Currently distributes 3 books on train rides in the Swiss Alps.

NOT IN THE MARKET

The dates in parentheses after these publishers' names are when they were last heard from or when mail was returned.

Adler & Adler (3/88). Out of business.
Almar (4/88). "We have not published any guidebooks."
American Council for the Arts (4/88). Mail returned.
American Studies (6/88). "We don't publish travel books as such."
And Books (6/88). "We do not have any travel books right now."
Australia in Print (7/88). "We wholesale only for many Australian publishers. We don't originate travel books ourselves."
Bala Books (6/88). "We specialize in children's stories from other lands."
Beaufort Books (6/88). Form rejection in response to questionnaire.
Briarcliff (6/88). "We do no travel books."
Contemporary Books (6/88). "We do not specialize in travel books."
Facts on File (6/88). "We publish virtually no travel books."
Granite Publishing (6/88). "We publish only regional rock climbing guides."
H. W. H. Creative Productions (4/88). Mail returned.
Harcourt, Brace, Jovanovich (6/88). "Our present publishing program does not include a line of travel titles."
Havin' Fun (6/88). "All of our books are done in house."
Lonely Planet (4/88). Not soliciting manuscripts.
Nick Lyons Books (6/88). "We publish no travel books."
Oak Tree (4/88). "We only publish children's books."
Octameron Associates (4/88). "We have decided not to develop a line of travel guides."
Overlook Press (4/88). Form rejection in response to questionnaire.
Pacific Trade Group (4/88). "We are no longer accepting manuscripts."

Routledge (formerly Methuen) (6/88). "No plans for further travel books under our new organization."

Shoe String Press (4/88). "We no longer publish guidebooks, as we have lost money on them in the past, and do not find the market congenial."

Slavica (4/88). "Sorry, we don't do guidebooks."

Wind River (10/88). Uses house-generated editorial material.

5

Record Keeping and Tax Tips

Robert B. Shapiro, E.A.

IT would be nice if writers only needed to worry about their craft and cashing their paychecks, but there are many other aspects of business they need to think about. One of these, of course, is our friend the Internal Revenue Service. The following information may help clear up some questions concerning the tax laws.

Assuming that you are in the business of writing, and are trying to make a profit, what kind of expenses can you deduct? The simple answer: You can deduct any reasonable and ordinary expenses of the business. But what does that mean to you? Here are some of the costs you may incur (the items with asterisks next to them are discussed further in this chapter):

- Postage
- Typing services
- Professional publications
- Dues in professional organizations
- Seminar costs
- Supplies (pencils, pens, paper, etc.)
- Automobile expenses for business-related mileage
- Copying costs
- Interest expenses
- Bank service charges
- Travel and entertainment*
- Advertising
- Professional services
- Rent
- Repairs
- Depreciation*
- Office in home expenses*

Travel Expenses

For travel writers, one of the most important expenses is the cost of travel. Is this a deductible expense? The intent of the travel is what determines the answer. Was this trip made for the purpose of writing an article that can be sold? If you take a two-week vacation, come back and decide to write an article about one of the places you visited, then the answer is no, and you will not be allowed to deduct the cost of the trip. If you want to increase the chances of being able to write off your travel expenses, I would suggest the following steps:

1. Decide where you want to go based on the marketability of articles about the destination.
2. Query possible markets about the article. If you can get an assignment or an expression of interest, that will help.
3. Make an estimate of how much you may be able to earn from sales of this article.
4. Make appointments with people in the area you are visiting for interviews, photo sessions, etc.
5. Spend more than four hours each day on activities that will contribute to the article. This can involve taking pictures that you can contribute with the article, interviewing people in the area, and taking notes on attractions, restaurants, and so forth.
6. Calculate the costs of your trip. If they come to more than you expect the article sales to generate, then you are going to have a hard time convincing the IRS that you were traveling for business purposes.

Depreciation

If you have purchased equipment for your writing (a computer, word processor, or typewriter are the most obvious possibilities), you may not be able to deduct the cost of the equipment as you buy it. Instead, you might have to depreciate it, which simply means that you are going to spread the deduction over several years. The rules for doing this are complex, especially for federal income tax, and even more especially for equipment purchased after December 31, 1986. If you are in this situation, tell your tax professional and let him or her take care of calculating the depreciation amount. Keep in mind that if you have purchased equipment that is used for both business and personal purposes, you must keep a written log that will enable you to come up with a business use percentage. If you do not do this, the IRS may well decide that no depreciation deduction is allowed. Again, consult your tax professional for help.

Office in Home

One other deduction possibility is office in home expenses. If you have an area in your home that is used *regularly and exclusively* for your writing business, then you may be able to deduct a portion of your home insurance, utilities, repairs, and so on, as well as a portion of your mortgage or rent payments. There are, however, some limitations and drawbacks.

First of all, starting in 1987, your office in home costs must be taken after you have used all your other allowable expenses, and these costs may not put you into a loss position. For example, if your writing income was $5,000 and your other expenses were $4,800, then you could take only a $200 office in home deduction. Any amount you did not use in the current year could be carried over into subsequent years.

One drawback of using the office in home deduction if you own your home is that if you sell your home, you may not defer the portion of the gain that arises from the section that was used as an office. This is a very complex area, and you should consult your tax adviser about it.

Hobby or Business?

Before you start deducting any expenses, there is one question you had better have an answer for. Are you writing for fun or profit? There are both advantages and disadvantages to either answer from a tax stand-point. If you are writing for the fun of it, and are not expecting to make money, then your losses cannot be used to offset other income. In addition, you will probably have to deduct your expenses as a miscellaneous deduction. This means that you will be able to deduct them only to the extent that they, along with your other miscellaneous deductions, exceed 2 percent of your adjusted gross income.

On the other hand, if you are writing to produce income, and you make a profit, your earnings are subject to self-employment tax. The rate for this tax is 13.02 percent for 1989 and 15.3 percent for 1990. In other words, if you make a $10,000 profit in 1989, you would have to pay $1302 in addition to your regular tax, and in 1990 the extra amount would be $1530.

Assuming that you are trying to make a profit with your writing, how do you make sure that the Internal Revenue Service agrees with you? If you have shown a profit in three out of the last five consecutive years, the presumption is that you are in a trade or business, which means the IRS must show that this was not the case. If you have not met this criteria, then the burden of proof is on you. The other considerations taken into account to prove you were in business include:

- The history of profit or loss from the business.
- The manner in which you carry on your business. If you maintain a complete and accurate set of books and carry on the activity in a businesslike manner, it is more likely that you are engaged in it for profit.
- Your financial status. What other financial resources do you have? If you have substantial sources of income from other sources, that may be an indication that your writing is a hobby.
- Amount of time and effort you expend on your writing. Do you spend much of your personal time writing or researching articles? Have you withdrawn from another occupation to have more time available to write? If so, it is an indication that you are trying to make a profit.
- Have you made a profit in similar activities in the past? If the answer is yes, then you may be expecting to make a profit in this activity even though it is currently losing money.
- The expertise of you or your advisers. Have you prepared for this business by studying its "accepted business, economic, and scientific practices"? If not, have you consulted with people who do have this knowledge? In either case are you following those practices?
- Personal pleasure or recreation. After considering other relevant factors, the fact that you do or do not get pleasure from writing may be taken into account. This does not mean that you must hate to write in order to have a profit motivation. If other factors indicate that you are attempting to make a profit, the presence of personal pleasure or recreation will probably not nullify that.

Unfortunately, there is no way of deciding which of the above criteria is the most important. Also, the regulation setting forth these factors states that this is not an all-encompassing list. Some of the conditions, however, you cannot do anything about. For example, there is no way to influence the success you have had with similar activities in the past.

If you want to show that you are in a trade or business, I would suggest that you concentrate on how you conduct your business and how much time and effort you expend on it. Be meticulous in keeping records of your income and expenses. Analyze these periodically (monthly or quarterly), and use what you discover to improve your profitability. It might be beneficial to hire an accountant to help you with setting up your books and analyzing your transactions. Also, you should keep taking courses and apply what you learn to your business.

Estimated Taxes

If you have made a profit for the year, you don't have to worry about proving that you are in a trade or business. Instead, you can worry about paying estimated taxes. In general, you have to pay your tax quarterly unless one of the following applies:

1. Your total tax less any taxes withheld is less than $500.
2. You were a citizen or resident for the entire preceding year, and you had no tax liability for the year.

If you do not meet one of these two criteria, and you have not paid in at least 90 percent of your total tax due, either by having taxes withheld (if you have anything to withhold them from) or by paying in estimated taxes, then you are subject to a penalty based on the amount you still have due.

How do you know what your taxable income for the year is going to be? If your income tends to be the same each year, you can use last year's amount and *probably* be safe. Keep in mind that you have to pay in only 90 percent of the tax for the year, so you do have a 10 percent leeway.

For many writers, however, taxable income fluctuates from year to year, so this approach won't work. In that case, the simplest answer is to take advantage of an exception that the law contains. If you pay in at least 100 percent of your prior year's tax, then there is no penalty.

Payments are due on April 15, June 15, September 15, and January 15, and you must pay the following percentages:

1. By April 15, 25 percent.
2. By June 15, 50 percent.
3. By September 15, 75 percent.
4. By January 15, 100 percent.

Let's look at two examples.

Example 1: Your total tax last year was $3000. This year, you expect your total tax to be $2500. Most of your income is from writing, but you have $500 withheld from wages you earned doing some temporary work during the year. To avoid a penalty, you must pay in at least 90 percent of the tax due this year or 100 percent of the tax paid in the preceding year. That is either $2250 ($2500 times 90 percent) or $3000 ($3000 times 100 percent). Clearly, in this case you would prefer to pay in the $2250, and in fact would be safer paying in $2500 if you are not sure of your estimated income for the year. Of the $2500, you have already paid in $500 by withholding, so you need to pay $2000 in estimated taxes. You make four payments of $500 each, on April 15, June 15, September 15, and January 15.

Example 2: Your total tax last year was $3000. This year, your income may be higher, but you are not at all sure by how much. All your income is from writing, so there are no withheld taxes. In this case, to avoid a penalty, you should make sure that you pay in at least the $3000 you paid last year. If you do this, then there will be no penalty, no matter what your tax due is this year. You should make four payments of $750 each on April 15, June 15, September 15, and January 15.

There is one other method you can use to figure out how much to pay; this is called annualizing. It involves figuring out your income and deductions for the year to date at the end of each estimate period. (An estimate period ends on the last day of the month before the estimated payment due date, that is, March 31, May 31, August 31, and December 31.) You then assume that the income and deduction stream will remain the same for the rest of the year, calculate your tax for the year, and multiply it by a factor to calculate the amount due each payment date. You would want to consider using this method if you can't estimate your income for the year but are sure that the tax due this year will be considerably less than last year's tax.

Contractor or Employee?

If you are doing your writing for someone else, then you must determine whether you are an employee or an independent contractor. If you are an employee you may not have to fill out a Schedule C or pay self-employment tax. On the other hand, as an employee, you cannot deduct many of your expenses that you could if you were an independent contractor, and when you do deduct them, they are miscellaneous itemized deductions. This can have a major impact on how much you can deduct since miscellaneous itemized deductions can be taken only to the extent that they exceed 2 percent of your adjusted gross income.

How do you determine whether you are an independent contractor or an employee? The first thing to remember is that what you call yourself or what the person you are doing business with calls you does not determine the answer.

There are 20 factors generally used for determination of whether someone is an independent contractor or an employee. In this discussion I use the term payor to designate the person for whom the services are being performed and writer for the person providing the services.

1. A writer who must take instructions on when, where, and how to work is probably an employee.

2. If a writer is being trained by or on behalf of the payor, there is an indication that the payor wants the services done in a certain way. This is an indication of employer control.

3. In general, the more integrated a person's services are into the business of the payor, the more likely he or she is to be considered an employee.

4. If services must be rendered personally, it indicates the payor's control over how the work is done.

5. If the payor hires, pays, and controls the assistants of the writer, there is probably an employer-employee relationship. If the payor performs these functions, there is probably an independent contractor relationship.

6. A continuing relationship is indicative of an employer-employee relationship.

7. If the payor sets the hours of work, then control is present.

8. If full-time work is required, then the payor has control over the amount of time the writer spends working and restricts the writer from doing other work.

9. Doing the work on the payor's premises is an indication of an employer-employee relationship, especially if the services could be performed elsewhere.

10. If the writer must perform services in the order or sequence set by the payor, this implies control and hence an employer-employee relationship. (According to Revenue Ruling 56-694, this holds true even if the payor does not set the sequence but reserves the right to do so.)

11. A requirement that the writer submit regular written or oral reports indicates a degree of control.

12. Payment by the hour, week, or month is generally an indication of an employer-employee relationship. Payment by the job, or

a straight commission, is an indication of independent contractor status.

13. If the payor ordinarily pays the writer's business or travel expenses, there is probably an employer-employee relationship, since this shows some control over how the writer conducts his or her business.

14. If the payor supplies the tools and materials used by the writer, such as a word processor and reference books, there is ordinarily an employer-employee relationship.

15. If the writer invests in his or her own facilities, such as an office, this tends to indicate independent contractor status.

16. If the writer can sustain a loss as a result of performing the services, he or she is probably an independent contractor.

17. Working for multiple unrelated entities at the same time is an indication of independent contractor status.

18. Making services available to the general public ordinarily implies independent contractor status.

19. The payor's right to fire the writer implies an employer-employee status.

20. If the writer has the right to terminate employment without incurring liability, there is probably an employer-employee relationship.

As with hobby or business considerations, no one of these criteria is determinative. But by looking at all of them, you can get an idea of whether you are likely to be seen as an independent contractor or as an employee.

Uniform Capitalization

In the Tax Reform Act of 1986, Congress inserted a section that, among other things, required authors to deduct expenses related to the production of articles and books only as the income for the writing came in. In practice this requirement—called uniform capitalization —was virtually impossible to fulfill since it entailed estimating how much income an article or book was going to produce.

During 1988, the IRS came out with a ruling that provided a simplified method whereby authors could deduct just a portion of their expenses each year, and carry the rest over to the following years. That is, they could deduct 50 percent of all their expenses in the first year and 25 percent in each of the following two years. Finally, in October of 1988, Congress eliminated the provision requiring uniform capitalization for authors.

Before you celebrate, however, you should be aware that not all states followed the federal law in this matter. California, for example, conformed to the law requiring uniform capitalization, but not to either the simplified method or the repeal. Theoretically, therefore, if you are filing a California return, you must calculate your state business income by applying the uniform capitalization rules and making an adjustment for the difference between federal and state income.

If you used uniform capitalization, or the simplified method of deducting expenses on your 1987 taxes, you can go back and file an amended return in which you deduct all the expenses incurred during the year, which should result in your getting some money back from the government. If you are going to do this, you have three years from either April 15, 1988, or the date on which you filed the return, whichever is later.

Appendix: Resources for Travel Writers

Magazines

These two magazines have information on markets and articles of interest to writers.

The Writer, 120 Boylston Street, Boston, MA 02116. Monthly.
Writer's Digest, 1507 Dana Avenue, Cincinnati, OH 45207. Monthly.

Newsletters

Markets Abroad, 2460 Lexington Drive, Owosso, MI 48867. Editor: Michael Sedge. Quarterly newsletter about overseas markets.
Travelwriter Marketletter, The Plaza Hotel, Room 1723, New York, NY 10019. Editor: Robert Scott Milne. Has news of free trips for established travel writers, market updates and tips.

Books

If no address is given, the books listed here are generally available at book stores.

Writer's Market. Writer's Digest Books. Yearly. Lists over 4000 markets for articles, books, fillers, gags, greeting cards, novels, plays, scripts, and short stories, plus information on how much to charge for different types of freelance writing.

The following two books have examples of successful query letters. Burgett has more information on queries specifically for travel writers.

Cool, Lisa Collier. *How to Write Irresistible Query Letters*. Writer's Digest Books, 1987.

Burgett, Gordon. *Query Letters/Cover Letters*. Communication Unlimited (PO Box 6405, Santa Maria, CA 93456), 1985

The following three authors have had many travel articles published, and all teach travel writing classes.

Casewit, Curtis. *How to Make Money from Travel Writing*. Globe Pequot Press, 1988. Special tips on writing for newspapers.

Garfinkel, Perry. *Travel Writing for Profit and Pleasure*. New American Library, 1989. Gives exercises for writing and a glimpse of the future of travel writing.

Zobel, Louise Purwin. *The Travel Writer's Handbook*. Writer's Digest Books, 1984. Information on general preparation for traveling.

If you'd like to go the self-publishing route, these two books will help you out.

Poynter, Dan. *The Self-Publishing Manual*. Para Publishing, 1984. Poynter also offers intensive seminars in self-publishing in Santa Barbara, California.

Ross, Tom, and Marilyn Ross. *The Complete Guide to Self-Publishing*. Writer's Digest Books, 1985.

A good source of information for writers on copyright, contracts, libel, taxes, agents, and publishers is:

Bunnin, Brad, and Peter Beren. *The Writer's Legal Companion*. Addison-Wesley Publishing, 1988.

Writers' Conferences

The Guide to Writers Conferences. Shaw Associates (625 Biltmore Way, Suite 1406, Coral Gables, FL 33134), 1988. Includes information on conferences devoted to travel writing.

Writers' Organizations

American Society of Journalists and Authors, Inc., 1501 Broadway, Suite 1907, New York, NY 10036. Open to qualified, professional freelance writers of nonfiction.

International Food, Wine and Travel Writers Association, PO Box 1532, Palm Springs, CA 92263-1532. Regular membership is open to persons actively engaged in writing, editing, publishing, or broadcasting about food, wine, lodging or travel, or related fields. Associate members are representatives of organizations engaged in the support and promotion of the industry, such as advertising and public relations firms, hotels, airlines, wineries, and so forth.

Society of American Travel Writers, 1100 17th Street, N.W., Suite 1000, Washington, DC 20036. Open to active travel editors and staff writers, freelance travel writers, travel radio and TV broadcasters, travel photographers, travel trade writers and editors, and travel video reporters and photographers. Associate membership open to persons regularly engaged in public relations in the travel industry.

Indexes

Magazines by Subject Matter

This index includes magazines listed in all three market categories: Active Markets, Marginal Markets, and Not in the Market.

Magazines by Title

This index lists all magazines mentioned in the book, including those that have gone out of business.

Subject Index